D1607563

THE POLITICAL FILMS OF ANDRZEJ WAJDA
Dialogism in *Man of Marble, Man of Iron,* and *Danton*

THE POLITICAL FILMS OF ANDRZEJ WAJDA

Dialogism in *Man of Marble, Man of Iron,* and *Danton*

Janina Falkowska

Berghahn Books
Providence • Oxford

Published in 1996 by

Berghahn Books
Editorial offices:
165 Taber Avenue, Providence, RI 02906, USA
Bush House, Merewood Avenue, Oxford, OX3 8EF, UK

Library of Congress Cataloging-in-Publication Data
Falkowska, Janina, 1951–
    The political films of Andrzej Wajda : dialogism in Man of marble,
Man of iron, and Danton / Janina Falkowska.
        p.   cm.
    Includes bibliographical references and index.
    ISBN 1-57181-005-6 (alk. paper)
    1. Wajda, Andrzej, 1926–   --Criticism and interpretation.
I. Title.
PN1998.3.W34F36 1995   95-16394
791.43'0233'092--dc20   CIP

British Library Cataloguing in Publication Data
A CIP catalogue record for this book is available from
the British Library.

Printed in the United States on acid-free paper

✥ CONTENTS

❀ INTRODUCTION

Andrzej Wajda is one of the greatest Polish film directors; indeed, he is considered by many film critics to be one of the most important masters of world cinema. Next to Krzysztof Penderecki and Witold Lutoslawski, he is also regarded as a distinguished ambassador of Polish culture and art. Moreover, he is said to have exerted a great influence on a whole generation of filmmakers not only in Poland but in other Eastern European countries and the former Soviet Union.

An artistic presence in Polish culture for thirty-five years, Andrzej Wajda has been extremely successful despite some setbacks – he has created many superb films but has also produced some of lesser quality. He has also been active in the theatre and in television. His artistic life has never failed to elicit violent responses from audiences. Wajda's films have always aroused emotions of both love and hatred, and stimulated long political discussions in the media. Most of his films deal with historical and political issues of importance to the Polish society, and, consequently, provoke never-ending discussions on the fate of Poland, its glorification and its restoration; the essence of the Polish character; the nature of political power; and the convolutions of Polish history.

Wajda has often said of himself, "I am a Polish film director," which is in his case not an empty declaration. His films, with few exceptions, can be read as an incessant contention: how to be a Pole. However, "Polishness" is not the only theme of his films. He deals with historical and political questions of his time and his country – the period after the Second World War; the moral concerns of the 1950s and 1960s; the rise of Solidarity; the overthrow of the Socialist system; and the Jewish question. His films never treat these historical processes in an impersonal or abstract way; people are always presented in context, both as political subjects and as ordinary human beings.

In Wajda's films an individual is shown as either trying to oppose the historical reality or as annihilated by it. Wajda defends humankind as an independent subject of history, not its passive object. In most of his films a protagonist faces specific moral choices within a defined historical reality. His or her internal struggle is always watched with tension by spectators who painfully negotiate the meanings of the images on the screen – images with which they identify or which they passionately reject. Wajda's films are controversial, painful, stimulating, and cinematically beautiful. The filmmaker knows how to build a narrative, how to construct a world on the screen realistically and how to draw the spectator into his protagonists' conflicts and personal tragedies. Rarely does the spectator, especially the Polish spectator, remain unmoved during the screening.

The nature of the director's artistic vision and narrative technique leads critics to describe both the director and his films as political. In this book I shall discuss the meaning of the notion "political" in relation to film in general, and to Wajda and his films in particular. As a result of this discussion we will see that Wajda is a political film director in many senses of the term: first, he is political because he usually deals with periods of Polish history during which the ruling class found its power abolished and dominant ideology repudiated; second, he is political because he uses flagrantly political tools – propaganda, docudrama, documentary film, or political collage – in the glorification of a new dominant ideology; third, he is political because he uses the individual in his films in an instrumental way – to prove one or another political credo; and fourth, he is political in the sense of making a subversive use of cinematic means. However, in all these cases, Wajda is a representative of society and proponent of a social cause. In all his films Wajda presents humanity's dilemmas within a complex historical and social reality.

The incorporation of the social and historical context in his films especially predisposes Wajda's filmic texts to be discussed within the context of the works of the great literary theorist Mikhail Bakhtin. Bakhtin's analyses of literary texts were based on the notion that these are deeply inscribed in the social fabric. According to Michael Holquist, the editor of many of his translated texts, and the author of many books on Bakhtin, Bakhtin has emerged as one of the leading thinkers of the twentieth century. Although Bakhtin's principal contributions were in the theory of the novel, he revolutionized the ways texts are interpreted as such, and he shed important light on the ways natural language functions. Of particular interest for this study of Wajda's work are Bakhtin's concepts of dialogism and polyphony in the context of a text's historical and social background, which help to elucidate the manner in which various semantic traits are interwoven in a text.

Bakhtin appears to be an ideal methodological choice for the discussion of Wajda's films, since they are all highly polemical in nature; all reveal multiple semantic and aesthetic glossia. The films' polemical aspect makes them ideal material for understanding the process of film reception as a constant negotiation and renegotiation of meanings by the spectator; and their multiple semantic glossia place the films within the concepts of dialogism and polyphony which arbitrate the internal structure of the films. This is especially the case for the three films I have chosen to discuss in this book, *Man of Marble, Man of Iron,* and *Danton.* All three illustrate the dialogical formation of meaning in the sense of Bakhtin's socially and historically inscribed dialogism. For the purposes of this study dialogism also will be treated as part of a universal dialogue between the spectators and the film author. In this sense, Bakhtin's idea of dialogue and its various processes will help to elucidate the negotiation of a film's meaning by the spectator.

There remains one other reason to incorporate the works of Mikhail Bakhtin and Andrzej Wajda in one book: both authors devoted much time and energy to the discussion of one of the greatest writers of the nineteenth century, Fyodor Dostoevsky. Bakhtin's first major published work was *Problems of Dostoevsky's Art* (1929), in which Bakhtin's revolutionary idea of "dialogism" was first announced to the world. Wajda's most important theatre productions concentrated on the texts of Fyodor Dostoevsky, too. Wajda's production of the play *The Idiot,* based on Dostoevsky's novel *The Idiot* (1935), at *Teatr Stary* in Cracow in 1977, is still remembered by theatregoers and European theatre theoreticians alike.

This historically inscribed dialogism is illustrated in *Man of Marble, Man of Iron,* and *Danton* by artistic approaches to the portrayal of history on the screen. In *Man of Marble,* Wajda seeks to portray a particular period in Polish history by dramatizing the story of a man living in one period – 1970s – within the framework of a narrative played out in a different – 1950s – period. By employing this technique of a story-within-a-story, the director can neatly incorporate historical events in the main story.

Man of Iron displays a collage of facts and fictional events, where the former play a more significant role than the latter. *Danton,* on the other hand, is a dramatized story which takes place entirely in the past, and only an interpretive approach to the presentation of the main *dramatis personae* creates references to the contemporary history of Poland. In all the films, the spectator takes an active part in the dialogical negotiation of the historical discourse presented on the screen. The three films force the spectator to determine the films' historical message within the background of his or her vision of history and the political reality of the post-war years in Poland.

In their texture, these films reveal multiple cultural discourses that blend with the overtly historical and ideological. The richness of the film's aesthetics, and its abundant layers of meaning, are a direct result of this mosaic of discourses.

I have chosen to divide this study into five chapters. The first chapter, *The Concept of "the Political" in the Films of Andrzej Wajda: Issues of Methodology*, presents a theoretical basis for the discussion of political film in general, and the films of Andrzej Wajda in particular. Through the analysis of possible uses of the notion "political" with reference to film and Bakhtin's dialogism I establish a methodological framework for the analysis of the political films of Andrzej Wajda. The films discussed in the book are interpreted within the framework of Bakhtin's theory of dialogism, which is used as a concept for this broad research project and as a discursive strategy, in a manner similar to other Bakhtinians in their analysis of literary and nonliterary discourses.[1] Bakhtin will serve here as "a kind of opening, or a crypto-syllogism, that can liberate or break down discursive barriers."[2] Bakhtin's dialogism is used as a mode of thinking – a *modus operandi* in my attempt to analyze the political films of Andrzej Wajda.

The second chapter, *Andrzej Wajda: The Carrier of the Political Message*, presents the artist in the context of his activities as a film director, theatre director, and cultural activist. Additionally, the chapter presents Wajda's role as a carrier of the political message in the films discussed in the book.

The third chapter, *Historical Dialogue in Wajda's Films*, in its theoretical part, introduces the concept of history in film analysis and discusses it in the context of Bakhtin's historically inscribed dialogism and Hans Robert Jauss's idea of *Erwartungshorizont*. Jauss's notion contributes to the understanding of the fusion of historical horizons of the producers and receivers of the cinematic message and explains the process of interpretation of history in artistic works. The later parts of the chapter present the concrete historical context of the films and examine historical discourse as the constitutive substance of the film text.

The fourth chapter, *Wajda and His* Dramatis Personae, is devoted to the *dramatis personae* in his films, who are directly shaped by Wajda's specific constitution as an artist and a director. Finally, the fifth chapter, *The Films' Dialogical Aesthetics*, debates the films' cultural discourses, which interact in the dialogical construction of the films' aesthetics. Additionally, *Appendix: Film Synopses*, introduces a detailed account of scenes and sequences in each film discussed in the book.

Finally, I have included in the book many quotations from Poish and French sources. In chapter 3, which deals with the historical discourse in the films, Polish and French press reviews are extensively quoted since they represent some of the responses of audiences whose voices are indispensable to the dialogical negotiation of the historical meanings in the films. Moreover, in the fifth chapter, several lengthy quotations are presented from the book *Socrealizm* (Socialist Realism), by Wojciech Wlodarczyk, which deals with important cultural phenomena under Stalinist rule. The publication of this book in Poland was only recently made possible thanks to the political changes in Eastern Europe. None of these important Polish sources has ever before reached the Western reader. They represent crucial cultural and social discourses evident in the three films discussed in this book.

Notes

1. I refer here to all the attempts at such an analysis presented in *Bakhtin and Otherness: Social Discourse. International Research Papers in Comparative Literature* 3, nos. 1 and 2 (spring–summer 1990).
2. R.F. Barsky and M. Holquist, "Dialogue," in *Bakhtin and Otherness*, 5.

✸ ACKNOWLEDGMENTS

In acknowledging the people who helped me prepare this book, I would like to thank the professors of the Comparative Literature Programme and the English Department of McGill University, in particular, Paul Coates, Brian Massumi, Marike Finlay, Darko Suvin, Paisley Livingston, and Sarah Westphal-Wihl. These persons demonstrated an exemplary level of decency and integrity in their teaching, in their studies, and in their personal interactions. Their teaching and research inspired me immensely; they were always helpful, understanding, and endlessly patient.

To Paul Coates and Susan Birkwood, who read this manuscript and provided many insightful and valuable criticisms, I am deeply thankful.

I would also like to thank professor Alicja Helman from the Jagiellonian University in Cracow, Poland, who provided me with recent publications on Stalinism, a period in Polish history that had not been discussed in official writings for a long time. She encouraged me in all aspects of my work, and her cooperation and support greatly enhanced my chances for success.

Many thanks are extended to professors Paul Gaudet and Alan Gedalof from the University of Western Ontario for their support and encouragement.

Finally, my thanks to my husband Janusz who has always offered me unconditional love and support.

1

THE CONCEPT OF "THE POLITICAL" IN THE FILMS OF ANDRZEJ WAJDA

Issues of Methodology

The Concept of "the Political" in Film Analysis

In contemporary film research the concept of "the political" is indiscriminately applied to all levels of film analysis. Films are often described as political or are said to imply and reveal political content. On the other hand, the analysts of the formal aspects of film refer to political film form or to films made politically. Andrzej Wajda's films are often described as political or as implying and revealing political content. Before analyzing Wajda's three films, it is worthwhile to concentrate on the term political in relation to film in general, and with reference to Wajda's films in particular.

The notion of political has been a subject of discussion for many authors. Among them are Nick Browne (1970), Peter Gidal (1976), Stephen Heath (1975, 1976, 1981, 1983), Dick Hebdige (1979), Paul Hirst (1979), Thierry Kuntzel (1980), Malcolm Le Grice (1977), James Roy MacBean (1975), Tania Modleski (1986), Laura Mulvey (1975), Bill Nichols (1981), Robert Stam (1989), Elizabeth Weed (1989), and, most recently, Douglas Kellner (1991), and Mas'ud Zavarzadeh (1991). All of these authors have dealt with various aspects of "the political" in cinema. The purpose of my analysis of the notions of "the political" is not to provide a critical analysis of the approaches taken by these authors – a task that awaits another occasion – but to introduce a basic conceptualization of the political with reference to films having political content.

The very word political in relation to film is used in several senses on two different levels of analysis. The adjective may be applied generally to film interpretation, or it may be employed in the definition of a particular category of films. Thus, on one level the concept political pertains to the process of interpretation of any film, and on another level the term political defines films that form a polyphonic heterogeneous patchwork of works variously described as "social problem films," "resistance films," "revolutionary films," "ideological films," etc., depending on the intention and focus of the film researcher. In employing the term political in relation to film, the film researcher ideally should indicate in which sense the word political is being used. This would save theoreticians from the inconvenience of Swift's Laputans, whose method of communication involves the physical display of concrete objects that they have to hold up to each other as a way of talking.

In the interpretive sense, the term political sometimes is used to indicate the radical nature of a new approach to an analysis of any film. The word political is applied to any film interpretation that differs from the interpretation established as a norm at a particular moment in the history of film criticism. "The political" implies contestation and revolt against the given, the existing; in addition, the term indicates a strong declaration of new values in opposition to the old ones.

Two examples of such a use of the term political in relation to film interpretation are those of a radically political (or "resistant") reading of film and the poststructuralist reading. These film readings are considered political from different epistemological perspectives: the first meaning of political signals a radically different interpretation of the film content; the second understanding of the term refers to a description of a radically different film form.

The term political, when used to refer to the interpretation of film content, is often employed in the context of seeing films politically. The politically radical theory that advocates this approach postulates that every film comprises certain ideological values not necessarily detected by an ordinary spectator. What is represented as visible in the dominant discourse is in fact made apparent by the intervention of the dominant ideology that postulates one and only one meaning for the visible constituents of the message. For instance, in his book *Seeing Films Politically*, Mas'ud Zavarzadeh,[1] a practitioner of a politically radical interpretation of films, demonstrates how a film's aesthetic impact conceals the ideological effects resulting from viewing films, especially the creation of the spectator as a subject of a particular social order. In this sense, films are read not as "aesthetic acts but as modes of cultural exchange that form (desired) social subjectivities."[2] Films, even the most trivial of films, constitute political spaces that "contest or naturalize the primacy of those subjectivities necessary to the status quo and suppress or privilege oppositional ones."[3] Zavarzadeh postulates that a dominant ideology is immanent in every film, and helps to establish an epistemological relation between the spectator (the subject) and the world. Through such relationships, the discourse of the dominant ideology creates meaning for the film's viewer. As Andrew Sarris had already stated without the methodological conceptualizations of radical politics:

> it can be argued that all films are ultimately political either as statements or as evasions. It is widely realized that films in general reflect the currents and attitudes in a society and its politics. The cinema does not exist in a sublime state of innocence, untouched by the world; it also has a political content, whether conscious or unconscious, hidden or overt.[4]

In this approach the viewer's interest is not so much in the film's aesthetics but in its politics: why do these films mean what they are supposed to mean in a particular cultural and historical context? Zavarzadeh, for instance, instead of focusing on the formal aspects of the film, concentrates on "the ideological conditions of the possibility of the formal, and chooses one specific site of the film to inquire into the way that film produces the kind of reality that is supportive of the existing socioeconomic arrangements."[5] In his analysis of "trivial" films such as *Desperately Seeking Susan*, *Terms of Endearment*, and others, he constantly constructs the tale of the films (the way that a film offers a narrative), which basically confirms that the ideological position of the films solidly remains within the dominant ideology of the ruling class. Seeing films, according to this theoretician, is part of the political struggle over cultural intelligibilities, subjectivities, and representations.

As Furhammar and Issakson[6] contend, such films serve the purposes of the government itself, propagating its views and reinforcing the values the government endorses. These "hidden propaganda films" (the term used by these theoreticians) are conspicuously political in that they propagate the values of the officially sanctioned status quo. They describe hidden propaganda in the following way:

> Hidden propaganda takes many forms. Every society which is built on a reasonably firm and homogeneous set of values, strives to reinforce and maintain them through times of change. Social outlooks and standards are passed on in upbringing and education, but attitudes can also be conveyed and implanted in ways which are more unsystematic and less intentional – for instance, through the various forms of entertainment. Here, myths and values are not

presented as such but camouflaged and, going unnoticed, are taken as self-evident and indisputable…. It is an active process of reinforcement: we watch the realization of our values in escapist drama with a sense of unreflecting emotional satisfaction. On the other hand, influences which openly conflict with established values are easily distinguished and rejected. Our defense mechanisms against experiences which run counter to our accepted ideas and attitudes are extraordinarily efficient; we safeguard our values as fiercely as if they were part of ourselves.[7]

Another kind of a political struggle is evident in a political reading of film often called the "ethical," which stresses the sovereignty of the subject. In this understanding of the word political, the subject behaves as a resisting agent while the dominance of the prevailing social order is not given most consideration (Barthes, 1975; De Lauretis, 1984; Foucault, 1980, 1988; Deleuze and Guatarri, 1983, 1987; Lyotard, 1988; Silverman, 1988). In this political reading "resistance," in Foucault's words, is situated everywhere in all the activities of producing and viewing film, from the aesthetic counterforces within the filmic text itself to the refusal of the spectator to support the subject positions offered by the film. This position has been especially strongly postulated in establishing the site of cinematic pleasure, particularly in works dealing with the theory of the "desire" of the spectator and its role in the formation of the subject. Radical theorists such as Laura Mulvey, who in the well-known article "Visual Pleasure and Narrative Cinema" (1975),[8] theorized cinematic pleasure from the feminist point of view, have seen the cinema mainly in patriarchal terms, as a political apparatus which subjugates the female body and presents it as a fetishized object of a pleasureful male gaze. The term political in this sense refers to the political strategy in which the functioning of desire is evoked for emancipatory practices: to critique the oppressive practices of mainstream cinema.

These examples of a political, interpretive analysis of film have to be dissociated from the notion of "the political" put forth by poststructuralism with regard to the interpretation of film structure. The poststructuralist sense of political refers to the film's discursive self-awareness, "a self-reflexivity that renders the 'meaning' of a text an 'undecidable' and contingent effect of the rhetorical tensions between containment and excess."[9] In poststructuralist film theory, ideology is a synonym for unproblematized representation and has very little to do with the radical notion of politics as diverse semantic practices serving class interests. In this reading, deconstructing the logic of representation is interpreted as being political. For instance, the films in which the continuity editing that marks the classic Hollywood film is subverted (so that the material discontinuity of the film is displayed as a means for showing the arbitrary connection of the signifier with the signified) are considered to be made politically, without necessarily displaying a political content by challenging or supporting the status quo in society. In this understanding of the word political, avant-garde and experimental films can be considered political because they subvert or transform classical film form.

The notion of the political in these radical readings of film would imply subversion of popular or widely accepted methods of film interpretation on the one hand, and subversion of the methods of film construction on the other. In other words, these two senses of the word political imply resistance or opposition to dominant ideologies in film content and film structure (for instance, the dictates of the capitalist market influencing the narrative form of mainstream Hollywood cinema).[10]

The concepts of "opposition to" and "resistance," in addition to a strong statement in favor of new values, lie at the basis of the political concept when it is applied to films with explicitly political subject matter. In a film that reveals political content or, in other words, which presents the political discourse explicitly, the dominant ideology may be challenged but it also may be reinforced. In opposition films, the dominant ideology is confronted more or less openly, its postulates are questioned, and the wrongdoing of the ruling class is exposed. In propaganda films that reinforce the dominant ideology, however, the currently dominant ideology or new emerging ideologies are presented in a positive light, openly praised and venerated. John Grierson's classic definition, "Propaganda is the art of public persuasion"[11] does justice to the concept of propaganda but also explains its political power.

As far as the political film as a category is concerned, in the theoretical treatises on film published so far there seems to be no consistent line of reasoning or mode of thinking regarding the definition of political film. The political film is alternatively called "confrontation cinema" by Lester Friedman, "social problem film" by Peter Roffman and Jim Purdy, and "ideological film" by Peter Rollins.[12] Other films, such as those produced in the Soviet Union of the 1920s, or those produced in Latin America, are referred to as being political because they have served as overt tools of revolution.[13]

The situation is similarly ambiguous when we consider the formal features characterizing political films. In fact, there seem to be none that specifically determine whether a film belongs to a possible film category called "political film." Neither can "political film" be considered a separate film genre. In film criticism, a genre is usually defined as a category or group of films about the same subject or marked by the same style, for example, gangster, war, science fiction, horror, or westerns. Films in the same genre tend to look alike and observe certain conventions, although there are exceptions to both rules even in classic Hollywood cinema. Why have not political films been widely recognized as a genre? One of the reasons is that as a group these films lack internal consistency. Although many films center on politics or social problems, the forms of these pictures vary widely, from comedy to melodrama.

As this brief discussion reveals, the challenge or reinforcement of the dominant ideology is characteristic of both the level of analysis that refers to the interpretation of any film and that which turns political film into a category. After all, the poststructuralist interpretation of film was also considered political at a certain time; its basic principles were considered threatening to the dominant ideology which, in the Western world, also implies male supremacy and heterosexual exclusivity. That is why on both levels of analysis we are speaking about "politically correct" or "politically incorrect" film interpretations and "politically correct" or "politically incorrect" films with political content. The word "correct" signifies acceptance or lack of acceptance by the dominant ideologies, depending on the perspective of the word's user.

There is, however, one additional category of political film that has not yet been discussed in this brief introduction. I would call this particular category audience-created political film. The entry of films under this heading would depend entirely upon an audience's disposition toward them. The film may be considered political not because a politically important historical event is presented on the screen but because the audience decides that the whole film or some of its aspects should be interpreted as political. In other words, at a particular point in time the audience decides that a film is "hot" in terms of the political message it transmits. Several years later its political aura slowly disappears, giving way to the core value of the film, that is, whether it is a good cinematic story. Moreover, the film may have done political work in the past, but its political value vanishes soon after the completion of the political task and no longer provides an alibi for aesthetic weakness. The film *Man of Iron* which is discussed in this book, is an example of a politically powerful film hastily produced and edited for political reasons, and thus very uneven in form. Several years after its production, the film lost its political appeal and was dismissed as a propagandistic attempt on the part of Wajda to publicize the Solidarity movement. In this case the political power of the film lay specifically in the discursive relationship with the spectator.

In the case of films interpreted as political by the audience, the concept of "the political" seems to be an empty vessel that is filled with semantic substance by audiences at a particular moment of film viewing. The act of negotiating the film's meaning becomes a continual process of accommodating and rejecting different ideological positions presented, not a process of instruction. The film does not inform the audience about how to make sense of the global reality of the culture, or how to fit together the details of reality to compose a coherent model of relations through which, as radical politics suggests, an all-encompassing picture of the real emerges.[14] The word political in this context is understood within its historical and material grounding, within what Bakhtin referred to as "the power of the word to mean."[15] This power evolves from concrete situational and ideological contexts, that is, from a position of enunciation that reflects time, place, and ideological values. The concept of "the political" is constituted in a language in which, as Bakhtin points out there have never been "'neutral' words and forms – words and forms that can belong to 'no one'; language has been completely taken over, shot through with intentions and accents."[16]

The contextual understanding of the idea of "the political," when grounded in the historical and sociological setting, is the aspect that mostly interests me in relation to Wajda's films. This negotiated, audience-dependent, communicative aspect of "the political" in his films binds the notion to Bakhtin's understanding of language as a contextualized, arbitrated phenomenon, the meaning of which is derived from various contexts, both those of the utterance's producers and its receivers. This notion originates from the Marxist view of language as a social phenomenon. In *The German Ideology*, Marx and Engels write that "language is the immediate actuality of thought"[17] and they point out that the empiricism of the world out there is mediated through language, which is itself a historical product. The notion of the intelligibility of the sign as the site of social contestation is further discussed in

Marxism and the Philosophy of Language by Volosinov,[18] whom many Bakhtinians regard as Bakhtin's disciple.

The notion of film as an act of communication implies that a film is a text written in a specific cinematic language and conveying a certain ideological message, while an act of film viewing is an act of communication. Consequently, the interpretation of a film relies on its audience, which is inscribed within a tangible, sociohistorical context. The interpretation of a political film thus situates its protocols within a broader historical inquiry. The process of interpretation of a film with a political message is reminiscent of a historical poetics introduced by David Bordwell in *Making Meaning: Inference and Rhetoric in the Interpretation of Cinema*,[19] not of the symptomatic or schematic interpretation that he so scrupulously analyzes in this influential book on film interpretation. According to Bordwell's explanation, what was political thirty years ago is no longer considered political today, but becomes, instead, a historical representation of power structures and ideological apparatuses frozen in a specific time and space. While analyzing a film produced in the past, one refers to a specific historical time and space and recreates the dialogue between the audience and the way the messages on the screen were presented in a political way in that particular time. The next step in the film's interpretation concerns the process of re-interpreting or finding inferences and possible explications of the discourse from the past by the audiences of the present. In this way, the process of film interpretation concentrates on the function of the film in a particular time as a vehicle of a political message. The historical poetics of film analysis accounts for the responses of audiences situated in different times and different historical and social spaces so that the final film meaning emerges as a polyphony of various historical voices. In this manner I will pursue the interpretation of Wajda's films. Historical discourse, a broad social and cultural contextualization, and, finally, a dialogue with the audience will illuminate the nature of Wajda's films as political.

The Concept of "the Political" in Andrzej Wajda's Films

Andrzej Wajda is a representative of Eastern European cinema, which has always depicted a highly politicized life in both its social and cultural aspects. In Eastern Europe, where ideological positions, political situations, and the whole sociohistorical context of viewing films changes every five or six years with new historical developments, the evaluation of any film as politically important depends greatly on the context of viewing. As the discussion of three of Wajda's films will show, such an interactive understanding of political has to inform my discussion of the three films. In all of them, a specific relationship is established between the film's message and the audience. My analysis will show how this relationship is played out and how the concept of "the political" is revealed in different contexts of interpretation. It appears that these films are political by virtue of the fact that they provoke a multiplicity of reactions on the part of the audience. The audience reacts to various aspects of the political discourse that is more or less explicitly presented in the films, and engages in its own discursive practice by either criticizing the director or approving of his presentation.

Following our introductory discussion of the political film along the Marxist line, it would seem initially that the three films discussed in this book, *Man of Marble, Man of Iron,* and *Danton,* observe the Marxist interpretation of political in that they present an opposition to the dominating ideology but also propagate an ideology of the dominated in an aggressive way. At first glance, these films represent what Andrew Sarris bluntly summarizes as a kind of political film in which "it is almost invariably People against Them."[20] In this sense of the political film, *Man of Iron* openly attacks the government for its totalitarian practices, criticizes the society for its consent to such practices, and sympathizes with the part of society that dared to oppose the dictatorship. Before this film arrived with its openly antagonistic stance, political film in Poland was represented by "the school of moral concern," which dared discuss only social problems, and to only indirectly criticize the government and its policy.[21] *Man of Marble,* another film that I feature in my analysis, initiated this trend. This film criticizes the dominant ideology in a less aggressive way than the later *Man of Iron,* but it has been considered by the general public and film historians as the most powerful Polish political film of the 1970s. *Danton,* by way of contrast, which was produced during martial law in Poland, symbolically refers to the general issues of power, and questions the discourses of the dominating and of the dominated.

Beside this obvious interpretation of the three films, it seems that "the political" manifests itself in a more complex manner. The audiences question the presentation of this openly political discourse from several angles. The following points are especially problematic. First, Marx's concepts of dominant ideology, class, and political system do not entirely explain the issue of the political in the films of Andrzej Wajda. In fact, Wajda's films do not question the political system itself nor the economic relations in Poland, but rather the practices of the Communist party apparatus and government members. In an analysis of Wajda's films as being political, Marx's concept of dominant ideology would have to be replaced by Foucault's notions of the "dominating" and the "dominated," and a fluctuating, discursive concept of power.[22] The ambiguous social relations in Poland are actually characterized by both the victims of the system and its executors, on occasions remaining within the same ruling class.[23] Consequently, opposition to the dominant ideology would have to give way to opposition to the dominating power residing within the same social class as the dominated.

In Foucault's postmodern interpretation of power, class as a separate entity is eliminated, while dominated and dominating coexist on the plane of the social as entities with movable and changing boundaries. John Fiske sums up the retreat from "class" in this postmodern social theory in the following way: "One of the many debts we owe to Foucault is his insistence that power relations cannot be adequately explained by class relations, that power is discursive and is to be understood in the specific contexts of its exercise, not in generalized social structures."[24] Foucault's interpretation of power relations accurately defines the political films of Andrzej Wajda in that Wajda basically questions a system of domination created within social structures by the party *nomenklatura* and members of the government.

The second problematic issue concerns the moral position of Wajda as a political filmmaker. In *Man of Marble* and *Man of Iron*, political opposition directly addresses the system of domination through the images of Wajda who, nevertheless, remains a convinced socialist at heart. In this sense Wajda's films are "political" because they reveal this internal contradiction: Wajda contradicts the wrongdoings of those in power while he remains inscribed in the very same political system. This issue is dealt with in detail in the chapter devoted to the analysis of historical discourse in *Man of Iron*.

The third problematic issue concerning the realization of "the political" in Wajda's films refers to the manner of the presentation of his political message. While criticizing old ideologies, Wajda propagates new, competitive ideologies in a politically aggressive way. In order to contravene the ideology of the dominating, Wajda presents a counterideology, that of the dominated, which he conspicuously dresses in propagandist garb. In this way, Wajda's films become political in the propagandist sense in that they communicate the set of values established and sanctioned by the ideology of the dominated. The rival ideology is not necessarily different from the dominant ideology in its principles, but it stresses its idealistic components. The propagandist elements in Wajda's films severely criticize the negative elements in the execution of power by the dominating while praising the positive elements of the dominated. Especially in *Man of Iron* Wajda openly uses most of the obvious elements of propaganda: glorification of the victims of the political system; condemnation of the authorities; the revival of mythical or religious beliefs; supersession of reality; direct address to the audience; and a black-and-white characterization of the protagonists, among others. These cinematic devices help convince the viewer of the legitimacy of the claims by the dominated, but because of their blatant propagandistic value they produce a contrary effect in audiences grown tired of the overt propaganda of Eastern European films. Thereupon, everything about this film is questioned by the public: Wajda's intentions, his version of events, his suspicious manipulation of the documentary material, his haste in film production. All these elements, of text and reception of text, contribute to the understanding or misunderstanding of the political intentions of the film director.

At this moment, it is necessary to point out that the three films discussed in this book are not the only political films which Wajda has produced. Other films, such as *Landscape After Battle* (1970) or *Rough Treatment* (1978), also can be called political, as is the case for almost all his films, with the exception of several comedies. The reason why I chose these three films is that they best represent the interactive and polemical aspect of the political in Wajda's films, and they are bound by a specific historical condition: the rise and development of the Solidarity movement.

The polemical aspect of the political is displayed in these films in three different ways. *Man of Marble* presents the reality in Poland in a slightly camouflaged way since the political situation in the 1970s did not allow for complete openness in the presentation of political facts. The audience must negotiate the meanings with what they know or are familiar with. *Man of Iron* is much bolder in the presentation of historical facts. Nevertheless, the reactions of the audience do not deal with the facts depicted on the screen, but with the modes of presentation and the intentions of the director. *Danton*, on the other hand, is an Aesopian tale that uses the events of the French Revolution as a smoke screen for its deliberations on the essence of revolution and the consequences it brings. The martial law introduced in Poland in 1981 and the historical facts leading to the disbanding of the Solidarity organization after the law's implementation have to be extracted from the historical facts referring to the French Revolution. These manners of presentation signify three different ways in which audiences actively participate in the construction of the films' meanings.

As far as the Solidarity movement is concerned, *Man of Marble* introduces the historical background of the movement by presenting the complicated political and social scene in Poland in the 1970s. The tense situation in Poland at that time erupted in anti-party and anti-government activities that led directly to the birth of the Solidarity organization (with 8 million members in 1980). *Man of Iron* presents the events of the momentous strike in Gdansk that initiated the official beginning of the Solidarity organization. *Danton*, in an Aesopian manner, presents an attempt at incapacitating Solidarity and eliminating it as a source of terror. The theme of Solidarity unites these three films and makes them a consistent whole, both in historical and diegetic[25] terms.

In their form, the political films of Andrzej Wajda constitute a site of contestation and unrest where various beliefs and opinions are openly revealed and challenged. The site of contestation is a collection of rich images that make up Wajda's sumptuous cinematic language. The concatenations of images in his films create distinctive political statements that originated both in Russian filmmaker Sergei Eisenstein's *Battleship Potemkin* (1925) and in the theatrical tradition of the Polish theatre. The language of these films demands an immediate emotional response, and instigates a polemical debate within the spectator.

In the subversion of the ideology of the dominating, Wajda's films, especially *Man of Marble*, use parody, pastiche, and irony. As postmodern film theory states, these are used as devices through which the connection between the signifier and the signified is deferred and the obviousness of established meanings is obscured. In Wajda's films, moreover, the subversion is met by the spectator halfway. The spectator recognizes the necessary referents and laughs because he or she knows what the object of irony is, or what

the filmmaker refers to. This variety of political subversion constitutes an important element of the films' semantic structure.
Although produced in the same country and relating to approximately the same historical period, *Man of Marble* and *Man of Iron* are different in that they present the social and historical contexts deeply inscribed in the Poland of the time of their production. The importance of society and history in meaning formation also explains the enunciative power of *Danton*, which relates the historical events of the French Revolution. All three films provoke a dialectical formation of meanings where the semantic synthesis is produced somewhere between the films' thesis and the spectators' antithesis. This dialectical formation of meaning and the inscription of the reader in the meaning formation in a political film would require a specific interpretive apparatus. A possible concept, an interpretive procedure, an interpretive device, could be brought to life by Bakhtin's theory of dialogism, which incorporates the indispensability of the reader/spectator to meaning formation. Bakhtin's understanding of language, inscribed in the class struggle, would provide an interpretive procedure accounting for the images on the screen in the sense of Bakhtin's "words," permeated by the historical and the social.

Bakhtin's Dialogism as an Interpretive Procedure

Bakhtin's dialogism provides us with the means to discuss film meaning as the consequence of an interaction between film texts and readers' responses to them in a broad historical and cultural context. In the following discussion I will try to use Bakhtin in order to do something that has not been done in film scholarship: to provide an analysis of the dialogical relations within the images of the political film of Andrzej Wajda, and to propose that the final interpretation of the images arises from a process of negotiation involving the spectator.

This kind of analysis has already been proposed by Lynn J. Shakinovsky, not for film, but for the poetry of Emily Dickinson.[26] As Holquist noted in his remarks about Shakinovsky's article, "Bakhtin is in fact being invoked not so much as a source of particular ideas that will advance a broader understanding of Emily Dickinson, but as a skeleton key opening the door to a set of connections that otherwise would have remained closed."[27] As in Shakinovsky's work, Bakhtin's dialogism is used here as an interpretive procedure and a mode of thinking, not as a concise and complete theory, which Bakhtin never intended for it to become anyway. By Bakhtin's model I do not mean a schematic super-structure of his writing alone, but also of the writings of the main members of his group, P.N. Medvedev and V.N. Volosinov. Some interesting additions and interpretations related to Bakhtin's notion of dialogism that made it possible to apply this concept to other fields of research also are quoted when needed.[28] Bakhtin's dialog-ism functions in this book as a gate opening onto new horizons and new possibilities in the interpretation of a work of art. In my opinion, the political films of Andrzej Wajda especially correspond to Bakhtin's understanding of language as an argumentative entity, a phenomenon which is meaningful only in relationship, only in the context of someone talking to someone else, even when that someone else is one's own inner addressee.

Bakhtin has inspired not only literary but also film and art criti-cism with his stimulating concepts of the carnivalesque, dialogism, and polyphony, among others. In the twentieth century, literary criticism has tended to become polarized between Saussure's abstract system of language on one hand, resulting in a conception of literature as a self-contained system,[29] and a Marxist sociologi-cal approach on the other. The synthesis of these poles that Bakh-tin attempted and the concept of dialogue in his works have posed a dilemma for a number of scholars working on a reevaluation of Bakhtin. The most important aspect of Bakhtin's model of analy-sis lies in his treatment of language as the center of the study of lit-erary discourse. His linguistic model is not a conventional one, however. Bakhtin argues in *Problems of Dostoevsky's Poetics*[30] that the analysis of discourse should be based not so much on linguis-tics as on "metalinguistics," which studies the word neither within the system of language nor within a "text" that is removed from dialogical intercourse, but within the sphere of the genuine life of the word. It is the word itself that Bakhtin profoundly redefines and attempts to infuse with its original Greek sense of *logos* as dis-course,[31] speech or reason. Language is understood by Bakhtin as a battle in the sense of an opposition and struggle at the heart of existence. His understanding of language does not imply system-aticity, but rather a process of constant creation and recreation of meaning. Language is a living, volatile entity, always dialogized and pulsating with rich, contradictory lives. Bakhtin postulates in *The Dialogic Imagination*, "The linguistic significance of a given utterance is understood against the background of language, while its actual meaning is understood against other concrete utterances on the same theme, a background made up of contradictory opinions, points of view, and value judgements ..."[32] This approach binds Bakhtin to the Marxist postulate that language is a social phenomenon. Marx and Engels write, "language is practical, real consciousness that exists for other men as well and only therefore does it exist for me; language like consciousness, only arises from the need, the necessity of social intercourse with other men."[33] In other words, Marx and Engels situate intelligibility in the social as a site of restlessness and semantic agitation. For Marx, the sign (intelligibility) is the scene of semiotic stirrings because it is the site of class struggle, the space where various social groups attempt to contest the established and assigned meanings of the sign.

While readily acknowledging the need to study "the specific object of linguistics, something arrived at through a completely legitimate and necessary abstraction from various aspects of the concrete life of the word,"[34] Bakhtin argued for the need to create an alternative approach that would incorporate a concern with how utterances and the voices producing them are organized in their sociocultural context. Bakhtin's original understanding of language as a set of utterances – a living, volatile entity – required a definition of the relation of movement between utterances and within them; this movement would mold utterances and semantically restructure them in a constant flux of ideas. Dialogue, dialogism, dialogicality, etc., were the terms that Bakhtin used to express this.

The very term dialogism has generated multiple interpretations and transpositions of its semantic and connotative content into the areas of literature. Krysinski notices the interesting fact that Bakhtin never really defines dialogue,[35] but creates a sort of "semantic field" around the notion of dialogism.[36] Krysinski sees Bakhtin's dialogism as a "convergence" toward the undefined notion of dialogue that is realized as a semantic field of such concepts as "dialogicity," "dialogical activity," "Socratic dialogue," "great dialogue," "dialogical attitude," and so on.

As Robert Stam explains in his introductory remarks to the chapter "From Dialogism to Zelig" in his book *Subversive Pleasures: Bakhtin, Cultural Criticism and Film*, Bakhtin's dialogism consists not in the passive meeting of two voices, but in the fact that every utterance is emitted in anticipation of the discourse of an interlocutor.[37] In Bakhtin:

a word, discourse, language or culture undergoes "dialogization" when it becomes relativized, de-privileged, aware of competing definitions for the same things. Undialogized language is authoritative or absolute ... Dialogism is the characteristic epistemological mode of a world dominated by heteroglossia. Everything means, is understood as a part of a greater whole – there is a constant interaction between meanings, all of which have the potential of conditioning others. Which will affect the other, how it will do so and in what degree is what is actually settled at the moment of utterance.[38]

Wertsch proposes a way of capturing and applying this theoretical perspective in concrete cases in the form of what he terms the Bakhtinian question. This question is: who is doing the talking? The pervasiveness of dialogicality in Bakhtin's view means that the answer will inevitably identify at least two voices. For example, in the case of parody, which was one of the phenomena discussed by Bakhtin in the context of dialogicality or multivoicedness that interested Bakhtin, the effect derives from the fact that two voices, speaking simultaneously, are discernible. On the one hand, the speaking consciousness producing the concrete parodic utterance is obviously speaking; on the other hand, it is only by populating, or appropriating the utterance of another, that parody comes into being. Hence the phenomenon is inherently multivoiced.[39]

Dialogical discourse has to be understood in opposition to monological discourse, which is single, unitary, fixed, finalized, univocal. It is the discourse of the single subject, the discourse of "definition, truth, denotation, logical analysis."[40] In the epic, for example, discourse is monological since it possesses no "dialogue of language" and since the narration remains "limited by the narrator's absolute point of view."[41] Dialogical discourse, on the other hand, is polyvalent, multidetermined, and multivocal. In contrast to the unity of vision implicit in monological discourse, the dialogical discourse is composed of "distances, relationships, analogies, and non-exclusive oppositions ..."[42] Dialogical discourse, emphasizing the double aspects of language and indeterminacy of reference, concerns itself with the tensions between multiple viewpoints, several narratives; it is a discourse in which "language parodies and relativises itself."[43]

McClellan stresses this twofold relation in his article, "The Dialogic Other: Bakhtin's Theory of Rhetoric."[44] As he notes:

> Nowhere is the rhetorical genealogy and basis of Bakhtin's discourse theory more evident than in his concept of dialogism ...

In double-voiced discourse the intentional movement is directed towards an object of reference and also another's utterance. In comparison, monologic discourse is oriented primarily towards a referential object and contains only a single, dominating intention.[45]

McClellan later elaborates on the theme by introducing the term semantic intention, which differs depending on the type of discourse, whether monological or dialogical. In the monological discourse, "even if it incorporates another's utterance – such as in direct quotation – this second utterance is completely subsumed under a single overriding intention,"[46] while the dialogical discourse has two semantic intentions or two voices residing and conflicting within the verbal utterance. In the dialogical discourse the authorial 'voice' infiltrates the original utterance from within; the two different voices or intentions cohabiting in the utterance may affect each other but neither obliterates nor subsumes the other.

Anne Herrman adds to the general explication of Bakhtin, according to which he distinguishes among at least five different types of dialogic relationship. Double-voiced discourse arises between individual words "if that word is perceived ... as a sign of someone else's semantic position, as the representative of another person's utterance; that is, if we hear it in someone else's voice."[47] It also arises between whole utterances, between language styles or social dialects, in relation to aspects of one's own previous utterance, and among different semiotic phenomena such as images belonging to different art forms.

A concept closely linked to dialogism and indispensable to its understanding is the idea of polyphony,[48] which roughly means the simultaneous existence of parallel discourses within one text, within the *logos* of a character, or even within a single word. Polyphony accounts for the hybridization of artistic images or words, which, to Bakhtin, present a mingling of one's own word with that of the other. This globalization of the dialogic sees every text as a polyphonous structure of cultures, languages, and ideological positions.

Polyphony (or heteroglossia) also refers to the shifting stratifications of language into class dialects, professional jargons (lawyers, doctors, academics), generic discourse (melodrama, comedy), bureaucratic lingos, popular slangs, along with all the other specific languages generated by cultural praxis. The languages composing heteroglossia represent "bounded verbal-ideological belief systems," points of view on the world, forms for conceptualizing social experience, each marked by its own tonalities, meanings, and values. The role of the artistic text, be it a novel, a play or a film, is not to represent real life "existents" but to stage the conflicts inherent in heteroglossia, the coincidences and competitions of languages and discourses.

Beside the concept of dialogism or the dialogic, Bakhtin introduced numerous other concepts and ideas that in their unpolished and intuitively formulated manner anticipated major poststructuralist themes: the denial of univocal meaning, the infinite spiral of interpretation, the unstable identity of the sign, the positioning of the subject by discourse, the untenable nature of inside/outside oppositions, and the pervasive presence of polyphony. In this way, Bakhtin's work anticipated the discourse of the art of postmodernism.

Bakhtin's contribution to the analysis of the literary text lies specifically in the fact that he considered the social, or interactive, factor as the most important element in the construction of meaning. This particular approach was later employed in so called "political criticism"[49] on the one hand, and linguistic pragmatics (pragmatics of discourse) on the other.[50] In both approaches, although taken from different methodological perspectives, the interlocutor, the reader, the audience or, in general, the recipient of the message plays an important part in the construction of meaning.

The importance of participants' interaction is also stressed by Volosinov,[51] Bakhtin's disciple, the pioneer of pragmalinguistics, whose works are considered by some researchers to have been written by Bakhtin himself.[52] Volosinov states that the functioning of any human society is deeply rooted in the mutual activities of individuals, described as social intercourse or social communication. Understanding the text becomes a pragmatic process, which, according to Volosinov, implies that, "To understand another person's utterance means to orient oneself with respect to it, to find some proper place for it in the corresponding context ... Therefore, there is no reason for saying that meaning belongs to a word as such. In essence, meaning belongs to a word in its position between speakers; that is, meaning is realized in the process of active, responsive understanding ..."[53]

Bakhtin's dialogism seems, then, to correspond to the basic concepts of pragmatics of discourse. In an elementary sense, pragmatics deals with the conditions of linguistic communication in terms of interactive relations between the sender, the receiver, the message, and the context. According to this definition, the sender is someone who sends the message, the receiver is someone who receives it, the message itself exists as a discrete, clearly defined object, and the context is a separate entity that conditions both the act of sending the message and its reception. The nature of the pragmatic relationship established between sender, receiver, message, and context is so rigid that it does not allow for any fluidity of semantic movement among the four components of the communication event.

Bakhtin's dialogism, on the other hand, seems to transcend the concept of a pragmatic understanding of the act of communication as something that occurs between the sender of the message and its receiver under the clearly defined conditions of the communication act. In Bakhtin's theory, the four concepts interact in a global process of dialogic struggle, which is more metaphorical and symbolic than a pragmatics of discourse dealing only with the real participants of the communication act. For instance, in Bakhtin, every utterance recalls earlier contexts[54] of usage, without which it could not mean anything at all. However, these contexts of usage are internalized in the utterance itself, and do not exist as independent constructs, as pragmatics of discourse proposes.

It would seem that, as in the pragmatic understanding of the speech act, for Bakhtin, the speaking subject, or author of the utterance, interacts with another speaking subject, or receiver of the utterance. Nonetheless, the Bakhtinian text as utterance has to be understood as existing on the boundary between two consciousnesses, not resulting from the actual communication between subjects, as it does in pragmatics. It seems suspended between the two while also reflecting other texts and interconnections in a multiplicity of ideas. While pragmatics deals with specific, natural language utterances, Bakhtin treats literature as an utterance, a discourse in action, which engages two consciousnesses (that of the writer/speaker and that of reader/listener) in active understanding. Although the dialogical nature of Bakhtin's word (*logos*) can be compared to a pragmatic understanding of the communication act with its sender, receiver, message, and context, Bakhtin's model seems to extend the concept of the communication act beyond the rigorous perception of it as existing in a single speech situation.

In Bakhtin, any utterance (text) is a link in a far-reaching chain of communication. Texts treated as utterances enact addressivity, awareness of the otherness of language in general and the otherness of given dialogic patterns in particular. Similar to pragmatics, they involve particular people in actual social and historical situations. But they treat their addressees as implicit objects immanent in the text, not existing outside the message, where pragmatics places them. Despite the differences between pragmatics and dialogism I would argue that Bakhtin unknowingly anticipated the extremely important role pragmatics assigns to response, an approach later employed by practitioners of the pragmatically-oriented spectatorship theory.[55] As Bakhtin insists:

> In the actual life of speech, every concrete act of understanding is active: it assimilates the word to be understood into its own conceptual system filled with specific objects and emotional expressions, and is indissolubly merged with the response, with a motivated agreement or disagreement.
> Therefore [the speaker's] orientation toward the listener is an orientation toward a specific conceptual horizon, toward the specific world of the listener; it introduces totally new elements into his discourse; it is in this way, after all, that various different points of view, conceptual horizons, systems for providing expressive accents, various social "languages" come to interact with one another.[56]

Krysinski also notes the similarity of Bakhtin's concepts to pragmatics. The following criteria for dialogue in Bakhtin's theory, as summarized by Krysinski, resemble the pragmatic foursome of sender, receiver, message, and context:

1. The alternation of two opposed roles: that of the speaking subject and that of the hearing subject ...
2. The construction of a communicative act as a situation in which two interlocutors participate ...
3. The interpenetrability of the two opposed worlds ...[57]

As Krysinski mentions, there can be a fourth feature added at this point, namely that "there should be a common elaboration of the code which the two speakers should share."[58] These four conditions are similar to the pragmatic conditions of a speech act. The first condition predicts the existence of participants of the communication exchange in a speech act, the second presupposes formation of the speech act itself, the third predicts the existence of felicity conditions, and the fourth one prescribes the common set of presuppositions.

Although he lived and worked earlier in the twentieth century, Bakhtin foresaw the major movements of literary and media criticism that occurred only in the second part of the twentieth century.

Moreover, Bakhtin allowed for the revolutionary concept of the reader's inscription in the work of art, and for a variety of relations between the two, in opposition to the rigid unilateral motion from the work of art to its receiver that exists in numerous approaches to reception proposed by Western researchers of the twentieth century such as Gibson, Eco, Riffaterre, Brooke-Rose, Prince, Culler, Holland, Fish, Jauss,[59] and others[60] who have lived and worked after Bakhtin's death. When Bakhtin's works finally reached the world of literary and philosophical research, contemporary literary theoreticians realized that the Russian scholar had already introduced the concepts of audiences, context, cultural and historical background, and pragmatics, though he never used these terms. Inventing names and providing a more rigorous scholarly shape for these concepts was to be accomplished by other scholars who came well after Bakhtin.

Dialogism and Film

Although the application of Bakhtin to film studies has been criticized or treated with distrust by orthodox Bakhtinians,[61] there have appeared on the academic scene a number of film theoreticians who have carefully grappled with the application of Bakhtin to film.[62] Critics of this application of Bakhtin to film analysis have postulated that film is a different means of enunciation than natural language, and that Bakhtin's concepts cannot be automatically transferred from the latter to the former. Also, Bakhtin and his revolutionary concepts always have to be seen within the Russian tradition and the philosophical tradition from which they emerged.[63] Contrary to the opinions voiced by those critics opposed to the use of Bakhtinian theory in film analysis, almost all of the Russian's concepts and ideas proved to be broad and explanatory enough to find application to film. So far, the most consistent analysis of film in the light of Bakhtin's theory has been presented by Robert Stam in his book *Subversive Pleasures: Bakhtin, Cultural Criticism and Film*.[64]

According to Stam, Bakhtin's approach seems to have a built-in place for film, since Bakhtin sees verbal language as part of a continuum of forms of semiosis that share a common logic. Purely linguistic definitions of an artistic language and its elements, Bakhtin suggests in "The Problem of the Text," can serve only as "initial terms for description," for what is most important "is not described by them and does not reside within them."[65] I agree with Stam here that if the cinesemiologists in the Franco-Italian tradition had known Bakhtin earlier, they would never have concentrated on the *langue* as a possible linguistic equivalent for film, but rather on *parole*, which is totally utterance-oriented. After all, "it is not phonemes and morphemes that enter dialogism, but utterances, and it is as utterance that the cinematic "word" acquires relation to the spectator and to life."[66]

In his book, Stam elaborates on the relevance of Bakhtin to cultural and mass-media critiques and shows how Bakhtinian conceptualizations can help analyze, teach and generate mass-mediated culture. The rightness of a Bakhtinian approach to film derives, Stam suggests, basically from the fact that Bakhtin's method allows for crossing the boundaries between various fields and disciplines. His dialogical style of analysis applies both to the center and to the borders of academic disciplines. Moreover, film as a medium seems to originate from the popular culture and the erudite culture as well, while it combines all the developments in literary theory and criticism, together with their new and often radical methodologies. Stam recapitulates finally that in view of all these developments "the encounter of Bakhtin with film might be viewed as virtually inevitable,"[67] a view that I share completely with Stam, and that I will try to explicate in this study.

In his book, Stam speaks not only about the critical use-value of "carnival" in the cinema, but also of other Bakhtinian concepts – his "politicized vision of language as pervaded by dialogism (i.e., the transindividual generation of meaning), heteroglossia (the interanimation of the diverse languages generated by sexual, racial, economic, and generational difference), and tact (the ensemble of codes governing discursive interaction)."[68] While chapter 1, "Translinguistics and Semiotics" stresses film as language, chapter 2, "Language, Difference and Power," addresses language in film, specifically the ways in which Bakhtin's non-unitary approach can help illuminate the impact of language difference (polyglossia and heteroglossia) on the cinema in terms of such issues as translation, postsynchronization, subtitles, and the like.

Chapters 3 and 4 of the book deal with diverse aspects of the Bakhtinian notion of carnival. In chapter 5, "The Grotesque Body and Cinematic Eroticism," Stam draws out the implications of Bakhtin's corporeal semiotic for an analysis of cinematic eroticism, emphasizing its potential for enabling both a critique and a transvaluation of pornography. In chapter 6, "From Dialogism to *Zelig*," Stam extensively discusses the concept of dialogism as applied to the analysis of rap music and Woody Allen's film *Zelig*. Mostly, Stam's application of the concept of dialogism refers to the cultural phenomena within the film itself. Stam treats film as another kind of literary fiction where characters take part in a multicultural dialogue. In this chapter, Stam has chosen a specific application of Bakhtinian dialogism to illustrate the presence of multiple cultures in the text of *Zelig*. He makes particular use of Bakhtin's method in explaining *Zelig*'s ideological mobility, cultural multivoicedness and historical complexity in the sociohistorical representation of a Jew. In interpreting *Zelig*'s chameleon personality, Stam applies the Bakhtinian view of the self as "a kind of echo chamber of socially orchestrated voices"[69] operating on several cinematic levels. The images, as well as the musical and linguistic phrases, operate side by side in *Zelig*'s numerous impersonations of the diverse synecdochic cultural figures with whom he comes in contact.

The chapter devoted to dialogism has drawn most of my critical attention and has produced a certain dissatisfaction with Stam's solutions. It is my impression that Stam has stressed mainly the multivoicedness of the film, and not necessarily its dialogic tension or struggle in the accommodation of the opposites that Bakhtin himself postulates in his definition of the dialogic.[70] Stam's analysis emerges as an enumeration of cultural and ideological traces but not as a presentation of the relational attributes of dialogization. Although he notices the potential for a variety of meanings and interpretations among multiple spectators who would, presumably, each interpret the film differently, he does not develop this idea in his analysis. Nor does he feature the pragmatic, communicative angle in Bakhtin's writing, dealing only with the semantic potential inherent in the Bakhtinian understanding of language as a system conveying a multiplicity of meanings.

It could be argued here that one of the reasons for Stam's rejection of (or disregard for) the interactive and dynamic property of dialogization in Zelig is that Stam does not necessarily see this dynamic in the film (or that the film itself does not invite such an interpretation at all). Woody Allen's film could be interpreted as an example of a multiplicity of discourses existing side by side in the film and not involved in any way in an internal struggle. This interpretation would be suggested by the chameleon characteristics of the protagonist Zelig himself, who does not allow for (does not care for) any dialogical tension in the flow of discourses.

Despite these methodological shortcomings, Stam's extensive analysis of *Zelig* is a clear attempt at a comprehensive application of Bakhtin's concept of dialogism to film. In general, his contribution undoubtedly lies in the fact that in *Subversive Pleasures* Stam discovered numerous possibilities for the application of Bakhtin's concepts to film and mass media analysis.

What Stam has also noted is that Bakhtin's concepts of dialogism and polyphony are especially inspiring when we consider the film's textuality itself. Bakhtin's ingenious understanding of the concepts of text and language allows for diverse interpretations of filmic textuality. Thus, based on Bakhtin's methodological approach to the latter, film can be treated in a variety of theoretical ways. One approach is to treat film as text. As Stam notes:

> What Bakhtin offers film theory and analysis is a unitary, transdisciplinary view of the human sciences and of cultural production, based on the identity of their common materials: texts. Bakhtin's broad definition of "text" as referring to all cultural production rooted in language – and for Bakhtin no cultural production exists outside of language – has the effect of breaking down not only the walls between disciplines but also the wall between "text" and "hors-texte."[71]

On the other hand, film is understood as constructed by a complex of signs in Bakhtin's understanding of language as any coherent complex of signs, meaning any communication system employing signs that are ordered in a particular manner, which encompasses everything from literature to visual and aural works of art.[72]

However, film can also be treated as an utterance, the reception of which is conditioned by the interlocutor of the communication event. This kind of approach, which gives credit to the spectator, is especially valued now in the writings of French and British film and media theoreticians, such as Stuart Hall, David Morley, Daniel Dayan,[73] and others. Bakhtin resembles these theoreticians in that he considers interactive discourse as an intrinsic aspect of text. Both the recipients of the discourse, prior discourses, and the author's voice form a polyphony of voices that themselves constitute an artistic situation, an event shared by the author and the reader. As Stam explains, "artistic speech is interlocution, the in-between of text and a reader, whose responsive understanding is sought and anticipated and on whom the text depends for its concretization."[74]

In this, Bakhtin's approach seems to intersect the concerns of the contemporary reception theory of Jauss and Iser and of the "reader response" criticism of Stanley Fish and Norman Holland. Especially Jauss's *Erwartungshorizont* (expectation horizon), the idea that all texts as all interpretations issue from a distinct vantage point but dialogically relate to each other, seems particularly promising for the analysis of historical discourses in films, an area I will deal with in detail in the third chapter of this book.

In the approach that views film as an utterance, the latter is perceived as situated within the pragmatic foursome of sender, receiver, message and context, but all of these elements are situated both within the film text itself, and within the situation of film viewing. Film does not exist in a vacuum, and is not understood as a finite, discrete text, an object as given, a product delineated by the spatial and temporal uniqueness of the act of production, but as a porous body of production and reception that allows for a process of out-and-in in the film utterance. Film is thus seen in the broader perspective of its intertextuality within which it functions as an element of a mosaic of both the producer's and the receiver's presuppositions and assertions.

The notion of the dialogic is pertinent to all the above mentioned concepts of film – film as text, film as a system of signs, and film as utterance. In all cases, Bakhtinian dialogism can be seen as a rewriting of the Saussurean view of language as the diacritical play of difference, a recasting of it as the play of difference within the text with all its others: author, intertext, real and imagined addressees, and the communicative context.[75] The irrevocable meaning (theme) of the film emerges as a final result of this confrontation.

Such an understanding of dialogism will be applied in the analysis of three films by Andrzej Wajda: *Man of Marble, Man of Iron,* and *Danton.* I will postulate that the films reveal multiple aspects of Bakhtin's dialogism. They involve a dialogistic use of cultural and historical events within the film text, and they attain a realization of dialogism in the film form itself. In all of the films the concept of dialogism elucidates a multiplicity of discourses along with the process of merging these discourses with the discourses of the responding audience.

This kind of dialogical understanding of political film necessitates a detailed discussion of, among other things, various contradictory voices in the interpretation of the role of the film director in totalitarian Poland (as in the explanations of the role played by Burski in *Man of Marble*); fighting discourses of truth and honesty as opposed to the discourse of fear and opportunism in the role of the journalist of Gierek's Poland played by Winkiel in *Man of Iron*; and the inner doubts and internal discussions of Robespierre in *Danton*. Moreover, a dialogical understanding of the political films of Andrzej Wajda would clarify the internal, formal tensions within particular films themselves. Perhaps, the stylistic unevenness of Wajda's films could be explained in terms of the dialogical tension within the films' complex aesthetics. After all, it is the combination of an image and sound that enunciates a film. The internal tensions between the two, as well as an attempt to adapt the films' aesthetics to the powerful, historical voices that try to disrupt or burst through the images, creates a dilemma for the artist who attempts to accommodate the historical glossia within the aesthetic requirements of the cinema.

Moreover, in terms of the films' images, understanding the political films of Andrzej Wajda means the negotiation of each of its images, scenes and sequences with the spectator armed with a set of cultural and historical presuppositions. The fundamental essence of cinematic language in the political films of Andrzej Wajda undergoes a transformation in the light of Bakhtin's dialogism. Bakhtin's methodology compels the researcher to consider the films' complex contextualizations and creates the possibility of introducing both politics and culture into film study.

It is worth remembering that the interaction with the audience takes place over the head of censors, an alternative audience which imposes its ruling on the ideological content of the film. The monological imposition of censorship must be counteracted, its scrutiny avoided. The exchange between the spectator and the message of the film negotiates the film's meaning in such a way as to distract the censor's attention. The innuendos and nuances in a political film of this kind, produced in order to deliberately mislead the official censors, would not be comprehensible without the active participation of an audience willing to decipher them; thus the audiences' interpretive reactions are considered the most important factor in the construction of meaning in the political films of Andrzej Wajda. Depending on the spatial and temporal circumstances of the film screening, and on the historical and cultural backgrounds of audiences, the images are transformed on the screen into multiple and varied segments of appreciation and understanding in the process of active reception.

Finally, I would like to point out that there exists one more reason which seems to link Mikhail Bakhtin and Andrzej Wajda. Both of them devoted a period in their lives to the analysis of Fyodor Dostoevsky's works, which the two masters considered the most accomplished achievements in the polyphonic novel and in the presentation of dramatic conflicts in human lives, respectively. Both Bakhtin and Wajda were fascinated by the complexity of Dostoevsky's fictional world, and both tried to unravel this complexity in their written (Bakhtin) and theatrical (Wajda) performances. Bakhtin wrote that:

> Dostoevsky's world is the artistically organized coexistence and interaction of spiritual diversity, not stages in the evolution of a unified spirit. And thus, despite their different hierarchical emphasis, the worlds of the heroes and the planes of the novel, by virtue of the novel's very structure, lie side by side on a plane of coexistence (as do Dante's worlds) and of interaction (not present in Dante's formal polyphony); they are not placed one after the other, as stages of evolution.[76]

Bakhtin analyzed Dostoevsky's work in his most accomplished treatises, such as *The Dialogic Imagination* and *Problems of Dostoevsky's Poetics* while Wajda directed many plays based on Dostoevsky's texts almost from the beginning of his career as a theatre director. Already in 1962 Andrzej Wajda directed an adaptation of Dostoevsky's short story ("Cudza Zona i Maz Pod Lozkiem" [A Different Wife and a Husband Under the Bed]) for a well-established and widely seen television production. In 1971, under his direction, The Old Theatre in Cracow presented an adaptation of Dostoevsky's *The Devils* in a brilliant performance. The same theatre presented a play, *Nastasja Filipowna*, based on Dostoevsky's novel *The Idiot* in 1977. In 1984, the Old Theatre in Cracow presented Dostoevsky's *Crime and Punishment* in another astounding theatrical interpretation by Andrzej Wajda. After directing the play in 1977, Wajda concluded in his conversation with Teresa Krzemien:

> I think that I can understand Dostoevsky better now. And this feeling will stay with me forever. The same feeling you have when you know someone exceptional, regardless of whether you like this someone or hate him.[77]

Notes

1. Mas'ud Zavarzadeh, *Seeing Films Politically* (Albany: State University of New York Press, 1991).
2. Ibid., 5.
3. Ibid.
4. Andrew Sarris, *Politics and Cinema* (New York: Columbia University Press, 1978), 6.
5. The filmic space or story is called by Zavarzadeh the film tale. He states, "This filmic space I have called the tale: the way that a film offers a narrative – and proposes that narrative to be a paradigm of intelligibility – not simply through its immanent formal devices but also by relying on historically dominant and contradictory assumptions about reality." Zavarzadeh, *Seeing Films*, 8.
6. L. Furhammar and F. Isaksson, *Politics and Film*, trans. K. French (New York, Washington: Praeger Publishers, 1971), 245.
7. Ibid.
8. Laura Mulvey, "Visual Pleasure and Narrative Cinema," *Screen* 16, 3 (1975): 6–18.
9. Zavarzadeh, *Seeing Films*, 70.
10. For a detailed discussion of all these positions, see Zavarzadeh, 31–89.
11. Robert Vas, "Sorcerers or Apprentices: Some Aspects of the Propaganda Film," in *Propaganda on Film: A Nation at War*, ed. Richard A. Maynard (Rochelle Park, N. J.: Hayden Book Company, 1975), 7.
12. The political film is called confrontation cinema by Lester Friedman in "The Necessity of Confrontation Cinema: Peter Watkins Interviewed," *Literature/Film Quarterly* 11, no. 4 (1983), 237–48; social problem film by Peter Roffman and Jim Purdy in *The Hollywood Social Problem Film: Madness, Despair, and Politics from the Depression to the Fifties* (Bloomington: Indiana University Press, 1981); or ideological film by Peter C. Rollins in "Ideology and Film Rhetoric: Three Documentaries of the New Deal Era (1936–1941)," in *Hollywood as Historian: American Film in a Cultural Context*, ed. Peter C. Rollins (Lexington, Kentucky: University Press of Kentucky, 1983), 32–48.
13. Argentinian film directors, Fernando Solinas and Octavio Getino, the founders of Cine Liberación in the 1960s, are typical representatives of ideological cinema. Their most famous production, the three-part agit-prop documentary *La hora de los hornos* [The hour of the furnaces, 1968] combines newsreel and documentary footage with dramatic reenactments and printed slogans which function as agents of ideological praxis.
14. Zavarzadeh, *Seeing Films*, 8.
15. M.M. Bakhtin,"Discourse in the Novel," in *The Dialogic Imagination: Four Essays*, ed. Michael Holquist, trans. Caryl Emerson and Michael Holquist (Austin: University of Texas Press, 1981), 352.
16. Ibid.
17. Karl Marx, *Collected Works*, vol. 5 (New York: International Publishers, 1976), 446.
18. I.R. Titunik, Appendix II,"The Formal Method and the Sociological Method (M.M. Bakhtin, P.N. Medvedev, V.N. Volosinov) in Russian Theory and Study of Literature," in V.N. Volosinov *Marxism and the Philosophy of Language*, trans. Ladislav Matejka and I.R. Titunik (New York: Seminar Press, 1973), 175–200, states that the three researchers constituted a closely knit group that consisted of "such people as his student, follower, and collaborator, V.N. Volosinov, the

literary scholars P.N. Medvedev and L.V. Pumpjanskij, the indologist M.I. Tub-
janskij, the biologist I.I. Kanaev, the writer K. Vaginov, and the musicologist I.I.
Sollertinskij." (p. 176, note 3).

19. David Bordwell, *Making Meaning: Inference and Rhetoric in the Interpretation of Cinema* (Cambridge, Mass.: Harvard University Press, 1989).

20. Andrew Sarris, *Politics and Cinema* (New York: Columbia University Press, 1978), 4.

21. For instance, B. Michalek and F. Turaj, *The Modern Cinema of Poland* (Bloomington and Indianapolis: Indiana University Press, 1988).

22. I am referring here to Foucault's discursive concepts of power as the basic principle of discussion in Michel Foucault's essays edited by Colin Gordon, *Power/Knowledge* (New York: Pantheon, 1980).

23. According to the official ideology proclaimed in socialist Poland, the workers constituted the ruling class. In reality, however, they were the real victims of the socialist system.

24. John Fiske, *Understanding Popular Culture* (Boston: Unwin Hyman, 1989). Fiske refers especially to Foucault's work *Power/Knowledge*.

25. The term "diegesis" indicates the total world of the story action (after the Greek word *∂inynsis* for "recounted story"). The diegesis includes events that are presumed to have occurred and actions and spaces not shown onscreen. See David Bordwell and Kristin Thompson, *Film Art: An Introduction*, 3d. ed. (New York: McGraw-Hill, 1990), 56, 409.

 Christian Metz interprets diegesis as "the film's 'represented' instance, that is to say, the sum of a film's denotation: the narration itself, but also the fictional space and time dimensions implied in and by the narrative, and consequently the characters, the landscapes, the events, and other narrative elements, in so far as they are considered in their denoted aspect." Christian Metz, *Film Language: A Semiotics of the Cinema*, trans. Michael Taylor (New York: Oxford University Press, 1974), 98.

26. Lynn J. Shakinovsky, "Hidden Listeners: Dialogism in the Poetry of Emily Dickinson," in *Bakhtin and Otherness*, 199–216.

27. R.F. Barsky, and M. Holquist, "Dialogue," in *Bakhtin and Otherness*, 4.

28. Bakhtin's theory has been discussed in the context of philosophy, sociolinguistics, psychoanalysis, feminism, and many other fields of research.

29. Ferdinand de Saussure, the founder of structural linguistics, is of prime importance for film theory. For Saussure, the meaning of any utterance is produced only in relation to a pre-existing system of linguistic rules (termed *langue*) that precede the individual speaking subject who must submit to them in order to become a member of society. This role of structures anterior to the individual subject is thoroughly discussed in his critical work, *Course in General Linguistics* (New York: McGraw Hill, 1966).

30. M. Bakhtin, *Problems of Dostoevsky's Poetics*, ed. and trans. Caryl Emerson (Minneapolis: University of Minnesota Press, 1984).

31. Discourse is understood here in the sense of a common theoretical usage where "discourse is shared by a socially constituted group of speakers or particular social practice,… and includes all those items, aesthetic, semantic, ideological, social which can be said to speak for or refer to those whose discourse it is." Christine Gledhill, "*Klute* 1: A Contemporary Film Noir and Feminist Criticism," in *Women in Film Noir*, ed. Ann E. Kaplan (London: British Film Institute, 1980), 13.

32. Bakhtin, *The Dialogic Imagination*, 281.
33. Karl Marx, *Collected Works*, 44.
34. Bakhtin, *Problems of Dostoevsky's Poetics*, 181.
35. Wladimir Krysinski, "Bakhtin and the Evolution of the Post-Dostoevskian Novel," in *Bakhtin and Otherness*,109–134.
36. Ibid., 110.
37. Robert Stam, *Subversive Pleasures: Bakhtin, Cultural Criticism and Film* (Baltimore and London: The John Hopkins University Press, 1989), 187.
38. Bakhtin, *The Dialogic Imagination*, 426.
39. James V. Wertsch, *Voices of the Mind: A Sociocultural Approach to Mediated Action* (Cambridge, Mass.: Harvard University Press, 1991), 70.
40. Martin Loy, *Browning's Dramatic Monologues and the Post-Romantic Subject* (Baltimore and London: The Johns Hopkins University Press, 1985), 56.
41. Julia Kristeva, *Desire in Language*, ed. Leon S. Roudiez, trans. Thomas Gora, Alice Jardine, Leon S. Roudiez (New York: Columbia University Press, 1980), 77–8.
42. Ibid., 78.
43. Ibid., 79.
44. William McClellan, "The Dialogic Other: Bakhtin's Theory of Rhetoric," in *Bakhtin and Otherness*, 233–49.
45. Ibid., 236.
46. Ibid.
47. A. Herrmann, *The Dialogic and Difference: "An/other Woman" in Virginia Woolf and Christa Wolf* (New York: Columbia University Press, 1989), 14.
48. Bakhtin's terms of polyphony, heteroglossia, or polyglossia originally mean "the simultaneous presence of two or more national languages interacting within a single cultural system" (*The Dialogic Imagination*, 431). Although Bakhtin's two historical models, on which the idea of heteroglossia is based, are ancient Rome and the Renaissance, the terms themselves proved to be so fertile that they have been used by many other theoreticians to describe complex cultural and sociological phenomena.
49. The term was used by Terry Eagleton to cover the analysis of Raymond Williams, Pierre Macherey, Cliff Slaughter, Tony Benett, Leon Trotsky, Mikhail Bakhtin, V.N. Volosinov, Georg Lukács, Walter Benjamin, Fredric Jameson, and others. See Terry Eagleton, *Literary Theory: An Introduction* (Minneapolis: University of Minnesota Press, 1983).
50. Wertsch, *Voices of the Mind*, 70.
51. V.N. Volosinov, *Marxism and the Philosophy of Language* (New York, London: Seminar Press, 1973).
52. Herrmann, in *The Dialogic and Difference*, 11, argues that Bakhtin published under his own name and assumed names borrowed from two friends, V.N. Volosinov and P.N. Medvedev. She agrees, however, that the extent to which Volosinov and Medvedev were authors, coauthors, or pseudonyms remains largely undecided. The texts in question are V.N.Volosinov, *Freudianism: A Marxist Critique*, trans. I.R .Titunik (New York: Academic Press, 1976); and *Marxism and the Philosophy of Language*, trans. Ladislav Matejka and I.R .Titunik (New York: Seminar Press, 1973); and P.N. Medvedev/M.M. Bakhtin, *The Formal Method in Literary Scholarship: A Critical Introduction to Sociological Poetics*, trans. Albert J. Wehrle (Cambridge, Mass.: Harvard University Press, 1985).
53. Volosinov, *Freudianism*, 102–3.

54. In Bakhtin, context is understood as the sociohistorical situation of the utterance which generates the word but also is an active participant in the word's interpretation. Pragmatics, on the other hand, postulates a more "passive" understanding of context. Context exists as a condition for the formation of utterances and not as an active participant, dialogically interacting with the word formation as happens in Bakhtin's understanding of the term.

55. The pragmatically oriented spectatorship theory approaches are represented, among others, by the Italian school of film theoreticians. This school is represented by G. Bettetini, V. Melchiorre, F. Casetti and A. Ferrara, all of them related in one way or another to *Scuola Superiore delle Comunicazioni Sociali* in Milano, Italy. Examples of their works dealing with the spectatorship issues are the following:

    G. Bettetini, "Partecipazione e comunicazioni sociali," *Comunicazioni sociali*, 1976, no 1–2.

    V. Melchiore, *Immaginazione simbolica*, Bologna 1972.

    F. Casetti, *Teorie del cinema dal dopoguerra a oggi*, Milano 1978.

    A. Ferrara, "A Few Considerations on a Pragmatic Component," *Versus*, 1977.

    As quoted by Tedeusz Miczka in "Pragmatyka tekstu audiowizualnego we wspolczesnej wloskiej teorii filmu" [Pragmatics of the audiovisual text in the contemporary Italian film theory], in *Autor, Film, Odbiorca* [Author, film, spectator], ed. Alicja Helman (Wroclaw: Uniwersytet Wroclawski, 1991), 38–50.

56. Bakhtin, *The Dialogic Imagination*, 282.

57. Krysinski quotes J. Mukarovsky "Dialog a monolog: Listy filologické LXVIII" [Dialogue and monologue: philological letters LXVIII] quoted from *Kapitoly z ceske poetiky I* [Theses of Czech Poetics I], Prague, 1948, as the originator of this idea. (Krysinski, "Bakhtin and the Evolution," 111.)

58. Kloepfer, "Grundlagen des dialogischen prinzips in der Literatur" [The foundations of the dialogical principles in literature] in *Dialogizität*, R. Lachman, Wilhelm Fink, München, 1982, 88. (Quoted by Krysinski in "Bakhtin and the Evolution," 112.)

59. The relation of Bakhtin's dialogism and Jauss's "fusion of horizons" will be discussed in the introductory part to chapter 3.

60. Most of the reception theory approaches have been discussed, for instance, in Elizabeth Freund, *The Return of the Reader: Reader-Response Criticism* (London and New York: Methuen, 1987).

61. See, for instance, a conversation between Robert Barsky and Michael Holquist in *Bakhtin and Otherness*, 1–22, where both interlocutors repudiate the application of Bakhtin to film studies. Barsky's statement is symptomatic of this kind of rejection:

    We have seen some applications of Bakhtin's work to film studies; although we don't have any representative examples of these studies in this issue, there have been some articles as well as a major book by Robert Stam published in this area. There seems to be a danger, however, in undertaking film studies with some of the general categories like polyglossia or heteroglossia in mind. Maybe this is because the theoreticians who have been studying Bakhtin with reference to film theory have not been placing Bakhtin into the Russian tradition or into the philosophical tradition from which he emerged. (p. 20)

62. Especially Robert Stam in *Subversive Pleasures*, and in his recently published book, *Reflexivity in Film and Literature: From Don Quixote to Jean-Luc Godard* (Irvington: Columbia University Press, 1991).

63. Bakhtin belonged to an anti-formalist movement in the Soviet Union in the late 1920s and early 1930s, which was opposed to a strictly structuralist analysis of the language but favored a more polemical approach. Titunik, a co-translator of Volosinov's *Marxism and the Philosophy of Language*, summarizes the historical appearance of this movement in the following words:

    As the decade of the 1920s ended and that of the 1930s began, the formalist movement and the controversy in which it was embroiled came more and more under the effect of changes occurring in the political and governmental life of the Soviet Union. In the interests of argument, of free-wheeling debate and polemics, were being gradually supplanted by the demands of dogma. Increasingly, formalism was put in the position of a "heresy" ... in the interim, though loyalty to the stand taken by a dogma was a prerequisite, it was still possible to contend with formalism in rational terms. During this period – the late 1920s and early '30s – a certain group of young, self-avowed Marxists ... were carrying out investigations in the theory of language and literature or, more broadly and accurately, in the field of semiology with particular emphasis on language and literature. The principal of this group was, apparently, M.M. Bakhtin; the membership included P.N. Medvedev and V.N. Volosinov. (I.R. Titunik, Appendix II "The Formal Method and the Sociological Method [M.M. Bakhtin, P.N. Medvedev, V.N. Vlosinov] in Russian Theory and Study of Literature" in V.N. Volosinov, *Marxism and the Philosophy of Language*, trans. Ladislav Matejka and I.R. Titunik [New York and London: Seminar Press, 1973], 176.)

64. Robert Stam, *Subversive Pleasures: Bakhtin, Cultural Criticism and Film* (Baltimore and London: The Johns Hopkins University Press, 1989).

65. Mikhail Bakhtin, *Speech Genres and Other Late Essays*, ed. Caryl Emerson and Michael Holquist, trans. Vern W. McGee (Austin: University of Texas Press, 1986), 60.

66. Robert Stam, "Bakhtinian Translinguistics: A Postscriptum," in *The Cinematic Text: Methods and Approaches*, ed. R. Barton Palmer (New York: AMS Press, 1989), 344.

67. Stam, *Subversive Pleasures*, 17.

68. Ibid., 18.

69. Ibid., 216.

70. See for instance Holquist's glossary in *The Dialogic Imagination*, 427.

71. Robert Stam, "Film and Language: From Metz to Bakhtin," in *The Cinematic Text*, 299.

72. This interpretation of film would basically conform with the structuralists' understanding of natural language as discourse, a speech act that is also a social utterance, understood through a social contract. Ferdinand de Saussure wanted to define semiology as "a science that studies the life of signs within society ..." in Ferdinand de Saussure, *Course in General Linguistics*, 16. Thus, for one of the more influential predecessors of contemporary linguistics, the act of speaking, i.e., "parole," is a historical, social act. However, as Janet Steiger notes, "this postulate was set aside as scholars concentrated on various media as self-contained, synchronic, semiotic systems. Consequently, in a large part for dominant literary and cinema semiotics, language theory moved through

a phase of ahistorical, nonsocial idealism in which meanings were assumed decipherable from structured oppositions or decoded via other strategies of analyzing textual syntagmas and semantics." (Janet Steiger, "Reception Studies: The Death of the Reader," *The Cinematic Text*, 355.)

Steiger's approach is corroborated by Tzvetan Todorov, for whom "discourse is the structural counterpart of the functional concept of language use." In Tzvetan Todorov, *Genres in Discourse*, trans. Catherine Porter (Cambridge: Cambridge University Press, 1990), 9. The social positioning of discourse, the dependence of its genres on "a society's raw material as well as on its historically circumscribed ideology" (Todorov, *Genres in Discourse*, 10) is important for understanding the film's plurivocality in an active negotiation of its meaning by the spectator. Film in this understanding becomes a fluid cultural and historical discourse and not a closed text.

73. See, for instance, Daniel Dayan, "Television Ceremonies and Their Multiple Audiences: An Austinian Perspective on the Performance of the Public." Series of lectures, Annenberg School, Los Angeles, November 1983; Stuart Hall, "Deviancy, Politics and the Media," in *Deviance and Social Control*, ed. P. Rock and M. McIntosh (London: Tavistock Publications, 1974), 261–305; David Morley, *The "Nationwide" Audience* (London: British Film Institute, 1980).

74. Stam, *Subversive Pleasures*, 20.

75. This analysis stands in contrast to what Dana Polan proposes, namely, that "Bakhtinian dialogism is seen as the diacritical play of difference between the text and all its others: author, intertext, real and imagined addressees, and the communicative context." In D.B. Polan, "The Text between Monologue and Dialogue," *Poetics Today* 4, no. 1 (1983), 145–52. Dana Polan's proposition, as Paul Coates suggested during a personal consultation in March 1992, at McGill University in Montreal, Canada, would reiterate Stam's failure to notice an internal tension within the text.

76. Mikhail Bakhtin, *Problems of Dostoevsky's Poetics*, 31.

77. "'Ostatnie miejsce, w ktorym ludzie jeszcze ze soba rozmawiaja' z Andrzejem Wajda rozmawia Teresa Krzemien" ["The last place at which people talk to each other": a conversation of Teresa Krzemien with Andrzej Wajda], *Kultura* October 30, 1977. Quoted in Wajda Wertenstein, *Wajda Mowi o Sobie: Wywiady i Teksty* [Wajda talks about himself: interviews and texts] (Krakow: Wydawnictwo Literackie, 1991), 210.

2

ANDRZEJ WAJDA
The Carrier of the Political Message

The dialogue initiated by Andrzej Wajda's films requires an active response on the part of the spectator and forces him or her to take sides, to negotiate meaning, to compare the images on the screen with his or her own conceptions of the reality represented in the films. As Krystyna Janda, the director's favorite actress who appeared in *Man of Marble* and *Man of Iron*, sums it up, "[Wajda] has a real flair for the social, for being a 'social activist,' a label which in Poland is sometimes used pejoratively. He envisions himself in the role of the teacher of the nation."[1]

As a film author who occupies a definite socioideological space, Wajda may be seen as the centering source of discourse, the personification of the discourse. He does not create this discourse in its totality, he only gives it a socioideological orientation and locates it in a historical context. He epitomizes Foucault's conception of the author as an embodiment of the discursive function, designating its subject's position(s).[2] Especially in *Man of Marble* and *Man of Iron*, Wajda forces the spectator to identify with the here and now in the images, and prompts him or her to take sides in the polemical presentation of the film's political beliefs. His role as film director is to juxtapose various existing social discourses in such a way that the manifestation and reinforcement of these discourses manipulates the spectator into an emotional reaction. By building a film message in this manner, Wajda seems to illustrate Bakhtin's individual role of the author who is understood to be "an architect of the plurivocal and pluridiscursive as well as plurinarrative structures."[3] In this context, Wladimir Krysinski's view, that the author should be defined as a "compilator" or "narrative voice," describes well the role of Wajda in these films.

Andrzej Wajda is one of the heirs to the Romantic tradition in Poland, but he also is a calculating artist who produces artistic effects in a highly determined and rational manner. At the same time, Wajda also is plurivocal and pluridiscursive in his own artistic activities, sharing the cinema with theater and television production. Each element of his artistic biography may be dialogically viewed in the light of others. His artistic activities are often highly disparate in content and style, but each of them contributes to the construction of the intricate polyphonic patchwork of Wajda's artistic sensitivity expressed in separate areas of his artistic experience.

Wajda combines the originality of a painter, a film director and a theater director. Andrzej Wajda was born in Suwalki on 6 March 1926. He spent 1939 to 1945 in Radom where he was employed as a simple worker and later as a draftsman at a railway design office. Wajda studied at secret underground sessions during the war. Because he wanted to become a painter he also studied at a secret underground session where professor Waclaw Dabrowski lectured on drawing, painting, and sculpture. During the Second World War, like many other boys of his age, Wajda performed the function of a courier in the National Army (AK).

In 1946, after the Second World War had ended, Wajda enrolled in the Cracow Academy of Fine Arts, where he studied until 1949. Soon he realized that painting did not completely gratify his artistic needs. The solitary act of creation on a canvas or on a piece of paper did not satisfy his temperament or his need to act. In 1949 he learned about the formation of the Lodz Film School and he decided to go, though he was not yet sure whether film would be his best medium of expression. He passed the entrance exams, and was accepted. He stayed at the film school until 1952. In the course of these studies he shot one brief feature film, *The Wicked Boy* (1950), based on a short story by Chekhov, as well as two documentaries, *The Ilza Ceramics* (1951) and *While You Sleep* (1950).

On completing his studies he worked as an assistant director on the film *Five from Barska Street* (1953) for another famous Polish filmmaker, Alexander Ford. Later, Wajda made his own debut as a filmmaker with *A Generation* (1955), which had an immediate impact upon other Polish filmmakers in the 1950s and provided the foundations for the nascent 'Polish School' of cinema. Along with Andrzej Wajda, another celebrated film director who was also considered a member of the Polish school is Andrzej Munk, with his film *Man on the Railway Track* (1956). Wajda and Munk became regarded as the most eminent representatives of the Polish School of Cinema.[4]

Within four years Wajda produced three other films which, like *A Generation*, dealt with the fate of the members of his generation as a result of the Second World War. These films are *Canal* (1956), *Ashes and Diamonds* (1958) and *Lotna* (1959). The first two films established Wajda internationally as an important Polish film-maker. In 1957 he was awarded the Silver Palm for *Canal* in Cannes, and in 1959 he received the FIPRESCI award for *Ashes and Diamonds* in Venice.

Within the same four years, Wajda also directed for the theater. He made his debut in the theatre in 1959 in Gdansk with *A Hatful of Rain* by Michael Gazzo, a realistic, psychological American drama about drug addiction, which had premiered in New York in 1955. From this point on, the paths of his creative work in both theater and film intersected and specific parallels may be observed in the development of his work in both areas, despite the very different demands of each art form.

As Maciej Karpinski, an author of a book dealing with Wajda's theatrical productions, notes, "In the beginning of his career Wajda had little respect for the stage, since the traditional style of presentation that characterized pre-1956 Polish theatre seemed irrelevant to current political and social problems."[5] The schematic style of presentation clashed with the artist's temperament, which required Romantic turmoil and passionate emotion. Wajda comments on his approach in those years:

> Looking back now I think that my views were provoked by the concept of theatre existing at that time, and which we suffer under to this day: that the theatre is a place of high ideals, a sort of salon where gestures are more precise, voices more melodious, and where people behave more elegantly than in real life (nothing could have been more false and less interesting for me at that time). I think that maybe I was so opposed to that convention of propriety, elegance and good taste because my films seemed to portray the very opposite.[6]

My book deals mainly with Wajda's film production, and this aspect of his artistic activity will be primarily discussed below. The only theatrical production we shall deal with in detail will be *The Affair of Danton*, which preceded the production of the film *Danton* itself. The theatrical aspect of Wajda's artistic creativity is a separate domain that requires a careful analysis far beyond the scope of this publication.

In terms of his film production, from 1955 to 1971 Wajda was related to or cooperated with the film units Kadr, Rytm, Kamera, Film, Tor, and Wektor.[7] From 1972 to 1983 Wajda was the artistic director of the film unit X, which produced many ambitious and politically provocative films. Wajda's films, as Karpinski notes, "are marked not only by changes in characteristic details of style and by particular moods, but also by vacillation of artistic intent, which resulted in an uneven standard."[8] The first films are *Generation* (1955), *Canal* (1957), and *Ashes and Diamonds* (1958), which mark the appearance of a controversial and politically courageous filmmaker. The three films made Wajda and his actors (especially Zbigniew Cybulski) famous and sought after. The fourth film of this period, *Lotna* (1959), is much weaker, although it significantly reveals Wajda's particular painter's eye in his construction of film images. These first films deal with the issues of war, occupation, and heroic sacrifice.

The films made in the 1960s examine a different area. After producing four films dealing with the subject of the Second World War, Wajda knew that he could not confine himself to war themes only. *Innocent Sorcerers* (1960) is an examination of the psychology of contemporary youth in post-war Poland. Before the celebrated *Ashes* (1965), a Napoleonic saga based on the controversial Polish novel written in 1904 by Stefan Zeromski , there are two other treatments of literary material, *Lady Macbeth of the Provinces* (1962) and *Samson* (1961). While *Ashes* brought Wajda success and stimulated fervent discussions in the press, the two latter films were largely ignored by the public.

In 1962 Wajda produced a twenty-minute contribution to *Love at Twenty* (1965), an internationally produced collection of short films on the same theme. Other directors taking part in this collaboration were François Truffaut, Renzo Rossellini, Marcel Ophuls and Shintaro Ishihara. The next film, *Gates to Paradise* (1967), proved to be a failure, and was never shown on the big screen in Poland. This film marks an end to an important period in Wajda's career, during which he produced ten films, directed five plays, and completed two TV productions.

The year 1968 starts another prolific period of Wajda's filmmaking. In this year he completed the film *Everything for Sale* (1968), about the real life of Zbigniew Cybulski, Wajda's favorite actor and the main protagonist of *Ashes and Diamonds*, who was killed in an accident. The film is based on Wajda's screenplay and combines both the elements of fiction and reality, a technique which would later be repeated in *Man of Iron* (1981). During subsequent years he produced two comedies, *Rolly-Polly* (1968) for television and *Hunting Flies* (1969); he returned to the theme of the

Second World War in *Landscape After Battle* (1970). Other films that belong to this productive stage in his life are: *Birchwood* (1970), *Pilate and Others* (1971), *The Wedding*(1972), *The Promised Land* (1974), and *The Shadow Line* (1976).

In *Landscape After Battle* Wajda returns to Polish problems and to the theme of the Polish character. *Birchwood*, on the other hand, presents universal themes of love, life, and death, while *Pilate and Others* depicts the Passion of Christ in a contemporary environment. *The Wedding*, based on the play by Stanislaw Wyspianski and one of the best films by Wajda, is seen as a vision of Poland and the Polish personality rendered satirically and bitterly. At the same time, the film is a beautifully composed fresco pulsating with rich social and cultural traits. Another social theme is presented in *The Promised Land*, which deals with the industrial development in the Polish town of Lodz in the early twentieth century. Finally, the last film of this period, *The Shadow Line*, based on the novella by Joseph Conrad, is about a young officer made captain and given the responsibility for all the men under his command.

The next films produced by Wajda initiated the trend of the films of moral concern in the Polish cinema. This kind of cinema represents a passionate attempt at defining the truth and sense of socialist Poland. The films of this group could not openly deal with the moral, ethical, and social anomalies of the Polish reality, so they showed in a camouflaged way the negative mechanisms and phenomena characteristic of the Polish reality of those times. Although the films could not openly attack the Communist Party, they clearly indicated its failures by undermining its propaganda of success and pointing to the problems of corruption and careerism in particular. These films are far more openly critical than any previous films in Polish history. Some of the most important films of this trend were Kieslowski's *The Scar* (1976), Falk's *Top Dog* (1977), Wajda's *Man of Marble* (1976), and Zanussi's *Camouflage* (1976). From these films a new sociocultural phenomenon came into being. Film directors tried to illustrate the real life of Poland, with its struggles and conflicts. Wieslaw Saniewski explains the historical context in which these films appeared in his discussion of the cinema of the 1970s in Poland,[9] "The historical events in the seventies not only deeply moved all of us and shocked our collective consciousness, but they also crossed certain psychological barriers. Double standards were attacked, and so-called *chutzpah* was discredited."[10]

Other Wajda films that belong to this period are *Without Anaesthetic* (1978), *The Young Ladies of Wilko* (1979), *Conductor* (1980), *Man of Iron* (1981), and *Danton* (1982). *Man of Marble, Without Anaesthetic, Man of Iron*, and *Danton* are rich in political and historical allusions, and they brought Wajda fame and respect. For all these films Wajda obtained prestigious international prizes.[11] *The Young Ladies of Wilko*, it should be mentioned, is an exception to his politically charged films and constitutes an escape into a world of feelings and emotions, the world of general questions of life and death shot in a masterly way by Wajda, the artist.

The last four films directed by Wajda were the result of his direct cooperation with French, German and British film producers. *Love in Germany* (1983) was shot in France and Germany, while *Les Possédés* (1988) and *Korczak* (1990) were produced with the help of Gaumont films and BBC Films, respectively. The only film produced at that time exclusively for the Polish audience was *Love's Accidents* (1986). Both *Love in Germany* and *Korczak* deal with the times of the Second World War; the first one tells a story of a love affair between a Polish boy and a German woman in Nazi Germany, while the second one tells of a famous Jewish doctor devoted to his orphaned Jewish children. Both films end tragically and both deal with the issues of honesty and human respect in the difficult times of Nazi Germany.

Finally, in 1992, Wajda directed *The Horse-Hair Ring*, a film which refers to the traditions and topics of the Polish School of Cinema and draws upon motifs from *Ashes and Diamonds*. Unfortunately, the film seemed ill-timed. The Polish public, disenchanted by "the war at the top," the infighting among leaders, turned away from politics and was no longer interested in political dilemmas presented in Wajda's last film.[12] In general, from the time of the production of *Korczak* in 1991, the interest in Wajda's political revelations seemed to wane and the Polish spectators perhaps felt that Wajda had fallen behind the times and no longer was able to present a dialogically negotiated political picture of contemporary reality in Poland.

Since 1978 Wajda has performed numerous political functions in cultural associations and political bodies that are related to or that originated in his artistic activities in film. In the years 1978 to 1983 he was the chairman of The Polish Filmmakers' Association (Stowarzyszenie Filmowcow Polskich), and in the years 1978 to 1981 the chairman of The Polish Federation of Film Discussion Clubs (Polska Federacja Dyskusyjnych Klubow Filmowych). In

1988 Wajda was a member of the National Committee established by Lech Walesa for culture and mass media. Since 4 June 1989 Wajda has performed the prestigious function of senator. Wajda also has been rewarded with many significant prizes for his theatre and film production, and for his cultural activities.[13] He was awarded an *honoris causa* of the American University in Washington in 1981, Bologna University in 1988, and Jagiellonian University in Cracow in 1989. As a celebrated and widely known film director both in Poland and abroad, Wajda has managed to retain a freshness of his outlook and to remain open to new influences and glossia, which he absorbed in his films and theater productions.

In Bakhtinian terms, Wajda emerges from his films as a truly discursive author, disseminating his hesitant, polemic concepts among numerous interlocutors. As William McClellan notes, "the difference between 'real' and discursive authors produces a gap which allows Bakhtin to expand his concept of authorship beyond the limited scope of a single individual."[14] Bakhtin's voice in a dialogical relation can represent a person, a class, a collective or a whole generation. Wajda in his artistic creations presents such a collective of voices, a multiplicity of internal splits, and a variety of discourses.

Wajda is a personality torn between reason and emotion, and this can be seen vividly in all of his films, which function as enunciatory carriers of this internal confrontation. The three films discussed in this book especially reveal repressed undercurrents in Wajda's assessment of historical and political truth.

In *Man of Marble* Wajda functions as a provocateur, an instigator of the discussion carried out between the protagonists in the film and film audiences. In watching the film, the spectator follows two stories at once, the story of the bricklayer from the 1950s, and the story of a young filmmaker who is making her diploma film about those times. Scibor-Rylski's script was based on the texture of genuine events, as Michalek and Turaj note in their book about Polish film, "In the early fifties, bricklayers, miners, weavers, and others with a rate of productivity exceeding five hundred percent of the norm became part of the propaganda landscape. The so-called 'work-emulation' movement, based on the Soviet Stakhanovite phenomenon, was cultivated, and chosen workers were exploited for publicity to inspire or pressure their peers to greater efforts."[15]

Agnieszka, a young filmmaker in the 1970s in Poland, is seeking to tell the story of a young Stakhanovite,[16] Mateusz Birkut (played by Jerzy Radziwillowicz), "a simple, good-natured bricklayer who becomes the subject of rampant propaganda and is hailed as a national hero."[17] His accomplishment was to lay thousands of bricks in record time. These kinds of events in the Poland of the 1950s were supposed to stimulate the rebuilding of the country after the Second World War. One of the propaganda shows in which Birkut takes part is sabotaged by unknown perpetrators. Someone, probably one of his co-workers, hands him a hot brick. Birkut cries with pain. The propaganda event stops and the security officers scurry to find the guilty party. This particular moment in the film changes Birkut's life, and also constitutes a turning point in the film diegesis. From an idolized worker Birkut turns into a character no longer loved by the authorities. When Witek, Birkut's friend and co-worker, is accused of causing the damage during the unfortunate propaganda event, Birkut takes his side in the political trial that follows the accident and is sent to prison himself. From then on Birkut is transformed into a victim of the system. He loses his status as an exemplary super-worker and suffers constant scrutiny by the security agents.

Agnieszka discovers the story of Birkut. She lives in the Poland of the 1970s and she wants to make her diploma film based on events of the 1950s. The film is to be devoted to the time period of her father's youth. While watching some old newsreels for her film research, she finds her interest sparked by a grandiose marble statue of a worker. She decides to look for the statue in the National Museum in Warsaw. When she finds it she chooses to use the statue as the starting point for her film. In order to tell the story of the man who was the subject of the marble figure, Agnieszka carries out a series of interviews with the people who knew him, and who now occupy positions of authority in the official Polish culture. They work to block her efforts to finish the film because in it Agnieszka is going to expose the mechanisms of power in the Poland of the 1950s, and, by extension, in the Poland of the 1970s, since nothing has really changed. The TV producer finally responsible for this decision explains that the film is not complete. In reality, the producer's decision masks a fear of revealing the dreadful facts concerning the mechanisms of power in the Poland of the 1970s. Still, the film ends on an optimistic note with Agnieszka walking down the corridor of the TV building with the son of Birkut, whom she met while conducting her interviews.

The complex structure of the film's ideological content is further renegotiated in the course of various film receptions, starting from the time of the first reading of the script (around 1967) until the early 1980s, when Solidarity was on the rise. The historical and sociological phenomena depicted in the film are literally relived by the Polish spectator together with the protagonists of the events taking place on the screen.

Man of Marble is at once a compelling detective story and a bitter satire on Stalinist-era propaganda and injustices. The film does not refer to actual historical events in such a direct way as *Man of Iron*. However, rich in allusions and political implications, *Man of Marble* presents all the historical aspects of the totalitarian system and the social atmosphere characteristic of the 1950s and pervasive until the 1970s.

At the same time the film serves as a reference point to the ideological discussion carried out between the spectators and the political subjects in the 1970s. Consequently, the film becomes a message in a global situation of pragmatic communication which takes place outside the film, within the domain of the spectator's world of beliefs, provoked by Wajda as the author. The dialogue transcends the textuality of the film itself. The film changes into a cavalry charge of ideas, where the actors, as carriers of the director's message, and the audience seem to carry on a continuous discussion with one another. The film carries on a political debate both with the supporters and opponents of Stalinism in Poland, with the censors at the time of the film's production, and with numerous strata of Polish society. The spectator witnesses here a diversified dialogue with audiences representing various political approaches to the reality represented in the film.

Wajda creates his own discourse in opposition to the existing sociohistorical discourse, engaging his camera in "a fierce social struggle"[18] in "the dialogic which represents the struggle between opposing discourses arising out of different contexts, either semantic or sociohistorical."[19] There is no dialectic in the film, however, no reconciliation in the transcending of oppositions by means of a synthetic third term. In the film the dialogic resists the reconciliation of opposites by insisting on the reciprocity of two or more antagonistic voices. Wajda appears as a "mono-dialogical"[20] author, bringing together numerous glossia into the film, constructing a framework for their performance, but also acting as one of the voices himself. Beyond the dyad Burski-Agnieszka, lies Wajda, the film director, whose film goes beyond this opposition. So, the film *Man of Marble* appears as an assembly of all the voices, the film director's included.

In *Man of Iron*, on the other hand, Wajda presents his monological conviction about the victory of the individual, but at the same time is perplexed by the dubious condition of the Polish intelligentsia. *Man of Iron* is a sequel to *Man of Marble*. Maciek Tomczyk, Birkut's son (played by Jerzy Radziwillowicz, the same actor who played the part of Birkut, the father, in *Man of Marble*) organizes a strike at the Gdansk shipyard. Agnieszka, the journalist in *Man of Marble*, is both his wife and political ally. The latter meets Maciek when she goes to Gdansk to find living proof that Birkut existed. Their meeting develops into a love affair (suggested already at the end of *Man of Marble*), and later ends in a marriage. The film's story begins during the historic strike at the Gdansk shipyard. Winkiel, a journalist from Warsaw, is sent to Gdansk to produce a broadcast on Maciek Tomczyk, the strike leader. Winkiel gathers the necessary information from a series of conversations he carries out with Maciek's friends and his wife, Agnieszka. In the process of gathering information on Maciek, Winkiel, initially representing the authorities in the film, becomes more and more involved in the lives of Maciek and the members of the opposition movement. Finally, Winkiel changes his political position and joins the striking workers. The strike ends with victory. However, Winkiel is rebuffed by the workers and leaves the shipyard disappointed and disheartened. On leaving the shipyard he encounters Badecki, the security official, who tells him that the agreement between the workers and the government is not valid.

In this film, Wajda seems to position himself diegetically in the place of Winkiel, since Wajda himself came to Gdansk only at the very end of the strike and, although he did not actively support it, he witnessed the event with sympathy and understanding. He seems involuntarily to position his presentation in *Man of Iron* within the boundaries of his own experience. His ardent depiction of the strike in Gdansk reflects his passionate feelings about the events, but also his ambivalence concerning his own participation. During the strikes in Gdansk Wajda did not actively join the dissident movement but watched it closely. He basically remained within reformist socialism,[21] hoping that within the basic structures of socialism the political and economic situation could be transformed and improved. However, as a sympathizer of Solidarity he suffered greatly after its defeat. While martial law lasted he was not only attacked by the government and the official press but also was forced to resign as president of the Polish Film Union, losing the directorship of the film unit he had led. This unit not only had been the vehicle for creating many of his own films, but had launched numerous young directors.

The choice of Winkiel as the protagonist of the film functions as a bitter reminder that Wajda himself was funded by the regime the Solidarity movement was trying to discredit. Winkiel's subjection to the reprisals of the regime also signifies the nightmare situation for film directors like Wajda whose presentation of the events could go only as far as the authorities allowed. The character of Winkiel could thus be interpreted by the spectator as epitomizing the worst scenario for the authors whose power of enunciation depended completely on the whims of the regime. This presentation, however, does not equate Wajda and Winkiel; it only reflects the undercurrent of hesitation and guilt in the creation of a mass-media representative in the film.[22]

In *Man of Iron*, the protagonist of *Man of Marble*, Agnieszka, forsakes the creative and enunciatory role of the artist for the quiet heroism of the wife of an opposition activist. Agnieszka says that she has abandoned her ambition to become a filmmaker, and now prefers raising a family, being politically active, and "speaking freely." But it seems strange[23] that Wajda, through Agnieszka, should denigrate filmmaking, since he and his films played a crucial role in defining and exposing Poland's growing crisis. Perhaps he merely wished to show that in the final analysis art must always take a back seat to direct political action. In this, Wajda makes his intention clear through the words and actions of his protagonists, who are representative of whole classes of people in Poland.

The critics often criticized Wajda's haste in the production of *Man of Iron*, claiming that the motive was the approaching Cannes Film Festival. Their predictions that it would win the prize were right – both the Cannes general public and the Cannes judges were stunned by the film's openness in the presentation of historical and social facts.[24] Thanks to the film's fame, Wajda could count on the positive decisions of the Polish sponsors of his films in the future. He also knew that due to the sensationalist aspect of his work in the context of the political events in Poland the public would be prompted to interpret his film not only as an artistic message but also as a premonition of things to come, including a possible threat to the Polish artist himself.

At the same time, Wajda wanted to win in Cannes because the Cannes Film Festival's reputation would not allow the authorities to deceive the Polish public and put *Man of Iron* away on the shelf. Wajda did not want the public to be deprived of this film as it had been deprived already of *Man of Marble,* which took several years to be widely released. The director hoped, in this way, that the quadrille led by the authorities would never again be repeated. After all, the lack of government permission deprived the public for a long time of another important film depicting the truth of those times, *Robotnicy* (The Workers, 1980) by Chodakowski and Zajaczkowski.

Although apparently monological (in the sense of Wajda's imposed voice in the creation of the global message of the film), *Man of Iron* depicts Wajda's inner tensions concerning the role of the artist at important moments of history, the function of the media, and the position of the political activist in the formation of history. The film functions as the director's exposé, but also as a presentation of events which, as a text, involuntarily entered a dialogical relation with the public. Everything about this film was questioned by the public: Wajda's intentions, his version of events, his suspicious manipulation of the documentary material, his haste in film production. All these elements, the film text as such, and its complex reception contributed to the understanding or misunderstanding of Wajda as a film director.

Finally, *Danton,* a film based on the volatile world of the French Revolution, is a careful reconstruction of the period, with the director's attitudes revealed through the words and staging of the film's protagonists. The action of *Danton* starts in the spring of 1794, four years after the storming of the Bastille. The government of Robespierre has achieved great military success in the ongoing war. However, Robespierre feels threatened by the opposition and decides to eliminate all opponents. A period of ruthless terror commences. At this time, Danton, the beloved orator and advocate of the people, returns to Paris. As a pragmatist and sybarite he yearns to end the chaos of revolution and bring bread and peace to the exhausted Parisians. Robespierre and his advocates consider Danton a threat to the revolution, which they want to continue, and decide to eliminate him. A mock trial ensues; Danton is silenced and condemned to death. Both Danton and several of his supporters die by the blade of the guillotine. Surprisingly, the film ends not with a triumphant but a terrified Robespierre who predicts his own death as a result of the terror which he has instigated.

As we shall see in the chapter devoted to historical discourse in the film, Wajda was rebuked by many French film reviewers because he took the side of Danton in the film. However, Wajda denies that he identifies with either of the protagonists. "As an author I have to stay a little on the outside of such a conflict. There can be no identification of the filmmaker with one of the characters."[25] In this way, Wajda states that he would like to avoid any personal statement on his part. He denies the film's ideological similarity or opposition to *The Danton Affair,* the Stanislawa Przybyszewska play upon which the film *Danton* was based. The author of *The Danton Affair* was a dedicated Communist in the 1920s who, according to Ophuls's interpretation, was a supporter of Robespierre. The film, to Wajda, did not display an obvious dichotomy. The historical truth is more polyphonous, he seems to say, not displayed in a monological opposition of white/black, univocal statements.

In *Danton,* Wajda as an author seems to be overwhelmed by the immensity of the historical and moral dilemmas in the choice between the two seemingly different positions of Robespierre and Danton. As a mature creator of artistic and moral truth, Wajda is careful not to present an idealistic picture of either protagonist, which would produce a monological statement prompting audiences to support a particular ideological position of the author's choice. None of the antagonists is presented as a clear-cut hero. Danton comes closest, with his yearning to end the terror that he is partly responsible for, and Wajda underlines this yearning by casting the charismatic Gérard Depardieu in this role. But the director refuses to downplay Danton's many eccentricities, and he allows Robespierre a streak of humanity, notably in his compassion for a doomed comrade.

Wajda proposes a duality of positions where the arguments of both protagonists seem convincing and justified. In this way, Wajda leaves room for a dialogical relation with audiences, which, depending on their own historical position and moment of interpretation, side with one or the other monological representatives of political truths. Both protagonists face death at the end of the film. The film ends with a wavering between the powers of reason and the powers of emotion, without, however, deciding in favor of one or the other. As David Sterritt notes in his review of *Danton*:

> in production notes for the picture Wajda apologizes for turning to such a familiar period (the French Revolution). But he notes that all his films address themselves to the issue of Man challenging History. He justifies his French foray by listing its main concerns: "how freedom operates as a motor of history; what things threaten history; and [whether] sacrifices [must] be made to protect freedom" ...[26]

The film is best seen as a wide-ranging meditation on politics and revolution rather than a coded commentary on specific Polish occurrences, the interpretation favored especially by the Polish press. Wajda seemed to support this view at the New York Film Festival in a press conference conducted by telephone from West Berlin, where he was completing his next picture, saying, "The reason for exploring history is to understand patterns and laws that underlie human affairs. For all its horror and bloodshed, the French revolution 'won' insofar as it brought about new social relationships – just as Solidarity won a 'moral victory' despite its failure to survive as an institution."

However, in France, Wajda's general and dialogical position is treated as a monological interpretation definitely in favor of Danton. Despite Wajda's claim that he wants to position himself outside the conflict, the French spectator suspects him of a monological voice, a uniform presentation of the revolutionary position from Danton's point of view.

Wajda: I try to do everything I can, really *everything* so that both sides can present valid arguments. Because what I am really interested in is the situation these two men place themselves in. There is a certain inevitability in that situation, a tragic inevitability. That's why I chose to make a very calm film in its form, a very "classical" film. You know?

Ophuls: Do you mind if I say something about that? My impression is that if you tried to be as objective as you say, then you haven't succeeded. That's not necessarily bad, as far as I'm concerned, because I think that subjective moviemaking is always vastly superior to any attempts at objectivity. But I do think you've made an extremely pro-Danton film, and a very anti-Robespierre one. You seem very lenient toward Danton's obvious corruption, his venality, his rabble-rousing, and very contemptuous of Robespierre's thirst for virtue.[27]

In Poland, the film was interpreted as "more Polish than French"[28] both because it was based on a play by a Polish author and also because it seemed to refer directly to the Polish "revolution" witnessed and experienced both by the Polish viewers and by Wajda himself. Such film reviewers as Leczek and Ostrowski,[29] for instance, suggest that Wajda, influenced by the very real, political situation of his own country, transfers his feelings onto the heroes of revolution. His sympathy seems to lie with Danton, the emotional and political equivalent of Walesa, the man who instigated the self-limiting revolution in Poland.

By stimulating a fervent discussion both in the Polish and French press (this discussion will be presented in detail in the third chapter in a section titled "Historical Discourse in *Danton*"), Wajda returned to his role as a discursive author, provoking a multitude of interpretations to his highly polemical political film. In *Danton*, Wajda no longer imposes a monological outlook on revolution as he had done in *Man of Iron*, but instead is skeptical of the revolutionary ideologies represented by both Danton and Robespierre. By making Saint-Just an incorruptible monster who is cruelly indifferent to Robespierre's suffering in the final scenes of the film, Wajda seems to articulate his pessimistic outlook on the course of any revolution: it will end with overpowering Terror carried out by the likes of Saint-Just.

By making the ideological conflict vibrant in human terms, Wajda stimulates a dialogical depiction of the historical truth of the French Revolution (and, in general, of any revolutionary effort). Both the ideologies of the two protagonists and the declarations of their opponents and advocates permeate the film with a multiplicity of polemical voices. These voices give credibility to our initial Bakhtinian definition of Wajda as a discursive author whose enunciative political power lies in a passionate, dialogical depiction of historical events and not only in their "objective" demonstration.

Notes

1. Michael Szporer, "Woman of Marble. An Interview with Krystyna Janda," *Cineaste* 18, no. 3 (1991), 14.
2. Michel Foucault, "What is An Author?" *Language, Counter-Memory, Practice: Selected Essays and Interviews*, trans. D. Bouchard and S. Simon (Ithaca: Cornell University Press, 1977), 113–38.
3. Wladyslaw Krysinski, "Bakhtin and the Evolution of the Post-Dostoevskian Novel," in *Bakhtin and Otherness*, 131.
4. Unfortunately, Andrzej Munk died in a car crash on 20 September 1961.
5. Maciej Karpinski, *The Theatre of Andrzej Wajda* (Cambridge: Cambridge University Press, 1989), 7.
6. Andrzej Wajda, "In Theatre ...," *Teatr*, no. 14 (1974).
7. The biographical information on Wajda and his films is based on *Wajda mowi o sobie: Wywiady i teksty* [Wajda Talks About Himself: Interviews and Texts], ed. Wanda Wertenstein (Krakow: Wydawnictwo Literackie, 1991), 259–96.
8. Karpinski, *The Theatre of Andrzej Wajda*, 7.

9. W. Saniewski, "Kino Polskie lat siedemdziesiatych: Dyskusja redakcyjna" [Polish Cinema of the Seventies: Editors Discussion], *Film na Swiecie*, no. 9 (1979).
10. Saniewski, "Polish Cinema of the Seventies," 63.
11. *Man of Marble* – Fipresci Prize at the 31st International Film Festival in Cannes, 1978; *Without Anaesthetic* – Ecumenical Jury Prize at the 32nd International Film Festival in Cannes, 1979; *Man of Iron* – Grand Prix "Golden Palm" at the 34th International Film Festival in Cannes, 1981; Oscar nomination in 1982; *Danton* – Louis-Delluc Prize for the best film of the year in 1982.
12. This opinion is shared by many Polish reviewers of *The Horse-Hair Ring*. Maria Kornatowska presented such a statement in her article "Polish Cinema," *Cineaste* 19, no. 4 (1993), 47–50.
13. The most important prizes and orders are the following: Krzyz Kawalerski i Krzyz Oficerski Orderu Odrodzenia Polski [The Knight's Cross and The Officer's Cross of the Polish Revival Order]; Francuska Legia Honorowa [The French Legion of Honour]; Bulgarski Order Cyryla i Metodego [The Bulgarian Order of Cyryl and Metody]; Nagroda Panstwowa I stopnia 1974 [The State Award of the First Degree 1974]; Nagroda Ministra Kultury i Sztuki I stopnia 1975 [The Award of the Ministry of Culture and Art I Degree 1975]; Premio David di Donatello – Luchino Visconti, Wlochy, 1978 [The Award of David di Donatello – Luchino Visconti, Italy, 1978]; Nagroda "César," Francja, 1982 [The "César" Award, France, 1982]; Nagroda Aten Fundacji A. Onassisa, Grecja, 1982 [Athens Award, A. Onassis Foundation, Greece,1982]; Nagroda im. G. Herdera, Austria, 1985 [G.Herder's Award, Austria, 1985]; Nagroda Pirandello, Wlochy, 1987 [Pirandello Award, Italy, 1987]; Nagroda Kioto, Japonia,1987 [Kioto Award, Japan, 1987].
14. William McClellan, "The Dialogic Other: Bakhtin's Theory of Rhetoric," in *Bakhtin and Otherness*, 239.
15. B. Michalek and F. Turaj, *The Modern Cinema of Poland* (Bloomington and Indianapolis: Indiana University Press, 1988), 156.
16. The word "Stakhanovite" comes from the name of the village Stakhanov in the former Soviet Union. The workers coming from this village reached the highest level of efficiency at their work in the 1950s. They became a symbol of workers who were always first in the Socialist competition to raise qualifications and exceed the productivity norms. From *Slownik Wyrazow Obcych* [Dictionary of Foreign Words], ed. Zygmunt Rysiewicz (Warszawa: Panstwowy Instytut Wydawniczy, 1959), 619.
17. Michalek and Turaj, *The Modern Cinema of Poland*, 156.
18. K. Hirschkop, "A Response to the Forum on Mikhail Bakhtin," in *Bakhtin: Essays and Dialogues on His Work*, ed. G.S. Morson (Chicago: University of Chicago Press, 1986), 73–79.
19. D. Bialostosky, "Dialogics As an Art of Discourse in Literary Criticism," *PMLA* 101, no. 5 (1986), 788–97.
20. The term "mono-dialogism" was introduced by Krysinski in his essay "Bakhtin and the Evolution of the Post-Dostoevskian Novel" (*Bakhtin and Otherness*, 120). As Krysinski states, "Within the multiplicity of voices, the lyrical voice has the central position, and its discourse is underlied by that what I would call 'mono-dialogism,' by which I mean that, although it is moved by dialogical intention, it tends to become a sort of cognitive filter of discourse." I find this definition extremely useful for the analysis of the role of the political film director.

21. According to Paul Coates, "... it is arguable, though, that at the onset Solidarity itself was a reformist socialist movement; moreover, the authorities' resistance and martial law drove Solidarity irrevocably into the arms of the Church." (Private discussions, McGill University, Montreal, March 1992.)

22. This hesitation and guilt on the part of the director was already involuntarily present in *Man of Marble*, when Wajda placed his name as assistant director on Burski's launch film.

23. Coates suggests at this point that this decision on the part of the director was not so strange after all. "Wajda might have been able to make a difference, by virtue of his prestige, but a real-life Agnieszka would have been forced out and would have been understandably cynical about the media world." (Private conversations, McGill University, Montreal, March 1992.)

24. *Nota bene*, Wajda himself admitted in numerous interviews the importance of having *Man of Iron* ready for Cannes.

25. Marcel Ophuls, "The Provocation and Interrogation of Andrzej Wajda on the Matter of *Danton* as Performed by Marcel Ophuls," *American Film* 9, no.1 (October 1983), 28.

26. David Sterritt, "*Danton*," *Christian Science Monitor*, 6 October 1983, 231.

27. Ophuls, "The Provocation and Interrogation," 94.

28. Wertenstein, *Wajda Talks about Himself*, 236.

29. Ireneusz Leczek, "*Danton*. Rewolucja francuska wedlug Wajdy" [*Danton*. The French Revolution according to Wajda], *Trybuna Robotnicza*, no. 39, 16 February 1983, 35. Marek Ostrowski, "Danton czy Robespierre" [Danton or Robespierre], *Polityka*, 5 February 1983.

3

HISTORICAL DIALOGUE IN WAJDA'S FILMS

Man of Marble, Man of Iron, and *Danton* embrace a discourse that encompasses the history of contemporary Poland from the period after the Second World War to the introduction of martial law in Poland in 1981. *Man of Marble* contains scenes from the early days after the Second World War, that capture the enthusiasm incited by the country's new freedom and manifested in an ardent reconstruction of the country. But these scenes also show the ever-present Stalinism and the growing role of the Communist Party. *Man of Iron* recounts the time of Edward Gierek's rule, the growing power of opposition movements, the strikes in Gdansk in 1980 and the Gdansk agreement between the government and shipyard workers in August 1980. Although its diegesis[1] reflects the times of the French Revolution, *Danton* dialogically refers to the introduction of martial law in Poland and debates the choice between the totalitarian power of reason and the passion of ordinary people in the formation of history.

In the treatment of the films' historical discourses, I will postulate a dynamic relation between historical fact and film, and discuss this relation in terms of their tensions and oppositions. The films of Andrzej Wajda presented in this book are conditioned by history. On the other hand, the films as carriers of meaning are representations of history. This approach conforms to Bakhtin's notion that textual historical traits constitute the substance of a work of art. In Bakhtin's opinion, history is ever-present in a metaphorical sense as it permeates every word of the text. For instance, in his discussion of the epic, Bakhtin refers to the "interrelationship of times"[2]

> [In the epic] the valorized emphasis is not on the future and does not serve the future, no favours are being done it (such favours face an eternity outside time); what is served here is the future memory of a past, a broadening of the world of the absolute past, and enriching of it with new images (at the expense of contemporaneity) – a world that is always opposed in principle to any merely transitory past.[3]

Julia Kristeva comments on this point:

> Although the Russian formalists were engrossed with the idea of dialogue as linguistic communication, for Bakhtin the significance was far greater. Bakhtin, born of a revolutionary Russia that was preoccupied with social problems, sees in dialogism the insertion of history (society) into a text and of this text into history.[4]

Thus, Bakhtin's notion of dialogism includes not only the complex relationships between writer, speaker, and addressee, but also the text's "intersection with the contemporary or earlier cultural context."[5] William McClellan interprets this issue in the following words:

> The important point is that Bakhtin grounds his theory of dialogics in the concreteness of heteroglossia, the socio-economic and the historical and not in a metaphysical order. "Truth" is not an eternal given but an evaluation that is historically determined and one that is subject to change ...[6]

In this sense, the films discussed in this study constantly relate to the past. For the spectators to understand the images properly they have to relate to the images, absorb them as their own, and interpret them in the context of their own lives. The border between the public and the private blurs, and the historical events presented or alluded to on the screen gain significance thanks only to the spectator's knowledge of history, which incorporates him or her into the historical discourse of the film itself. In this manner, a merging of historical horizons, a fusion that Hans Robert Jauss called the *Erwartungshorizont* (expectation horizon) is created.

The findings of Jauss seem especially crucial in the context of Bakhtin's understanding of the historical as an indispensable element for the contextualization of the message. It was Jauss who ascribed particular importance to historical context in the interpretation of a literary work within the area of reception theory.[7] In 1967, Jauss presented his study "Literaturgeschichte als Provokation der Literaturwissenschaft"(Literary History as a Challenge to Literary Theory)[8] as a suggestion for salvaging the historicity of literature by radically curtailing event-oriented historiography. His goal was to "establish a new relationship between the historical and the aesthetic perspective."[9] One of Jauss's seven theses reads:

> If literary history is to be rejuvenated, the prejudices of historical objectivism must be removed and the traditional approach to literature must be replaced by an aesthetics of reception and impact.

The historical relevance of literature is not based on an organization of literary works which is established *post factum* but on the reader's past experience of the literary data.[10]

This model postulates a definition of historicity in which (in contrast to the history of events), present and past comprise a unity; consequently the mediation of the past and the present becomes the true task of writing history. Just as Heidegger states that "an interpretation is never a presuppositionless apprehending of something presented to us,"[11] so Jauss's emphasis on the communicative aspect of the aesthetic experience within its historical dimensions offers a crucial point of departure. By theorizing the indispensability of historical contextualization to the interpretation of the literary work, the innovative Jauss made a contribution to the reception theory so far unacknowledged by his fellow reception theory scholars.

Rather than reconstructing the past, Jauss seeks an integration of past and present, of reader and text, thus allowing a hermeneutically reflected approach to the historicity of literature as well as its readers. In this approach, although reception theory concerns itself "with the historical conditions of the aesthetic effect of works of art,"[12] it does not exclude the subject, as Jauss states in an interview:

[reception theory] does not exclude the standpoint and the activity of the subject, but rather includes him as the condition of knowledge, and this concept is to that extent specific to all sciences which would understand meaning, which proceeds from the assumption that meaning is a yielded truth – and not a given one ...[13]

For Jauss a subject is every bit as time-bound as a given text; an encounter between these two elements gives rise to a dialogue, an exchange Jauss describes as a relation between history and (literary) effect. The concept informing Jauss's project, *Erwartungshorizont* (expectation horizon), a notion borrowed from Karl Mannheim,[14] signifies that all texts, like all interpretations, issue from a distinct vantage point. Fundamentally dialogic in nature, literature stands within, questions, and often seeks to revise the shared assumptions and accepted traditions of a given point in time. The literary historian's task – and Jauss speaks here with this audience, not a wider readership, in mind – involves not only recreating the *Erwartungshorizont* of author and contemporary audience, but also opening these up to a conversation with present and past interpreters. The advantages to be gained are many: reconstructing the expectation horizon enables one to discern the questions for which a text provided an answer; and it allows one to establish how previous readers understood the work as well as to apply it to the present reader's situation. This procedure makes it clear that there is no single definitive reading of any given work, but it implies placing a text within the context of its multiple possible meanings and interpretations.[15] In Jauss's approach, interpretation is an interaction between the contextualized spheres of aesthetic and other factors. The explication of meaning results from an intermingling between the social and historical, which produces a particularized reading dependent on the actual context of reading and on the world of the interpreter's beliefs and convictions. The contextual positioning of the interpreter greatly determines the interpretation of the text itself.

Bakhtin seems to have foreseen Jauss's theory and its postulate of the importance of the historical in the analysis of a work of art. However, while Jauss disregards the possibility of internal tension in the text itself, Bakhtin's dialogism seems to offer a more interesting approach to its interpretation. The passive existence of a work of art is dispensed with, giving way to a pulsating interaction of discourses within it. The meaning of the literary work becomes structured around internal tensions between differing ideologies and points of view within the text itself. Reception theory as represented by Jauss seems static by comparison, with the work of art remaining a stable construct. The Bakhtinian approach allows for tensions to exist within the text, thus permitting a development, a movement, and greater possibilities for its interpretation than the rigorous reception theory of Jauss does.

Jauss's reception theory accepts the work of art as a ready-made product to be appreciated and deciphered by the reader in a unilateral relation. The reader engages in an interaction with the work of art based on a set of presuppositions inherent in his or her own world of beliefs, which he or she then matches with particular discourses in the work, trying to decipher or deconstruct its meaning. The work of art itself, however, is treated as a finished product, an aesthetically polished result of the artist's work. Jauss's theory tackles only the interpretative relations between the receiver of the text and the text as it exists as a final product in the sense of the historical conditioning of the process of interpretation.

Bakhtin's model of dialogism, by contrast, encompasses a multiplicity of incomplete voices and unconcluded positions and assumes an active participation on the part of the reader in the dialogical formation of the meaning, and in the appropriation of the work's multiple discourses. In Bakhtin, history is ever-present in a metaphorical sense as it permeates every word of the text. Bakhtin thus postulates a dynamic relation between history, society and text. As in the literary text, history is the very fabric of the film text as well; it exists in the text in the form of images, soundtrack, and the particular voices of the protagonists. In *Man of Marble,* memories from the Stalinist era, given in the accounts of the protagonists, are transformed into stylized images combining the moments of the past glory and its horror. Stalinism is alive in the bluish hues of the security officer's office and in the low-angled presentation of the terrified Birkut. Stalinism also persists in *Man of Iron* in the ubiquitous subliminal presence of the powerful authorities evoked in the words of Agnieszka in the prison, or in a powerful scene in which the human relations officer from the shipyard forbids Maciek and Agnieszka to start an exhibition in their apartment of photographs depicting the events of 1970. The totalitarian system introduced by Stalin is later echoed in the totalitarian system of the French Revolution in *Danton.* A color palette similar to that used in some scenes of *Man of Marble* constitutes the atmosphere of the whole film. *Danton* is thus filmed in bluish and grayish tones from beginning to end, thus depicting the overpowering gloom of terror. By such a use of color in his films, Wajda imposes his own interpretation of history. The rhetorical devices he uses create a specific interpretation, a set of figurative statements relating to the past. History in these films is a highly subjective undertaking, the perception of which has nothing to do with an absolute truth of the presented events.

There are scenes, however, in which the representation of reality in the historical discourse becomes almost transparent, without any intrusion of rhetorical devices. Such transparency is seen in the scenes of *Man of Iron* where documentary footage coalesces with the fictional narrative. Even then, although the style of this footage seems to be almost devoid of the personality of the filmmaker, the camera angle in particular shots creates other meanings for the spectator. For instance, the bird's-eye view of the Catholic mass in the documentary footage in sequence six in *Man of Iron* is stunning in its simplicity and enunciative power. The purpose of this "objective" shot produced by Zajaczkowski and Chodakowski in their film *Robotnicy* (The Workers, 1980), and included by Wajda in his film was to present the Catholic mass with its crowds of people, in juxtaposition with the shot of the stunned Winkiel who watches the mass from the hotel window. The sequence clearly marks the power of the Catholic religion in the formation of opposition movements in Poland.

In general, however, Wajda is no historian in the literary sense of the word. His historical language in the cinema is not utterly lucid, but rather resembles "a focusing lens, but an uncolored one."[16] The historical discourse in his films is part of the whole cinematic experience, not devoid of the personality of the filmmaker. The rhetorical effect of his presentation of history is unique; and the factual knowledge his films present is rendered in such a way that each film tells its own story instead of presenting bare historical facts.

The rhetoric of his films constitutes a specific "politics of discourse"[17] that creates a historiography that is far from politically innocent. In his films depicting stories deeply ingrained in the history of Poland, Wajda presents his version of events and his interpretation of those times. The fact that the spectators identified with these stories and read them as their own version of events (especially *Man of Iron*) contributed to the enormous success of the films. Wajda's version of history, however, must not be considered an objective truth, a full reconstruction of the events, historically proven and rationalized. Nevertheless, his presentation of the events creates a specific political impact. The artistic manipulation of the facts and their brilliant cinematic presentation opens a dialogue with the spectator, who identifies with the images, painfully negotiates them, and finally accepts them, embracing, in this way, the political message of Wajda himself.

It is with an understanding of history as the constitutive substance of the film text and not an abstract entity on its own that I offer analyses of the three films. In the following section I present historical facts that have found their representation or have been alluded to in *Man of Marble*, *Man of Iron*, and *Danton*. Later, I concentrate on particular scenes in the films in which historical discourse is explicitly realized.

The Historical Context of the Films

In this part of the chapter I shall present the moments of Polish history that are directly reported, alluded to, or commented upon in all three films. The films *Man of Marble*, *Man of Iron*, and *Danton* refer to the time between Stalinism in the 1950s and the implementation and execution of martial law in Poland in 1981.

In Poland the term "Stalinism" refers to the historical period after the Second World War up to 1956. Boleslaw Bierut, the Polish advocate of the Soviet dictator, governed the country following directives from Stalin himself. Stalin implemented a Soviet-style communism, preached and practiced in the Soviet Union from the late 1920s to the early 1980s. The totalitarian political and ideological system espoused by Stalin demanded not only a complete psychological subjugation of Soviet citizens to his dictates but also required that every Soviet citizen remain under total government control in all areas of his or her life. Every human activity, whether public or personal, was monitored by "The Great Leader" and his followers. The party controlled industrial growth, agricultural and cultural activity, but also watched the individual through constant political meetings and propaganda sessions. Ideological argument was swamped by the cult of Stalin's personality, and all discussions were brought to a close with a timely or untimely quotation from "The Great Leader" himself.

An attempt was made to establish the same system in Poland. In those years, Poland was a one-party state under direct Soviet control. The Polish economy was directed to serve military purposes. On the pretext that the socialist bloc was about to be attacked by the forces of American imperialism, Poland and other countries of Eastern Europe were collectively turned into an armed camp.

Stalinism was also a mode of thinking, and, as Davies describes it, "a doctrine, a system, and an attitude of mind."[18] Davies summarizes Stalinism in Poland in the following way:

> the habits of Stalinism penetrated into every walk of life. Statues of Stalin appeared in public places. Everything and anything, from the Palace of Culture in Warsaw downwards, was dedicated "to the name of J.V. Stalin." Soviet Russian civilization was upheld as the universal paragon of virtue ... In art, "Socialist Realism," once described as "the orchestra of the concentration camp," gained exclusive approval. In the sciences, Russian names such as Lysenko superseded Mendel, Newton, and Einstein. In the humanities, Soviet "Diamat," the allegedly scientific analysis of all human problems, was indiscriminately applied. Nonconformity of any sort was promptly punished. The militiaman and the petty Party bureaucrat walked tall.[19]

In this totalitarian sense, Stalinism in the three films appears as a political and cultural trait continuing into the present, not as a distant, completed, and closed past. Stalinism of the 1950s merges with the 1960s and the 1970s and imposes its dictatorial voice on the 1980s.[20]

As a political and historical phenomenon, the Stalinist system remained intact in Poland until October 1956. The thaw that started after the "secret speech" by Krushchev to the 20th Congress in the Soviet Union in 1956, in which he recounted a selection of Stalin's crimes against the party and the people, rocked the entire communist world. Krushchev's speech and the death of the Polish Communist Party leader, Boleslaw Bierut, opened wide the doors to internal party conflict in Poland between revisionists and dogmatists. Intellectuals seeking cultural independence and political change attacked the doctrinaire party leadership. Also, the first serious social conflict occurred in June 1956, when industrial workers in Poznan, protesting revised production norms that reduced their take-home pay, demonstrated in the streets to express their grievances. The government used force to end the demonstrations and caused scores of deaths but failed to strengthen the party's authority or bring about its unity.

This first Polish crisis after the Second World War revealed a serious disagreement between the workers and the party and started a slow demoralization process in all layers of Polish society. Absenteeism and alcoholism were common phenomena. Workers did not feel any emotional attachment to their places of employment since the plants belonged to the state, which was represented by the party bureaucrats who enjoyed their privileges. From that moment in the post-war history there was an observable separation of post-war ideals from socialist reality. The post-war enthusiasm to rebuild the country after the Second World War changed into disillusionment and cynicism. Workers observed the emergence of a new class, a bourgeois elite of the party officials. Enraged by the schizophrenic disparity between the party principles (equality, democracy, and equal distribution of goods) and a reality that stood in obvious contrast to these ideals, workers took matters into their own hands and tried to organize their lives accordingly. The state plants ceased to be important, so the workers purloined them and supported their own thriving private concerns. (It is worth noting that the party apparatus also took active part in embezzlement, forgery, and simple theft, and orchestrated these crimes in a more sophisticated way than the workers did, as recent documents on this phase of Polish history reveal.)

The demoralization of the whole population caused by the disillusionment concerning the role of the party in the country's development was also reinforced by an inertia in the political, economic, and cultural policies in the 1960s. Consequently, other crises followed. The first one, in 1968, was preceded by a political event that revealed a deep disparity in the Polish society between intellectuals, especially Jewish ones, and official party representatives. The stimulus was the Six-Day War in the Middle East and the victory of Israel over the Arabs. Poles reacted sympathetically to this victory, which, in turn, precipitated an official reaction from Wladyslaw Gomulka, the first secretary at that time. Using the party's anti-Zionist policy to accuse Jewish communists and non-communists of Zionism and revisionism, he bluntly told the Jews that they had to choose between two fatherlands. After a quiet time that had followed the Second World War, when the Jews who wanted to contribute to Poland's reconstruction and wanted to live in Poland stayed in the country, an open persecution of Jews started in 1968. Many Jews who found Poland a somewhat bizarre country but one in which it was possible to live and prosper were forced to emigrate to Israel, a country they neither knew nor desired to inhabit. They left behind their cultural heritage, friends, and members of the family who decided to stay against all odds (despite possible retributions in the future). This second important event in the post-war history indicated a divergence between government policy and the wishes of the people. The public was outraged but feared persecution if it expressed its reactions at that time.

This event was followed by another important crisis in the same year. In March 1968, intellectuals and students protested the party's cultural policy, especially the premature closing of the play *Forefathers' Eve* by Adam Mickiewicz,[21] because anti-tsarist observations mouthed by the protagonists within the play were taken by the audience to be direct references to Soviet oppression. It is worth remembering that Poland remained in the orbit of Soviet influence long after the death of Stalin. Poland "cooperated" with the Soviet Union on economic and cultural levels; compulsory Russian language classes were taught in schools; and various forms of pressure were exerted on Poles from the Soviet side. This constant presence of the Soviet spirit irritated Poles, so Mickiewicz's nineteenth-century verse functioned as a stimulus that revealed a long buried hatred. The audiences reacted in a spontaneous way. Students and young professors in particular, with the Romantic tradition of revolutionary protests behind them, took part in enthusiastic street demonstrations in Warsaw. These were promptly crushed by Mieczyslaw Moczar, the ambitious minister of internal affairs. A wave of arrests followed.

These two events, together with a third one that occurred in Gdansk two years later brought about the downfall of the party secretary, Wladyslaw Gomulka, who was unable to develop an economic policy that would improve the standard of living for the Polish people. The nature of this crisis, followed by the next one in 1976, was mainly economic, but both events prompted serious changes in the country's political life, and, later, led directly to the abolition of the existing political system and introduction of a market economy in the 1990s.

The first event, in 1970, occurred because of an unfortunate decision of the party to publish a list of food and consumer items with new higher prices effective on 13 December, just before Christmas. The prices were published on the front pages of the newspapers and produced a reaction of the utmost rage and despair in conservative, traditional people who spent most of their savings on Christmas food and presents. Confrontations erupted in Gdansk, on the Baltic Coast, and these were followed by similar confrontations in Gdynia, Szczecin and other towns. Hundreds of workers were killed and injured in this conflict. The event led to a change of political figures. A group led by Edward Gierek, the provincial party leader in Silesia, overthrew Gomulka and his closest associates. The new leader carried out a series of talks with the striking workers and finally agreed to the workers' primary request concerning food prices.

Gierek's early attitude, his willingness to listen to complaints and grievances, and his show of respect for interlocutors from any level of society were widely welcomed. Party membership increased, and the party's legitimacy seemed to grow. However, although Gierek in the beginning of his leadership significantly increased the workers' standard of living, he did it mainly through loans from the West. The party's policy of modernizing and expanding industry did not yield the anticipated dividends. By 1975 Poland's debt to the West had reached nearly eight billion dollars, and numerous investment projects were still unfinished. When Gierek himself tried to increase the prices of food in 1976, several protests occurred. As Nicholas Andrews, a historian, relates:

> a major protest occurred at the Ursus tractor manufacturing plant on the outskirts of Warsaw, where workers pulled up the railroad tracks of the Warsaw to Poznan line, a primary east-west transportation link. Another incident occurred in Radom to the south of Warsaw, where workers spontaneously took their grievances to the provincial authorities and were met and forcibly dispersed by internal security

troops. Rioting broke out, and several workers were killed or injured and many arrested.[22]

This time, however, there was no change in the government or the party positions, and Gierek was slowly consolidating his power base. He did it by strengthening the party apparatus and making all economic decisions dependent on the final word of party officials. At that time the hated *Radiokomitet*, the media institution governing the shape and content of any piece of information coming from TV, radio, and other sources, was created. *Radiokomitet* bred such cultural and sociological phenomena as "newspeak" and the "propaganda of success."

During Gierek's period of tenure, the Communist Party became extremely corrupt. The phenomenon of corruption was widespread in every sector of the economy and governed almost all the areas of human life. Allocation of state living quarters, better food, better industrial products for homes, and all services, such as medical, telephone, etc., depended on the "good will," meaning bribery, of officials. Generally speaking, the late 1970s were characterized by disenchantment with government policies, stagnation of the standard of living, a worsening party reputation, and general discontent by people in the whole country.

As disenchantment with government policies grew, formal opposition movements began to emerge. One of the most powerful was KOR (Komitet Obrony Robotnikow), the Workers' Defense Committee, which was created in 1976. This was an underground dissident organization with Adam Michnik and Jacek Kuron as its leaders.[23] This organization and others led an active opposition to the authorities. In 1980, the authorities decided to introduce further price increases on food. Unlike 1970 and 1976, the government did not plan to make public announcements that all newspapers would headline on their front pages. The authorities seemed to believe that if they did not draw attention to the price increases, their actions would pass almost unnoticed. Gierek seemed to have made the same mistake as his predecessor. This time, however, the Polish opposition was much better organized, and immediately after the price increases work stopped in several plants. The workers demanded wage increases to compensate for the increase in food prices. Since there was no response from the government, the strike started.

Strikes erupted in the whole country. In Lublin they were potentially most dangerous because the railway workers who joined the strike of the truck plant workers blocked the railway lines between Lublin and the Soviet Union. This created a risky situation by jeopardizing the safety of the lines of communication between the Soviet Union and the Warsaw Pact's western-most state, the German Democratic Republic. On 14 August 1980 an historic strike began in Gdansk. Historians such as Andrews, Taras,[24] and Ash,[25] describe the beginning of the strike in a similar way. In Andrews's words, "At 6 a.m. on 14 August 1980, the workers in sections K-1 and K-3 of the Lenin Shipyards in Gdansk put down their tools and left their machines. By the end of the day the entire yard – 17,000 people – had stopped work, and a 13-person strike committee had been formed."[26]

The strike was an event of extreme importance. The shipyard workers were widely respected for their uncompromising attitude during the 1970 strike. At that time they had risked their lives to express their distress. Polish citizens also felt that the strike was extremely important because the Gdansk shipyard workers decided to take part in it again. The strike extended to other cities on the Baltic coast like Gdynia, Elblag, and Szczecin, and later to *voivodship*[27] capitals such as Lodz, Wroclaw, and Warsaw. In Gdansk, the workers drew up a list of demands that included wage increases, approval of the erection of a monument devoted to the memory of the workers who were killed in 1970, and the reinstatement of Lech Walesa and Anna Walentynowicz, active members of the opposition who had been fired just before the strike started.

The Gdansk shipyard was a major employer in the region and an important source of political opposition. Consequently, the authorities wanted to end the strike as soon as possible. Two days after the strike began, the government seemed to agree to the Gdansk shipyard strikers' demands. However, workers from other plants protested that their grievances had not been taken care of yet. Both the Gdansk strikers and the strikers from other plants felt that the time had come to deal with the whole political situation of the country in a conclusive manner. From a job action for a particular cause in a couple of plants, the strike changed into a general event of great political significance. On 16 August an Interfactory Strike Committee of thirteen persons representing striking workers from plants in Gdansk, Gdynia, and Sopot drew up a list of demands. The most important ones included acceptance of independent trade unions; the right to strike; freedom of speech, press, and publication; restoration of rights to persons dismissed in 1970 and 1976 and to students expelled from schools for their beliefs; full public disclosure of information about the economic crisis; and selection of managerial personnel on the basis of qualifications, not party affiliation. Unlike the crises of 1970 and 1976, the representatives of the intelligentsia joined the workers. The members of the Gdansk Writers' Union lent support to the workers' effort in the strike, and one of them took part in the meetings of the Interfactory Union Strike Committee on 21 August. Warsaw intellectuals brought an appeal signed by writers, journalists, and artists from other parts of the country, with a request to reach a compromise through negotiations and avoid a repetition of the bloodbaths of 1970 and 1976.

The final agreement between the government and the striking shipyard workers was signed on 22 August and it had a tremendous effect on the political situation in Poland. The strike revealed that workers could display a high level of organization and discipline when needed (e.g., drinking of alcohol was banned during the strike); it signalled a close cooperation between the intelligentsia and the working class; and it revealed the important part played by the Catholic Church in Polish political life. A new trade union, Solidarity, which promised democratic changes in all areas of society, emerged after the strike. Although the Polish Communist Party insisted on its leading role even throughout the sixteen months of Solidarity's existence, its actual domination ended as the so-called "dictatorship of proletariat" proved to be a fictitious construct. On the other hand, although Solidarity was careful never to call itself a political party, in reality it seized psychological power in Poland after the strike.

The strike also influenced the country's neighboring countries. The news of the strike spread all over Europe. The workers in Eastern Europe especially felt excited and encouraged by the course of events in Poland. Consequently, the ruling parties in those countries placed tighter controls on their own media and on the flow of information. As Andrews comments, "In an era of deepening economic problems, they (the authorities) were more concerned than ever about the stability and popular acceptance of the Communist system ..."[28]

After the registration of Solidarity as the first independent trade union, which was accomplished thanks to the support of Cardinal Wyszynski, the primate of the Catholic Church, the movement consolidated. However, it became increasingly militant and no longer could accept the privileged position of the party. In December 1981, Solidarity was planning to hold a referendum on important political questions. The first query concerned confidence in General Wojciech Jaruzelski, prime minister; the second asked whether a provisional government should be established and free elections should be held. The third and the fourth ones asked whether people were in favor of providing military guarantees to the Soviet Union and whether the Polish United Workers' Party could be the instrument of such guarantees in the name of Polish society. Moreover, Solidarity's National Commission[29] demanded new elections to the Sejm (national legislature) in 1982.

The referendum would have touched upon crucial political problems, such as Poland's dependence on the Soviet Union and the role of the Communist Party in the formation of Poland's political fate. In fact, the referendum would have undermined the role of Wojciech Jaruzelski as the country's leader and definitely would have jeopardized the country's political stability. This call for a referendum aggravated the tense relations between the union and the government; activated a process of deterioration of the political and social situation; and finally led directly to the implementation of martial law on 12 December 1981.

Sixteen months passed between the strike in Gdansk and the introduction of martial law. This period was considered to be the most productive for the government opposition and most similar to the ideal of freedom Poles had always nurtured in their hearts. Lack of censorship produced a variety of new publications that openly denounced the regime. Poles indulged in a process of purification of their national history, trying to reveal all the atrocities of Stalinism and the hypocrisy of the government in hiding unpleasant historical facts. In this atmosphere of unrest, during the night between Saturday, 12 December and Sunday, 13 December 1981, General Jaruzelski had the Council of State introduce martial law in Poland.

During the first days of martial law Jaruzelski's forces arrested most Solidarity leaders and other opposition members. They also imposed severe organizational measures, such as cutting off telephone and telex lines between Poland and the outside world, establishing a curfew, banning travel between cities, suspending all trade unions, and closing universities and schools. Moreover, all government media and certain industrial facilities were militarized.

In an address to the Polish nation on 13 December Jaruzelski tried to justify martial law by pointing to the danger presented by Solidarity and its strike threats and protest actions, which he said would have paralyzed the country for months to come. In fact, before martial law was implemented constant strikes all over Poland had produced chaos and risked a breakdown of the economy. Jaruzelski presented himself as the savior of the country who could do nothing else in this situation but introduce the toughest measures possible to save the country from impending chaos and from the ensuing Soviet intervention. Jaruzelski could not afford to forget the Soviets' concern. Their continuous pressure simply could not be disregarded. Their ability to influence Poland's economy could not be dismissed. Finally, the Soviets had a capability for military intervention they had previously demonstrated they were not afraid to use, and Jaruzelski recognized it was his goal and duty to do whatever was necessary to avoid such a catastrophe.

It is worth noting that the possibility of Soviet military intervention in Poland reminded Poles not only of the Soviet smashing of the Hungarian revolution of 1956, the invasion of Czechoslovakia in 1968, and the intervention in Afghanistan in 1979, but most particularly of the Russian tsarist occupation of eastern Poland throughout the nineteenth century, up to the First World War. It summoned the fear that during the next occupation the Polish state might well lose its sovereignty; that the Polish people could see their standard of living reduced to the Soviet level; that Polish culture could be gradually destroyed; and that Polish traditions could be suppressed. Polish experience with Russian rule during the last century was strengthened by the judgement of most Poles that the Soviets were responsible, at Katyn and elsewhere in 1941, for the massacre of Polish officers captured during the Soviet military occupation of eastern Poland in 1939. These experiences hardened Polish determination to avoid providing the Soviets with sufficient motive for military intervention.[30]

However, as recent documents on the introduction of martial law in Poland handed to Lech Walesa, Polish President, by Borys Jelcyn, Russian President, during his official state visit to Poland in spring 1994 confirm, Jaruzelski played a much more sinister role in bringing the Soviets over. The so called "Suslow's file,"[31] handed to Lech Walesa during this visit, contains documents on the very elaborate intelligence work of both Polish and Soviet security agents concerning the leaders of the Solidarity movement before the implementation of martial law. The documents also verify the suspicions of many Polish citizens that the implementation of martial law was a carefully orchestrated and very well prepared operation monitored by the highest representatives of the Communist Party in the Soviet Union and supported by other leaders of former Eastern European countries, such as Eric Honecker in the former East Germany. In the context of these documents, the self-image of a savior of the nation that Jaruzelski tried to present to the outside world long after the end of martial law seems to have been unjustified.[32] However, in 1981, long before these documents were known to the public, the momentous decision to implement martial law in Poland was fiercely debated by Polish citizens. It cannot be denied that it brought military order out of civilian chaos. Martial law lasted seventeen months – from 13 December 1981 to 22 July 1983. During this time Jaruzelski followed a consistently repressive policy. In October 1982 Solidarity and other trade unions were banned. Many union activists remained in prisons long after an amnesty law was passed in July 1983. A military style was introduced into all areas of life, administrative, industrial, and cultural. Representatives of the military were present at each level of the government, administration, and medical institutions. Every walk of life was scrutinized and remained under constant control of the military forces. Cultural life was especially seriously affected. Journalists were purged; theater directors, actors, and filmmakers were dismissed; and the autonomous powers of academic bodies were reduced. In every area of life both military presence and party supervision were painfully visible.

Psychologically, martial law caused irreparable damage to Poles because it destroyed their confidence in the army, which was a tool for martial law's implementation and maintenance. Also, the brutality and acts of terror perpetrated by the riot police during the first days of martial law were never forgotten.

This period of Polish history, 1945 to 1982, constitutes the historical discourse in the three films under discussion. *Man of Marble* incorporates Stalinism and the time of the 1970s in Poland. *Man of Iron* embraces Polish history at the time of the August strikes in Gdansk. And *Danton*, although situated in the time of the French Revolution of the eighteenth century, makes significant references to the implementation of martial law in Poland. The three films signify and present the development of the Solidarity movement – *Man of Marble* in forecasting Solidarity's imminence through the presentation of opposition movements; *Man of Iron* in presenting it in action, with the political opponents involved in an actual political struggle; and *Danton* in its depiction of a political struggle between Danton and Robespierre, (interpreted by Polish spectators as a conflict between Walesa and Jaruzelski, respectively).

In the rest of this chapter I shall present an analysis of scenes in the films that specifically engage the spectator in his or her appropriation of the films' historical discourse. The analysis of these films can be helped by referring to the film synopses in the appendix. These synopses present the content of the films in the form of summarized sequences.

The Historical Discourse in *Man of Marble*

The historical discourse in *Man of Marble* takes place in stories about the past and the present that form two interchanging discursive chains. The historical events are seen through the eyes of participants from the past, through the eyes of the protagonists of the film in the 1970s (Agnieszka, her crew, and, except for the deceased Birkut himself, all the characters from the stories of the past), and through the eyes of the spectators.

Some scenes in the film seem especially rich in historical digressions and allusions, and they prompt the spectator (especially the Polish spectator) to dialogically interact with the filmic discourse and to connect it to the context of his or her own experience. The following analyses illustrate how the historical discourse reveals itself in a dialogical negotiation of the scenes' meaning by the participating, active spectator.

One of the first examples of such an interaction is the work's fourth sequence[33] which takes place in the TV studio, where Agnieszka, the protagonist of *Man of Marble*, sees films from the 1950s. Most of the people taking part in the screenings of the films in the studio are older than Agnieszka. The times depicted are well known to them or to their families. They are full of doubt about Agnieszka's attempts to make a film based on the forbidden past. However, a series of significant glances are exchanged between the woman who assists with the reels and Agnieszka. She seems to understand fully the risk Agnieszka is taking. Her look is motherly, full of pity for the aspiring young director, but, at the same time, full of admiration. The exchange of looks signifies a rich historical discourse on the totalitarian system, which allows for such an unspoken exchange but forbids an open verbal exchange. It also is seen by the Polish spectator as a form of the spectator's involvement in the implied historical reality behind the women's looks – the reality shared by the protagonists on the screen and the spectators in the cinema.

In the same sequence, the recreations of films from the 1950s, which the woman shows to Agnieszka, dialogically involve the spectator in the appropriation of their meaning in the context of cultural and historical discourses well known to Polish spectators. In particular, the scene of the fight for food leads the spectator into a discourse on a similar scene in Eisenstein's *Battleship Potemkin* (1925), which also featured the workers' discontent and distrust of the authorities. Huge paintings of prominent workers, on the other hand, lead the spectator to the historical area of the machinery of Stalinist propaganda.

The fifth sequence in *Man of Marble* presents Agnieszka's conversation with Burski, the director of the films she has seen. The sequence depicts Burski (played by one of the most famous artists in Poland, the late Andrzej Lomnicki) as the director of a film about Birkut. By the 1970s, Burski is a well established artistic personality living in a villa with his family and a woman servant who attends to the family's needs. The villa bears all the signs of luxury and comfort. Agnieszka does not fit in here. The class difference and the status difference are all demonstrated by Agnieszka's dress, lack of any material belongings, and her inelegant behavior. The meeting between the older director and the younger one is read by the spectator as a contrast between the old and the young, the powerful and the weak, the upper and the middle class, and the opportunistic and the rebellious in the course of Polish history. After all, class differences, although officially absent in the socialist Poland, were nevertheless present in a society where the distribution of power and influence was no longer dependent on family background or material assets but on position in the party ranks or on a relation to party officials. As a consequence of this power structure, the representative of artistic circles often compromised his or her artistic autonomy in exchange for party favors, which guaranteed a comfortable life equivalent to that lived by the upper classes in the West.

It is worth noting that the indicators of luxury so clearly read by the Polish spectator were read differently by the Western spectator, for whom possession of a house with a yard and a car is a fact of everyday life. In this case, the Western audience cannot understand the class implications of the unusual dialogue between the two directors, one who belongs to the older generation and the other starting her career. In Poland, where most of the members of the intelligentsia used to live in ugly housing projects or old, neglected houses (such as the one occupied by Agnieszka's father), the luxury of a single home meant either relations with the security (Sluzba Bezpieczenstwa), connections with the black market (illegal dealing in dollars), or a very comfortable position within party circles. Wajda here refers to the fourth possibility, the privileged position occupied by famous artists (such as Wajda himself) who were kindly allowed decent living conditions in return for sympathetic depiction of the regime through their art. It was rare for artists well known to the outside world to present their own views in their work, and only then under the constant threat of retribution and persecution.

Wajda was trying to describe this mosaic of contrasts through acting technique; the actor playing the older director is careful not to be too blunt with the young rebel and he tries not to offend her. The scene was considered by many critics to be Wajda's repentance, but also an attempt to explain the artistic cynicism and opportunism on the part of any director in socialist Poland. That is probably why the scene is full of symbols: Burski wears a black shirt and a white suit; his villa is full of old Polish paintings; and, in the beginning of the sequence, there is a striking conversation between him and his maid reminiscent of old, gentry times. These symbols tell the spectators, among many other things, that Burski serves as a symbol of the contemporary artist in Poland – a rebel at heart (black shirt) who had to compromise his position (become white in the eyes of the authorities, thus the white suit) in order to start producing films. In this way, Burski tries to lessen the negative impact of Burski's film about Birkut; the director says he had to invent a tour de force in order to survive on the artistic and political scene, since no one, in the Stalin years, could accept his films about poor food rations for workers.

Burski continues to cultivate old traditions in his own home, as if trying to indicate that there is a certain continuity in the historical and artistic tradition in Poland, and despite all the misfortunes of history (Stalinism, socialism, etc.), the Polish tradition stands above everything. On the other hand, the director produces a dialogical tension between the aristocratic image Burski promulgates in his house, and the historical understanding on the part of the spectator and Agnieszka, who know the degree of subjugation to authority required for such luxury to be enjoyed in the home of a private citizen of socialist Poland.

But the idealistic historical discourse of Polish nobility overshadows a more skeptical reading of the scene on the part of the Polish spectator. The spectator dialogically interrelates all the tensions and historical contradictions within the scene itself. He or she senses the irony in this presentation, and also detects a certain helplessness in the director who tries to present a positive picture of the Polish artist as someone who, despite the impositions of the system, tries to preserve the continuity of Polish history. Wajda emphasizes this wish in his remark on the film itself, "Poland did not start today, its reality was created after the Second World War; the country went through all kinds of stages, and endured many difficulties. The film introduced this theme, people started to talk about it, and interpret it in many different ways."[34]

A non-Polish spectator, on the other hand, who knows little about the discourse on Polish history but something about the artist's position in a socialist state, definitely would react to the skepticism and irony in the scene to a greater extent than the Polish spectator, who is often affected by sentiment and historical idealism.

The Polish spectator, moreover, interprets this scene in the film in terms of a cultural discourse. Andrzej Lomnicki,[35] the actor playing Burski, has played in Henryk Sienkiewicz's *Trilogy*, which presented an idealistic picture of the Polish nobility. In the eyes of most Polish viewers, Lomnicki is always associated with Michal Wolodyjowski, a famous and amorous nobleman who fought for an independent Poland in the seventeenth century. The fact that Wajda used this particular actor for such a dubious and ideologically suspicious figure might mean that he wanted to be forgiven in the name of all the Polish artists who compromised their artistic integrity in Poland for not telling the whole and unquestioned truth to the spectator, the truth that Agnieszka wants to reveal. Even the timbre of Burski's voice, especially in the scenes with his child and maid, reminded the spectator of Wolodyjowski so much that he was more likely to be forgiven for anything he could have done in the past.

I consider this particular scene a kind of subliminal manipulation by Wajda of the Polish spectator. It reminds me of the election scene later in the film when Birkut says that, despite all the wrongs he has suffered, he does not want revenge because this is Poland, after all, his beloved native country. The same kind of sophisticated manipulation of nationalistic feelings, especially in the older generation of Poles, is seen in the scene with Burski. On the other hand, this scene could also be interpreted as depicting an internal dialogical split in Wajda, the director, who identifies both with Burski and Agnieszka.

The diversity of discourses, historical, cultural, and literary, produces an emotionally disturbing combination that interacts with the spectators' sensitivities in their own assessment of the historical viability of Burski's explanations. The scene itself becomes a vibrant combination of voices interacting with each other, where each particular voice conditions others. The historical discourse of socialistic Poland, familiar to the spectators, becomes relativized and de-privileged in its interaction with the cultural icon of nobility and the ideal of historical continuity that Burski/ Lomnicki portrays.

The scene with Burski opens up a retrospective scene from the past (the 1950s) when Burski was making his film about Birkut. This sequence transports the spectator into another world, compelling him to compare the historical discourse presented by Wajda with whatever he knows, thinks, or realizes concerning the 1950s. The reaction of older spectators, upon the film's release, was especially violent in regard to this scene since they recognized whole areas of associations that they dialogically related to their own experience.

In this sequence, Burski decides to produce a tour de force, a staged screening of the workers' race for the best construction results. The first secretary, Jodla, the security members, and the film director all take part in the conspiracy. However, the final word concerning the arrangement of the *mise en scène*, the action, and the choice of actors belongs to the director. Party corruption goes hand-in-hand with a cynical manipulation by the media. The event Burski orchestrated was the construction of a wall of 35,000 bricks within one day. Such an event had to be carefully prepared, and a worker had to be chosen who would not jeopardize the propagandist value of the whole event. He had to be extremely naive, young, and strong. Birkut served this ideal in the best way imaginable. As a young man from a village, he knew nothing about the manipulation by the media; in his naiveté he just wanted to be a good worker and comrade. Birkut was presented as a very naive person, a peasant who believed in the ideals and purposes of the Marxist ideology.

This depiction of Birkut as a representative of his society at that time contrasts strikingly with the scenes in the beginning of *Man of Marble*. Certain ominous signals of social awareness had already appeared in Burski's early films from the 1950s: the cutting of cherry trees, mud at the construction site, lack of food, forced labor, and a party official running away from furious workers constitute a kind of overture to forthcoming events.[36]

As this dismal reality dialogically clashes with the party's slogans and propaganda shows, there is a sudden improvement in Birkut's living conditions. This change infuriated members of the older generation in Poland who took the propaganda of the 1950s seriously, and really believed in the progress of Poland's reconstruction under Boleslaw Bierut's[37] rule. The film's reality was perceived by them without any irony. Z. Zaluski expressed this view, writing

> Why did Wajda spit in our faces, the faces of retired people, the ham he fed the Stakhanovite, showing no concern for our hard work, hunger, rheumatism, chronic tuberculosis and wasted youth.[38]

As Wieslaw Godzic[39] mentions, older spectators reacted with an emotional reading oriented toward an entirely referential discourse that was related to their own experience. Such an interpretation allows for an entrance into the world of the diegesis at its referential level only, not at the level of articulation. As spectators they rejected the irony in the film which resulted from the dialogical clash of the discourse of historical truth and the discourse of its presentation.

Birkut naively believes in the good intentions of Burski and in his positive presentation of the workers' effort as a joint effort of his team.[40] At the end of the dramatic race in which 35,000 bricks are laid, the spectator is exposed to the twisted face of Birkut, whose eyes are filled with an animal-like exhaustion. At the moment of extreme fatigue no ideals are important, and the propaganda machine shows its real face.

The scene is striking because of another emotionally loaded concatenation of images, that is, the faces of the viewers of the humiliating spectacle, the older workers, tired and disinterested, looking with disbelief at the circus.[41] The image of the party officials – dressed up and businesslike – is later juxtaposed against the image of the sick and mutilated hand of the worker. This dialogical juxtaposition of images created a feeling of repugnance and hatred in the spectator at the time of the first screening of the film, or rather brought to the surface a feeling that had already been present in the Polish spectator for almost two decades.[42]

On the other hand, some Polish spectators considered Wajda's Birkut to be a caricature of a worker in the 1950s – an unsophisticated individual who enthusiastically accepts the exposition of his image in the Social Realist monuments.[43] They detected a dialogical coexistence of several discourses in such a presentation: a discourse of bitterness in Wajda fighting for the upper hand against the discourse of historical presentation in the depiction of Birkut's heroism and naiveté, and the discourse of irony that made Birkut a comic strip figure of the Social Realist drama[44].

Some official reviewers in Poland interpreted the scene at the artist's studio, where Birkut's marble figure was made, as playing an important role in the explanation of the film's title. They also added that, in this way, Wajda made a symbolic gesture toward the greatness of the worker's toil itself. By immortalizing Birkut in a marble figure, Wajda pays homage to all the oppressed, naive, and abused workers of the 1950s. Thus, as they said, *Man of Marble* restored the spectator's belief in a cinema of great passion and reminded them, in a drastic way, of the continuity of Polish history. For instance, Krzysztof Klopotowski, more sympathetic to Wajda than other official critics were, wrote about this film in 1981:

> It was the only film which claimed the blood, sweat and tears of the working people. Although the film was seen by 2.5 million viewers, all Wajda got for his efforts was a bag of insults ... It is not a film about a Stakhanovite, as the official critics were trying to convince the general public, it is a film about the idea of the dictatorship of the proletariat. In those years, the proletariat was given the conditions indispensable for their taking part in governing the country, but, on the other hand, a gigantic propaganda manipulation machine and terroristic security apparatus were initiated to control them.[45]

Other reviewers, like most Polish spectators, sensed a great deal of irony in the pompous erection of Birkut's monument, which was abandoned later in the dusty cellars of the National Museum in Warsaw.

In *Man of Marble*, the sequence of the production of Burski's film about Birkut serves as a carrier of the historical discourse into other parts of the film. The spectator who is prepared by the film's exposé of the truth of the historical discourse in the 1950s is not surprised by the monstrosities depicted in Wajda's presentation of the authorities in the 1970s. The chilling picture of the discourse of great manipulation serves as an ideological and moral explanation for the atrocities committed by the officials and of the moral degeneration of the people surrounding Birkut. Thus, the moral degeneration of the decisionmakers of the Polish culture in the 1970s – the TV producer who makes decisions about Agnieszka's film, and Burski, now a famous director – is an inescapable consequence of the moral depravity in those early times of socialist Poland. The historical past and the historical present within the film, that is, the 1950s and the 1970s, produce a strong dialogical encounter since both of them dialogically interact with the historical present of the spectator at the time of the film viewing.

One of the most important aspects of the historical reality that Wajda displayed in the film was the frightening and oppressive presence of the security forces, which inevitably introduced the discourse on Stalinism. Stalinism is alluded to especially often in *Man of Marble*. The Stalinist totalitarian spirit is referred to in every discursive layer of the film, and it monologically conditions and manipulates the spectator's reaction toward the film. The Polish spectator, living most of his or her life under the influence of the Stalinist aura, felt especially overwhelmed by the hopelessness and oppressiveness of some scenes.

In the film the discourse concerning the totalitarian threat of Stalinism is revealed especially in the scenes presenting the security forces. Both in the contemporary discourse and in the discourse from the past the *Bezpieka* (the derogatory name for the security forces) is presented as a threatening force and tool of total oppression; mere acquaintance with it can be harmful. The discourse of *Bezpieka* (security) dominates Burski's film about Birkut, where the security officials take care of the safety of the participants and keep a close eye on any opposition movements by potential subversives. This sequence is read by each generation of Poles in a different way, depending on the political circumstances and the knowledge of the real conduct and misconduct of the security. An example of this is the fifth sequence, which constitutes a flashback describing the activities of *Bezpieka* from the security agent's point of view. Michalak, the security agent assigned to Birkut and Witek during and between their propaganda shows, describes the building event and the fate of Birkut as a social worker, which Birkut became after his accident. Birkut emerges from Michalak's retrospective as an idealistic and naive social worker, not frightened by the apparent sabotage during the fateful event. This made Birkut a dangerous type, impervious to any kind of political and ideological influence from the authorities.

As Michalak shows it, Birkut's naiveté was challenged when Birkut's friend, Witek, was arrested for "probable contacts with the West" (a lie fabricated by the authorities). Birkut goes to the Central Security Office in Warsaw to ask about Witek, despite warnings from his wife and his friends, who begged him not to jeopardize his future. He is received by the security official with patronizing nonchalance but gets no promises. In its ambiguity, the scene is similar to the scene when Witek "disappeared," somewhere in the office of the security official to which he had been invited for a talk. Birkut had accompanied him to the secretary's room and had waited endlessly for his reappearance. When after several hours he demanded to see his friend, the secretary pushed him into a prison-like room, a cool and frightening interior. The security official sitting in the room cynically tried to convince him that nobody had entered the room before.

At this moment, the spectator dialogically enters the discourse of Witek's trial as he or she confronts the historical fact that even in 1976 any contacts with the West were considered suspicious. In the early 1950s these contacts were severely treated "on the doubtful pretext that the socialist bloc was about to be attacked by the forces of American imperialism."[46] Also until the early 1980s, letters, telephone conversations, and trips to the West were usually heavily scrutinized and anybody could suffer unpleasant consequences (interrogations at the security office, withdrawal of one's passport, or talks with the party officials at one's place of work). Therefore, Witek's trial was doubly unpleasant to all the spectators who had suffered in similar circumstances. Although no trials of the type that were common in the 1950s took place in the 1980s, that is, no flimsy evidence of the sort presented at Witek's trial could throw a person into prison, still the Kafkaesque paranoia of those trials was vaguely reminiscent of other historical, more recent trials that took place after the workers' revolts in Poland.

In the 1950s, Witek's abduction by the security symbolizes a common practice performed by the Stalinist regime, which considered human life irrelevant. Czeslaw Milosz's words in *The Captive Mind* convincingly relate the atmosphere of fear which such actions of the security apparatus provoked, "a long period of terror demands an established apparatus and becomes a permanent institution ... Fear is well known as a cement of societies. [Under Stalinist rule], if all one hundred thousand people live in daily fear, they give off a collective aura that hangs over the city like a heavy cloud."[47]

This collective aura of overpowering and ever-present fear is vivid in all textures of the film: the linguistic texture (ambiguous statements, remarks based on common knowledge), the texture of imagery (the exchange of looks between Agnieszka and the woman in the screening room, the exchange of looks between the security official and his secretary, and many other instances), and the musical score.

Michalak's relation in sequence number seven functions as an alternative discourse, presenting the historical truths from the position of the authorities in the 1950s. Together with Burski's depiction of the events and the scenes from authentic propaganda films of the period, the pictures from the 1950s form a polyphony of discourses in a dialogical turmoil. The 1950s period presented itself to the spectator as a mosaic of voices regulated by the monological oppressive power of the totalitarian regime.

The trip to Warsaw ends the first part of the film and also marks the end of the old Birkut as naive, and sometimes even stupid in his idealistic belief in people and ideology. Birkut leaves Warsaw as a man full of bitterness. The man of marble is no longer an ideal statue; the events in the second part of the film start to chip away its idealized contour.

The second part of the film starts with Birkut at a meeting with his comrades, where he begs them for help to release Witek. The comrades do not answer his plea; they start singing workers' songs from the 1950s and Birkut's words are no longer heard. From then on there is a downward spiral in Birkut's career. He is deprived of his apartment in Nowa Huta and has to move to the slums on the outskirts of the city.

Birkut is thrown in prison. After his release, he is told that his wife, Hanka, has left him. He then decides to leave his job to search for her. This romantic, unhappy love, senselessly broken by cruel fate, is typical of Polish culture, which is full of knights errant hopelessly looking for lost love and lost ideals. The Polish spectator interacts here with numerous cultural discourses and wanders through a vast field of texts belonging to the Polish Romantic literary tradition.

Birkut sees his wife in a nouveau-riche restaurant with an older man, her present husband, in snobbish, rich Zakopane.[48] This juxtaposition of the degraded Hanka and her former idealistic husband reinforces the black/white dichotomy of character formation. Hanka is ashamed of her betrayal and does not want to return home with her former husband. Birkut disappears after his trip to Zakopane. Nobody knows where he is. Only later does the spectator learn from his son, Maciek, that he remained faithful to his ideals and fought for the rights of workers. It is only in the last sequence of the film, with Birkut's son, that we learn about his death after the Gdansk demonstrations. Even after his death, Birkut remains the man of marble, invincible in his convictions. The most important sign of his moral invincibility is the fact that he decided to take part in the national elections even though he had suffered so much at the hands of the authorities. His statement, "ludzie, tu roznie bywalo, gorzej, lepiej, ale to jest nasz kraj" (Folks, fortunes have varied here – they've been up and down, but this is still our country), serves as the final credo of Birkut and of Wajda himself, who despite many offers from abroad, decided to stay and make his films in Poland, against all odds.

The reference to the Gdansk demonstrations in 1970 reinforces the historical discourse in an abrupt and painful exposition at the very end of the film. This reminds the spectator that the fictionalized story is convincing only thanks to its dialogical relation with the real: the world of historical facts and events involving real people.

One of the most striking sequences in *Man of Marble* is sequence number ten, in which Agnieszka carries out her third interview, this time with Vincenty Witek, Birkut's former friend and ally. Witek, a former political prisoner, is now a director of one of the numerous Polish "industrial miracles," the gigantic construction site of Huta Katowice. Witek seems to enjoy the role of a successful manager, and, full of satisfaction, tells about his own achievements. Not much is said about Birkut, however. The statement uttered by him: "O, Birkut to byl prawdomowny czlowiek. Dzisiaj juz malo takich, a przydalby sie na budowie" (Oh, Birkut was a truthful man. There are not many like him nowadays, he would be useful at our construction site) is shockingly banal, and it jars the ears of the Polish spectator with its ideological "newspeak."[49] This sequence constitutes an historical recapitulation of the 1970s, with its fascination with industrialization, the technocratic propaganda system, and the subordination of human needs to the requirements of "historical necessity" as propagated by the power system.

The sequence presenting the Huta Katowice site has been widely criticized by film analysts in Poland. Alicja Helman from Cracow University, for instance, considers this sequence (especially the part in which Wajda presents an idealistic picture of the industrial landscape from a bird's-eye view) as an act of capitulation to the system on the part of Wajda, and a final proof that Wajda basically did not reject socialism, and found some of its phenomena (industrialization, for instance) fascinating and worth showing.

Wajda produced an interesting effect in this scene, a dynamic presentation of Huta Katowice. Human values and feelings, violated in the time of the fierce construction of the socialist state, looked especially bleak and unimportant. After all, the cause was important:

the rebuilding of the impoverished country, its industrialization and progress. Another witness from the past, Jodla, the party official in Nowa Huta, whom Agnieszka meets later in Nowa Huta while assembling her fragmented picture of Birkut, summarizes the situation sharply for Agnieszka: "What do you know about those years? It [Nowa Huta] wasn't built by itself, was it?" This justification of rough measures by the party clashed unsympathetically with the presentation of life in those earlier times in the film, although at the same time, it introduced an unsettling note that perhaps the party official was right after all. The lack of response by Agnieszka allows the discourse of the totalitarian regime to creep in and introduce a discordant note of doubt. This is why the Nowa Huta sequence and the conversation with Jodla were so fiercely debated by ordinary spectators and by film critics.

Spectators reacted very strongly to this scene in the film, which takes place in the 1970s. Godzic[50] notes, for instance, that the sequence creates a "fiction the wrong way up," and that this creates a new context, reformulating or putting in ironical quotations the connotations of the underlying diegesis of the reality in which Agnieszka exists. The scene in the context of the whole film looks like an example of an internal polemical discourse. It caused confusion in the spectator; the position of the director seemed self-doubting or self-questioning.

The Poland of the 1970s in this particular sequence seems to be a country of success (in line with the official line of state propaganda) marked by the modern, contemporary buildings of Warsaw, the Lazienki route, and the enthusiasm of the builders of Huta Katowice. Poles are seen as active, industrious people. This optimistic presentation of Polish reality in the 1970s is ironically contrasted with the discourse of the Poles' own experience. Seeing this sequence, Polish viewers looked at themselves in disbelief and wondered how Wajda dared include a typical official success"story in his film. In the context of the 1970s in Poland – a country of gray and neglected cities, impatient and unhappy people working without enthusiasm or belief in the good of the cause – a colorful scene from Huta Katowice introduced a dissonant note into the film.[51]

Wajda is more faithful to his public in the presentation of the historical discourse when he shows one of the last sequences in the film, the Gdansk shipyard. A kind of grimness is vividly apparent in the shipyard early in the morning, when the workers go to work. The atmosphere of apathy gives way to growing dread and the imminence of final solutions to the political crisis. (Although Wajda claims that there is no causal relationship between the film and the strikes in Gdansk, he thinks that "it's not unreasonable to see a connection between them, if only of mutual concern."[52]) As Godzic notes, the presentation of the Gdansk shipyard reminds one of the famous fog sequence in the port after the murder of Vakulinchuk in *Battleship Potemkin*, when the imminence of final dreadful solutions to the crisis is equally threatening.[53] The scene is monologically clear to the spectator; the pervasive discourse of fear comes to the surface again as the dominating overtone of the historical discourse in *Man of Marble*.

The examples of scenes in *Man of Marble* given above illustrate how the historical discourse is present in every layer of the film, in the film diegesis, the construction of *mise en scène* and the film dialogues. It is revealed in the dialogical clash of the ideological positions of the protagonists, in the concatenation of semantically opposing images, and in the linguistic commentaries of the representatives of all the film glossia.

Moreover, the historical discourse in *Man of Marble* evokes certain reactions in the spectators who, in their attempt to match their personal historical truth with the history on the screen, try to appropriate the latter in the act of spectatorship.

The Historical Discourse in *Man of Iron*

In *Man of Iron* history is no longer delicately alluded to or presented in the form of multiple glossia in the film's content and form. In *Man of Iron* history is unmercifully present in almost every scene of the film. It is recalled in flashbacks, it is quoted in the form of original footage, and it is present in the artistic interpretation of the events of 1980.

The interpretation of the events of the shipyard strike is imposed on the spectator as the first synthesis of August 1980, the time of the strikes in Gdansk, and the time of the beginning of significant changes in Polish political life. Wajda's position is monological in the film in the sense of the uniform ideological position that he propagates through the authoritarian voices of his protagonists. The world of the "dominating" will be gone soon, he seems to say, and the world of the "dominated" with its own dominant ideology is approaching. In presenting this monological position in the film, Wajda communicates his message "divested of its language diversity,"[54] and his authorial language inevitably resembles "an awkward and absurd position of the language of stage directions in plays."[55] In *Man of Iron*, Wajda is no longer a ventriloquist; he no longer speaks "through (the) language"[56] of his characters as he had done in *Man of Marble*, but practices "an authoritarian enforced discourse"[57] whose purpose is to support the main thesis of the film. Through flashbacks, a crude enforcement of documentary footage, staged and fictionalized interviews, propaganda techniques, and other cinematic methods of the documentary tradition, but also deeply ingrained in Socialist Realism, Wajda produces a film depicting history at the moment of its creation, a passionate and one-sided depiction of the Gdansk strike.

Wajda created his own artistic vision of the historical event before anybody proposed another one. Since he was the first to present this vision to the public at large, he became the co-author of a specific version of history that would later proliferate in other parts of the country. Wajda produced his perspective on history for both aesthetic and moral reasons, and not necessarily for its epistemological value.[58] Other discourses, such as newsreels, BBC programs, radio broadcasts, and television programs prepared by other foreign TV crews existed as historical documents but they never reached the general public, especially in Poland.[59] In fact, censorship was still so strong in August 1980 that, although the TV-viewing public knew that something was happening in Gdansk (TV reporters reported work stoppages in the Gdansk shipyard), the public had no idea what was really going on. Filmed six months after the strike, Wajda's text became a proto-text, a singular artistic source for establishing the discourse depicting these events, one that the Polish public could trust. Although the Polish audiences were aware of the fact that Wajda's film was a fictionalized account, not an analysis or a document, they accepted this as an artistic presentation that communicated not only the historical truth but the spirit of the August strike as well. Consequently, Wajda's film was not only an artistic event but also a social event, and was extremely important for the people of those times who were never properly informed about the strike by the authorities. As Andrews notes, "Party propaganda was to stress the hardships that work stoppages caused and the costs of the Baltic strikes in terms of idled ships and consequent foreign trade losses, production shortfalls, and market-supply interruptions. Party editorials were to play on the themes of responsibility, domestic peace, common sense, and the need for self-discipline and normal, productive work."[60]

The party's propaganda created its own version of history in an attempt to counteract the revolutionary impact of the strike. Both ideological opponents, Wajda and the party apparatus, presented their own historical account. These two political discourses, one by the party apparatus, and the other Wajda's film, created two different historical narratives which, as Hayden White explains, are always "a mixture of adequately and inadequately explained events, a congeries of established and inferred facts, at once a representation that is an interpretation and an interpretation that passes for an explanation of the whole process mirrored in the (historical) narrative."[61]

To a greater extent than the narrative of the party apparatus, Wajda's narrative reflected the feelings of Poles, and it addressed them in a more emotional and direct way than the orations of party officials did. The propagandistic presentation that Wajda initiated in *Man of Iron* dealt with the basic feelings of oppression and the fight for freedom on which the rebellious Poles always set a high value. In this, Wajda violated the delicate balance between the private and the public that had existed in his far better *Man of Marble*. In the earlier film, social and political events gained meaning only by virtue of their connection to private life; in *Man of Iron*, on the other hand, the private life of the protagonists serves only as a pretext for Wajda to proclaim a political credo of the dominated.

One of the important historical processes that *Man of Iron* initiated was the partial defiance of censorship. This had already gotten underway in the earlier *Man of Marble*, but in the later film Wajda openly revealed the facts without resorting to his earlier stylistic obfuscations. *Man of Iron* favored a direct presentation of facts over the elaborate formal figures that had cushioned facts and dates in *Man of Marble*.

In *Man of Iron* the events of the plot are constituted by the very course of the history itself, which is too fresh and too painful to coexist with the cinematic stories of the heroes on the screen. *Man of Iron* provoked a painful confrontation with the spectators' memories. Wajda combines the fictional and factual discourses in the film, causing a dialogical tension in the spectator's appropriation of the message. The spectator compares the image on the screen with what he or she knows, has heard about, or what he or she directly experienced. There are several ways in which Wajda combines the fictional and factual discourses. The most revealing are:

voicing of historical facts by fictional protagonists; appearance of real historical persons on the screen; and a combination in one sequence of the fictional and factual footage describing particular historical events.

The following scenes illustrate the dialogical presence of historical and fictional discourses in the film that together constitute a polyphony of voices making the fabric of the film vibrant, making it pulsate with a life of its own. In particular the glossia, the relation between the fictional and the factual, the presentation of authority, and the presence of religion in the film reveal most significantly the tensions in the dialogical negotiation of the film's meaning by the spectator.

The voicing of historical facts by fictional characters, is present in the beginning sequences of *Man of Iron*. For instance, in the first scene of the third sequence,[62] at the office of the police official, Badecki, an interview on a TV screen introduces the spectator directly into the problematic of the strike. The scene begins with a close-up of a television screen. In the following shot the camera zooms back to the room in which the TV monitor is situated, and where Badecki briefs Winkiel on Maciek Tomczyk, the strike leader. The historical event of the strike is presented within the framework of the official media, a fact that the Polish spectator always scrutinizes carefully. Used to years of propaganda manipulation, TV "newspeak," and the political announcements of Polish party leaders on the TV screen, the spectator senses an emotional tension in the presentation of the discourse of the revolutionary ideology in the official media. Could it really happen, or was it Wajda's idealistic wishful thinking that the discourse of the strikers could be established with full power on the screen of official TV? This juxtaposition of two discourses, the discourse of revolution and the discourse of the "dominating," creates a dialogical tension in the film text that has to be negotiated by the spectator and accommodated by him or her depending on the political orientation.

In its monological simplicity the revolutionary discourse presents historical facts, historical names (e.g., Anna Walentynowicz), the names of the Gdansk shipyard (K3), and the name of the real leader of the strike (Lech Walesa). Unlike other official presentations on Polish TV, usually full of more or less concealed lies, the discourse of the revolutionary ideology established its authoritarian power simultaneously on the TV screen, and on the diegetic plane of *Man of Iron*. The presence of the police official, Badecki, in the room where the screening takes place introduces an element of ironical tension, while the whole scene is undergoing a process of hybridization, "contain(ing) mixed within it two speech manners, two styles, two 'languages,' two semantic and axiological belief systems,"[63] that of the "dominating" and the revolutionary. This imposition of the conflict of ideologies onto the fictional diegesis makes the didactic monologism of Wajda overpowering in its initial enunciation. The spectator is immediately exposed to historical fact, which requires from him or her careful attention in the appropriation of images on the screen. The spectator is in the discourse of the film and becomes an inherent part of it. On the other hand, the placing of the factual in the mouth of the fictional hero produces an additional dialogical tension that generates disbelief. The spectator wonders whether there is any disparity between the historical fact and the voice of the fictional character relating the historical narrative. Where does the truth lie? In a sense, this alternation of the fictional and the factual forces a recognition of the way the film constructs historical reality for the spectator. Like the staged documentaries of Michelle Citron (especially *Daughter Rite*, 1978), the film "challenges assumptions about the 'reality' of documentary in relation to narrative."[64] The spectator rationally acknowledges the power of such a presentation but emotionally reacts with a dose of skepticism.

Another way the factual is realized in the film is by the presentation of real, historical persons. For instance, Lech Walesa and Anna Walentynowicz appear in *Man of Iron* several times. However, while their appearance in the historical footage or in the staged scenes related to the strike itself strengthens the enunciative power of the message, their artificial incorporation into the film fiction, as in the scene of the wedding of Agnieszka and Maciek, strikes a false chord. As Mariusz Muszkat noted:

> The proportions of ordinariness and sublimity have been obliterated, especially in the scene of the wedding in which Walesa and Walentynowicz took part as witnesses. They were not the same people as they had been before August. Confidence, caused by an unprecedented victory, was all too clear on their faces. In this theatrical scene two times were mixed. This was a serious dissonance.[65]

In this case, the spectator could not dialogically come to terms with the proximity of fiction and reality on the screen. He or she seemed unnecessarily manipulated into a forced combination of two disparate discourses in one scene. The feeling of uneasiness on the part of the spectator and his or her inability to negotiate the meaning of such a convergence is best expressed by Jedrzejewski, who concludes:

In *Man of Iron* the insertion of some staged sequences is morally equivocal, both in relation to the spectator, and to the documentary footage. This device has another consequence as well. The combination of documentary footage with fictional footage causes the fictional layer of the film to become superficial and sketchy.[66]

The spectator reacts with uneasiness especially to sequences that combine fictional and historical footage. The ninth sequence is an example of this device; in it, Wajda liberally mixes documentary footage from the past, documentary footage from the strike of August 1980, and fictional events. In this sequence, from the moment of Dzidek's and Winkiel's meeting in the studio where Dzidek works, the film diegesis is presented in the form of two parallel temporal paths: the present and the past. The present path carries the discourse of the society in August 1980, during the strike. The past discourse, on the other hand, contains numerous flashbacks, explaining the development of Maciek Tomczyk as a political activist and referring to historical events that have shaped him.

In the first flashback, the documentary discourse is simple and frightening in its power. The film shows authentic shots of walls with dissenting slogans; demonstrations of workers, tanks dispersing them, tear gas, and then the shipyard wall, frightened faces of the workers, and crying women. This documentary sequence is echoed by fictional images of the workers ten years later: the images of the workers, their wives and mothers in front of the shipyard. Both factual and fictional discourses function as a unity and strengthen the monological discourse of presentation of the striking people.

A fictional flashback later in Dzidek's relation recalls Birkut, Maciek's father, and the protagonist of *Man of Marble*. Dzidek witnesses the quarrel between the two. Birkut does not allow his son to join the students who have decided to go on strike to support the liberal protests in Warsaw in 1968. He justifies his decision with the supposition that this would provoke the authorities. Birkut summarizes the 1968 demonstration as the intelligentsia settling accounts, and he also thinks that students are being used by party factions as pawns in party infighting.

Another fictional flashback leads the spectator to the demonstrations of 1970. The scene shows the room in the students' hostel from which Maciek, Dzidek, and other students watch the workers demonstrating in the street below. This time it is the workers who call the students to demonstrate. Dzidek shouts back that they do not agree to join the workers. In the following dead silence the two students see the events unfolding from the window. The window frames the workers under attack, the tanks, and it structurally frames the sounds of shots and cries. The Polish spectator thus recalls the historically documented tension between the workers and the intelligentsia. The window in the students' dormitory functions as a metaphorical framework that symbolically alludes to the conflict.

The third flashback in the same sequence introduces one of the most powerful scenes in *Man of Iron*, which is partly fictional and partly documentary. The fictional restaging of the procession of the workers with the body of a dead worker on the door board is accompanied by a documentary soundtrack recorded by the police. On the soundtrack the policemen monitoring the procession relate in a matter-of-fact voice where the procession is heading and what should be done about it. One of them suggests that the corpse should be disposed of because the impression is horrible and the procession could instigate a series of demonstrations.

This mixture of historical footage and fictional footage was openly rejected by some spectators not only because of its emotional impact but also because of historical inconsistencies in the film. For instance, Surdykowski treated the film as a very real statement and a serious portrayal of the events. He reacted to *Man of Iron* as if the film were a documentary, different from the pseudo-documentaries of propaganda pieces on television.

> ... the scene of the carrying of the young worker's body ... was shot in a completely different place. This fact impairs the credibility of the documentary footage for the inhabitants of the Gdansk-Gdynia-Sopot region (Wybrzeze), and especially for the inhabitants of Gdynia, afflicted most tragically in December. The people carrying the body walk along a tramway track while in Gdynia there is not a trace of one on the streets! ... One should not do that![67]

The spectator demands from the director a journalistic scrupulousness and precision in the presentation, and places little importance on the need for consistency of cinematic diegesis and for the aesthetic compactness of the cinematic image. It is worth noting at this point that this lack of precision of place was noticed only by Gdynia and Gdansk viewers. Some of them were witnesses of the

December event; others knew about the place and time of this event from spoken and written communications. The violent reaction of the audience led to a questioning of every single detail of the film, and blurred the border between the fictional and the factual.

The scene of Birkut's death was also debated by the participants in the event. The place where Birkut supposedly died was full of people, so no militiamen could have passed through the crowd. The victims died on the other side of the overpass, where no students could see them. These and other examples of journalistic inconsistency (e.g., the appearance of the gate at the shipyard, the presence or absence of certain topographical points in the film image) were ferociously questioned. The film was supposed to perform the function of a truth tester, a counterbalance to the hypocrisy of the mass media and historical treatises describing earlier strikes in Poland. The viewers' demands for factual accuracy disregarded the requirements of the filmic metaphor, metonymy, and parable. Viewers were not interested in the effect of condensation that required Wajda to put together the images of Birkut's death and students witnessing it from the windows of their residence when this condensation violated the logic of the real place of the action in December 1970. The spectator demanded documentary truth of the presentation and, like Surdykowski, considered the factual inconsistencies as "the screeching of iron over the marble."

This fascinating debate concerning the fictional and the factual is reminiscent of the controversy regarding the relation of the poetic function to the referential function. Roman Jakobson notes, "the supremacy of the poetic function over the referential function does not obliterate reference ... but renders it ambiguous,"[68] while Paul Willemen explains for film:

> Many of the more assiduous filmmakers have become aware of this contradiction, complaining that it is impossible to shoot slums and misery without somehow aestheticizing them – a paradox generated by the widely held but nevertheless false premise that images represent more "accurately" than other forms of representation, and that the choice is between imprecise (poetic) "pictorialism" and precise, referential "photography of record."[69]

Thus, devices that fulfilled the poetic function for many non-Polish spectators, breached the referential function for the Polish spectator, especially the spectator constrained by geographical positioning within the site of the *mise en scène*. The Polish spectator reacted first and foremost to the inconsistencies within the referential function, treating the poetic function of the cinematic image as secondary.[70]

This imposition of the discourse of fact in the film means that the spectator is forced to negotiate every image on the screen with his or her own factual experience. The result was that from the very beginning of viewing the film the truth on the screen was ferociously negotiated with the historical truth of the time. The spectator appropriated and reappropriated the images on the screen in an attempt to render them acceptable to himself or herself. Consequently, at every moment of viewing the film the spectator also negotiated the credibility of Wajda's presentation of the psychological motives of his protagonists in the context of the historical reality of the strike. For instance, in the thirteenth sequence the historical discourse imposes a fictional unreality onto the scene in the car when Dzidek and Winkiel go to see Mrs. Hulewicz at her house. Winkiel should not have gone to the house of a person sympathizing with the opposition movement because such an action posed a danger of exposure for the representative of the official press. The facts of those times contradicted the fictional reality on the screen.

On the other hand, this improbable scene had to be artificially introduced by Wajda in order to give the spectator a chance to see the next events in the diegesis, which were to be related by Mrs. Hulewicz, the representative of "real, simple people." In any case, the spectator forgives Wajda for the impossible dialogue between Winkiel and Dzidek, in which Winkiel totally exposes himself, and Dzidek pretends that he has not noticed.[71] My reaction as a spectator was that Dzidek could have badly jeopardized the safety of the families of the striking workers. Still, I understood Wajda's intention in this improbable positioning of the fictional discourse. If the monological truth of the fighting worker was to be presented, no obstacles, such as improbable dialogues and situations, could prevent the director in his imposition of the authorial truth. This moment was noted by Czeslaw Dondzillo, who stated:

> *Man of Iron* obtained a (Cannes) prize primarily because it appeared at all, and, because it appeared in the form it did. This includes its political message and its artistic form; its documentary layer and fictional (staged) layer; more or less successful dramaturgic solutions; successful and less successful, and rich or one-dimensional, psychological profiles; and, finally, the intentions and preferences of the film authors.[72]

In order to make the factual in *Man of Iron* more credible, Wajda also positioned it within the monological framework of the voice of the people. The historical facts voiced by simple people from the street reinforce the enunciative power of the presentation. According to Czeslaw Dondzillo, situating the film's discourse in the minds of the people was intentional, since Wajda wanted to reveal the mass character of the reform movement (masowy charakter ruchu odnowy).[73] In particular, history seen from the point of view of the most vulnerable observers – old women – strikes the spectator as an extremely powerful device. Mrs. Hulewicz, an old woman at whose house Maciek rented an apartment, is introduced in sequence thirteen, which serves as an insertion into the past to describe Maciek's life. Technically, the sequence consists of several flashbacks relating the life of Maciek, and, accompanying them, bitter commentaries.

One of the flashbacks triggered by the monologue of Mrs. Hulewicz describes the search for Birkut's grave on the first of November the following year. This annual Day of the Departed is devoted to the memory of the deceased, when families traditionally gather at graves, light candles, and lay flowers. Birkut's grave is nowhere to be found. In response to the brutal and inhuman desecration of the grave, Maciek puts an iron cross at the place where his father died. The coarse symbolism of this act is monologically direct; a cross made of iron, and polished by Maciek in the shipyard serves as a symbol of Maciek himself, but also as a premonition of times to come. Neither Maciek nor any other participant of the 1970 events was ever going to forget them. The cross functions symbolically as a solemn reminder of the dead, but also as a reminder of the power of the opposition unified under the banner of Catholicism in Poland. At this point, Mrs. Hulewicz introduces the historical discourse of Gierek, the Communist Party chief at the time, in an attempt to explain the political twists of his decisions, which always remained a mystery to common people like her.

Another flashback reported by Mrs. Hulewicz (the fourth in sequence thirteen) refers to Maciek's discussions at the shipyard, where he tries to convince fellow workers that they should officially support the 1976 strikes in Radom. At that time, the workers of the Radom factories were striking in response to food price increases. The disillusioned workers from other parts of the country did not believe in active support of the common cause; there was resignation among the Polish workers, who did not believe that anything could be changed. This resignation is appropriately displayed by the shipyard workers as well. When approached by Maciek and his argument to support the strikes, shipyard workers say that they want to live quietly as long as possible, work hard, and feed their families. The atmosphere of defeat is blandly pessimistic, shared by all members of the Polish society at that time. It is present in the workers' words, "we shall always be defeated (by the authorities)" and in the union official's threats toward Maciek. When Maciek approaches the shipyard union official with a request for formal support for Radom, the latter threatens him with dismissal.

The conversation between Maciek and the union official comprises a whole array of historical details that, in the diegetic time of 1980, are restated in a different context. Maciek asks for support for Radom and Ursus, stating that this is "the last chance for the unions" (meaning the officially sponsored unions). He adds that if they do not support the strikes, they can simply terminate their existence. The only reply from the union official is that the shipyard does not need rabble-rousers like Maciek. The following day Maciek is fired.

This part of the flashback is dialogically related to the historical discourse of the dissolution of the official unions in 1981, following the establishment of the Solidarity Union. The official unions proved to be obsolete when the new unions came into being. The scene also provides a dialogical insertion of the historical truth behind the numerous firings or harassments suffered by countless workers and representatives of the intelligentsia in the whole country who jeopardized their livelihood whenever they voiced any opposition in the workplace. When juxtaposed against the final scenes of the film, this scene seems to be a reminder of past events, and it marks ensuing steps in the fight for the rights of the people.

The scene of Maciek's firing is a shocking and violent illustration of the methods used by the authorities at that time in Poland. Maciek is stopped by the shipyard official guards at the gate to the plant and refused entry. He is physically stopped by them while the payroll clerk gives him his pay and the human resources official hands him his notice. In the general atmosphere of confusion and shock the spectator watches the scene with a vague feeling of déjà vu. Both Maciek's violent reaction and the comment of the human relations official ("If I do not give you the notice, I will be fired as well") are familiar to the spectators, who either witnessed similar events or heard about them.

Mrs. Hulewicz finishes her account with a statement that is almost the credo of a fighting artist. In simple, naive words Mrs. Hulewicz says, "We must win. If not now, then the next time." She adds that Agnieszka, Maciek's wife (and the protagonist of the film *Man of Marble*) brought her many Polish history books that taught her interesting things. "There must be justice," she says, "the one which is described in the history books, in the constitutions, in the monitors, at least this kind of justice." Wajda introduces the discourse of history in this scene by drawing a direct reference to a body of written work, the confirmed discourse of history books. The film becomes a process of gathering evidence on the rights and wrongs of history. Allusion to the history books strengthens Wajda's argument concerning the rights of the striking workers and places it in a more general historical context.

An interesting voice that dialogically relates to the enunciative power of the discourse of the people is that of Agnieszka, a representative of the intelligentsia, introduced in sequence sixteen. This sequence changes the spectator's reaction from slightly distrustful of the monological, authoritarian presentation of the opposition movement in Poland to an enthusiastic acceptance of a living, real protagonist on the screen. Agnieszka's laughter and lack of fear are shared by the spectators. Her voice is, additionally, a comment on the life of simple people, real workers who, although deprived of party privileges, live a life that is a little freer than career life in Warsaw. The discourse of alternative lives – the life of the workers, and of the opposition in Poland – is described with humor and warmth. The activists' adventures with the security agents remind the spectator of escapades of school children who are not afraid of anything. "It is a great pleasure not to be afraid of anything," she says. "And when you are in prison you cannot be put in prison again, can you?" Agnieszka's monologue introduces the discourse of liberation, and her optimism and stamina infuse the spectator with a feeling of hope.

Agnieszka's discourse introduces a sense of humor into the historical depiction of the life of the opposition in Poland. It is difficult for the spectator to accept deadly seriousness in any approach to the opposition activists in general. This aspect of the film was especially challenged by representatives of the opposition movement itself. Mariusz Muszkat from *Tygodnik Solidarnosc* openly questions certain scenes in the film from the point of their historical credibility:

It is true that there were violent incidents [initiated by the authorities – JF], but almost every search ended with bantering and jokes about the police. Everybody was bragging how he or she fooled them. It is a pity that nothing of this was present in the film, as it was a significant phenomenon at the time which could have been a windfall for a screenplay writer.[74]

According to this author, then, the rare humorous moments in the film are too scarce to properly depict the historical truth of the events. This comment by Muszkat raises an even broader issue of the extent to which the film director should have remained "accurate" in his presentation. In *Man of Iron*, after all, the monological power of a serious depiction of historical events completely supersedes reality, a phenomenon that was constantly questioned by suspicious spectators.

The same suspicion concerning the presence of the fictional and the factual characterizes the reception of the last scenes in the film. Here, the documentary footage presents the hall of negotiations, where the final agreement is being signed by a government representative and Lech Walesa. However, this documentary footage is later combined with the fictional one. Consequently, on the way to the hall the spectator sees a triumphant Lech Walesa and Maciek in a fictional shot; an enthusiastic Winkiel and Anna Hulewicz; and Agnieszka and Maciek, who finally meet after Agnieszka's stay in prison. The historical soundtrack carries the speech of Mieczyslaw Jagielski, who describes the painful negotiations and announces the signing of the final agreement.

The spectator reacts to the closure of the fictional strand with uncertainty. The sentimental, melodramatic scene of Maciek's and Agnieszka's meeting in the hall, where the famous Gdansk agreement between the workers and the government was reached, leaves a feeling of a narrative closure that is too simplified and too didactic in its monological power. The rhetoric of the revolution may have required this kind of closure, an impersonal crowd with backs turned to the spectator, and the loving couple immersed in their feelings.

In the next sequence, the documentary footage continues in its presentation of Walesa before the shipyard facing a huge crowd of enthusiastic people and, later, show Walesa carried upon the arms of the workers and the crowds chanting thank you. In the context of this historical footage, the fictional story of Winkiel, unfolding after the historic agreement in Gdansk, introduces a discordant and pessimistic note. In sequence nineteen Winkiel is denounced by

Badecki's driver, who wants him to see Badecki in front of the shipyard. Dzidek uncovers Winkiel's microphone with the words, "This
you can carry openly now." Winkiel will not be forgiven easily by
everyone, definitely not by Dzidek nor by any of the shipyard
workers, since in their eyes he still belongs to the hated regime.
Winkiel then encounters Badecki, who smilingly tells him that
the agreement is not important because it was signed under duress. In this statement it looks as if Wajda doubted the persistence
of the workers' stubborn resistance to the government's impositions of power and also foresaw a pitiful end to the victory. "It is
only a piece of paper," Badecki said, as if he knew that only sixteen months after the agreement the government would decide to
introduce martial law.

With this final scene, Wajda seems to say that the post-talks *raison d'état* will decide the outcome of the Gdansk victory. In a way,
the later events of martial law confirmed Wajda's suspicions. So,
Wajda did not have to suppress his own historiosophy and his
artistic temperament after all in producing *Man of Iron*. Without
the final scene of the talk between Winkiel and the security agent,
Wajda would have had to consider the course of events in August
1980 as meaningful and just, and would have had to change his
own pessimistic view of history. The tragic historiosophy was not
replaced by an optimistic one, and a sequence of passionate portraits subordinated to one optimistic trait has not produced a convincing synthesis.

To recapitulate, the fictional and the factual clash dialogically in
the film in many ways. The predominance of the factual in *Man of
Iron* makes the negotiation of meaning more violently polemical
than in the case of a more fictionalized approach to history, as
depicted in *Man of Marble*. The images in *Man of Iron* deeply affect
the spectator and almost completely eliminate the distance between himself or herself and the reality on the screen. The spectator has to relate dialogically not only to the fictional discourse but
also to the factual one. Moreover, he or she has to negotiate the
relation between the two.

Within the fictional discourse in *Man of Iron* Wajda establishes
two voices: "us" vs. "them," in which the former refers to the discourse of opposition, and the latter to that of the authorities, the
government, the hated and the distrusted. Already at the outset of
the film, in its first sequence, the poem by Czeslaw Milosz[75] initiates
the discourse of the opposition movement in Poland. Thus, in the
beginning of the film, Wajda makes poetic discourse a linguistic

carrier of the historical revolutionary message. "Maybe they will not notice it," the radio technicians say, referring to the censorship officials. Milosz's text serves as a blatantly subversive message directed to the striking workers and to the representatives of the opposition in Poland from the official radio network. This discourse is commented upon by Winkiel, who appears in the first scenes of the film as the person representing the worst aspects of the authorities. As a representative of the infamous *Radiokomitet*, the radio and television media organization in Poland, he constitutes a combination of all their vices. He is cynical in his remarks, slightly threatening, drunk, and unwieldy. In the opening scenes of the film, Winkiel undermines the monologic voice of authority he is supposed to represent with an appearance and behavior that make him repugnant to the spectator.

This presentation of Winkiel produces a dialogical tension in the spectator, who reacts with disgust to the image of the drunken Winkiel on the screen. As Surdykowski indicates, Winkiel became the whipping boy through Wajda's caricature-like presentation of the persona of the journalist. The journalists in Poland reacted violently to such a demeaning portrait of a representative of their profession, arguing that Winkiel's cynicism and alcoholism are only screens that hide acute moral dilemmas much more convoluted and interdependent than a simple fear of incrimination by security agents.[76] In Surdykowski's words:

> Although one dreams of seeing the real face of the journalist, Winkiel, and his psychological roots, one is aware of the fact that the cheap caricature of the journalist presented in *Man of Iron* functions and will continue to function, copied in the thousands by standard literature and screenplay writing. Society needs its whipping boys.[77]

Winkiel is in the process of producing a radio broadcast in which three young women greatly upset by the strike present their opinions. However, while the women are trying to show their support for the strikers, Winkiel tries to make them present the version that he prepared, a censored text supporting the position of the government. The opposition of discourses signaled in the first few images discussed above is strengthened by the linguistic opposition of the two statements. The women finally present the version Winkiel wants. But when Winkiel leaves the room for a moment, his departure is illustrated by a comical musical motif that sums him up as a person and as a representative of the authorities.

Winkiel is notified about a telephone call from his supervisor, through which he is informed that he has to see him immediately. The frightened journalist is taken there in a business car. In the car, Winkiel is presented as a little man belonging to the system but frightened of it at the same time. He is comical in his fear but also pathetic. His total subjugation to the system is openly revealed. At the office of the chief Winkiel is accepted as part of the gang. The court-like scenario of the chief's office, with lackeys waiting at the door, begins to envelop Winkiel as well. Winkiel gets an order to go to Gdansk, the heart of the revolution, and produce a broadcast about the events. He is given money and radio equipment and is ushered to the door with a smile and the remark "everything remains between us." The impression of conspiracy and blackmail is blatantly present in this discourse of authority. It is monologically powerful, and unquestionably evokes in the spectator an immediate reaction of contempt and opposition. The conspiracy aspect in particular, was correlated with the personal experience of the audience, the fact that ordinary people were often unaware of the historical decisions regarding their fate. Such decisions were never openly discussed with the society at large, but were exacted through government decrees. Blackmail meant that the authorities had something on Winkiel and used this information to send him to report on the leaders of the strike; blackmail is often used by the government in recruiting their agents.

The same aspect of the discourse of the authorities as the bad guys is later reinforced in the conversation between Badecki, an official in Gdansk, and Winkiel. In a brutally honest monologue, Badecki states that the interview with Maciek Tomczyk that he and Winkiel saw on TV can serve as basic material for a smear campaign that Winkiel is supposed to start with his radio broadcast. When Winkiel expresses his surprise and revulsion, he is immediately reminded of an event from his past when the very same official helped conceal evidence after a car accident in 1971 in which Winkiel killed an innocent passerby. An obvious blackmail plan by Badecki places Winkiel in a deadlock, and immediately introduces the discourse of submission and dependence within which Winkiel will operate and from which he will try to escape later on.

The discourse of authority situates the government exclusively within the framework of the bad guy, unlike in *Man of Marble*, where the position of "them" could still be debated, questioned, and, in some cases, reluctantly accepted.[78] Here, the representative of the authorities, Badecki, is presented as a drunkard who shouts that the party will not share power, and that the only way to get rid of the workers is to dispose of Tomczyk. This aspect of Wajda's presentation irritated many spectators in Poland. They doubted especially its excessively literal quality. As Szpakowska states, "In general, *Man of Iron* is over-explicit ... the bad guys ooze anger, sweat and vodka. If one is bad, one is also ugly and badly brought up; if one is on the right side, then one is also subtle."[79]

In the context of this clear-cut discourse of the bad guy Winkiel emerges as a schizophrenic embodiment of oppression, as both the victimizer and the victim. The short conversation with Badecki, full of the oppressive monologue of the authorities, makes the victimization of Winkiel clear and obvious. But the conversation also signifies a first faint sign of dissent in Winkiel. He reacts with disgust to Badecki's exposition. Finally, he agrees to the order and leaves the office with a bottle of whisky the official gives him on his departure. This subjugation of Winkiel is carried out without any reservations on the part of the officials. They know they own Winkiel as they had owned *Radiokomitet* and the innumerable journalists who had to succumb to the authorities' power to keep their jobs.

Some voices in the Polish press tried to justify such a presentation of Winkiel. Among them was Andrzej Bernat, who tries to understand Winkiel's position, "The most authentic problem with which each of the protagonists has to grapple is the realization of certain basic truths about reality and along with that: how to define one's position against the authorities and the choice of one's way of acting. This related unambiguously to one's rejection or acceptance of basic moral norms."[80]

In general, however, Wajda was criticized for the monological presentation of the authorities. Both Badecki and Winkiel (the latter in the first half of the film in particular) revitalize the negative discourse concerning the behavior of the people in power in socialist Poland. Every spectator in the cinema related to the images on the screen, which produced a violent feedback based on memories, hidden facts revealed by the underground publications of the opposition movements in Poland, and the underground discourse of social knowledge circulated in the form of gossip, conjectures, and personal experiences. As Pawel Jedrzejewski states, "In *Man of Iron* reality is cold and autumnal. Security agents are dressed in leather jackets or have their hats pulled down over their eyes. The so-called decision makers and VIPs are repulsive and recognizable from one hundred metres away. The world is unequivocal. The appearances of normalcy, so characteristic of earlier Wajda's films, were missing."[81]

The discourse of the authorities as bad guys is reinforced by the discourse of widespread alcoholism in the Poland of those times. The spilled alcohol in the bathroom serves as a pathetic symbol that leaves Winkiel vulnerable and subjugated to the two supplementary discourses: authority and alcohol. The widespread consent to alcohol in every area of life produced a social phenomenon of camaraderie that subjugated all the opposing discourses and made them feel at home with the authorities. Alcohol blurred the differences between good and bad, honest and dishonest. Not surprisingly, the declared abstainers were treated with suspicion and distrust by their colleagues. Alcohol leads Winkiel to the bar in the hotel, where he tries to get some despite the ban imposed by the striking workers. The discourse of the striking workers functions here as an alternative monological power clashing with the discourse of alcoholic permissiveness in Poland.

The underlying discourse of violence and of the frustration of authorities no longer able to use such violence strengthens the monological depiction of "them" as the "bad guy." Sequences fifteen and seventeen illustrate this undercurrent perfectly.

In sequence fifteen, Winkiel, who is beginning his convoluted journey of revolt against the authorities, faces his boss, who has come to Gdansk to personally supervise the smear campaign against Maciek that Winkiel was supposed to start. This sequence immediately introduces an atmosphere of idolatrous respect and paternal leniency. The boss gives Winkiel a glass of vodka to calm his craving for alcohol and, in the next move, demands the journalistic materials. The conversation between Winkiel and his boss introduces the discourse of power and reminds the spectator of the existence of the discourse of fear that was present in *Man of Marble*. The boss demands to know whether Winkiel has had any contact with the striking workers in the shipyard. When Winkiel tries to dodge the question the boss answers with the threat that Winkiel will be beaten some day by somebody if he does not answer correctly. In language that reminds the Polish spectator of the rude and absolute power of the party apparatus in ordering people around, the boss tells Winkiel that his first piece of reporting will be on the air the following day. When Winkiel tries to interrupt with an objection that the material is not finished yet and that he needs some time for editing, the boss intervenes rudely and says that Winkiel will not edit the material. Here, the Polish spectator is reminded about the years of manipulation of information, its transformation and distortion by the media.

The boss reminds Winkiel that the party secretary is mostly interested in the people from the "second line," and when Winkiel, surprised, asks him what that means, the answer the boss gives is an example of the hated and ridiculed "newspeak.": "There are hidden antisocialist elements which feed on the healthy response of the working class. These elements act with a definite purpose in mind." This ambiguous and ridiculous statement, which is so characteristic of the party officials and journalists representing the official media at that time, generates laughter in the audience but also sums up the policy of divide and rule that, up to 1980, helped the authorities dissipate the imminent danger of uprisings and strike actions in the country.

Laughter as a dialogical reaction to oppression seems the only weapon that the audience could use in its appropriation of these images on the screen. It originated from a rich context of historical resistance that forced Poles to employ any weapon they could, whether irony, a political joke or the outright laughter of ordinary people, to fight violence.

The undercurrent discourse of violence permeating sequence fifteen only as a mood is depicted with full force in sequence seventeen. On his way out of the restaurant where he had met his boss, Winkiel passes the gym at the police headquarters where Wirski, the security officer, whom he had encountered earlier in the hotel, notices him and demands information on Maciek. Winkiel tries to explain his delay and squirms under Wirski's eye like a worm. Wirski, in a sports outfit, looks with contempt at Winkiel, who tries to escape the tension by smoking. When Wirski forbids him to light a cigarette, Winkiel suddenly takes a police truncheon and begins to hit the wooden mannequins on which the police train, to develop the power and the precision of their beating methods. At first slowly, later ferociously, Winkiel hits the mannequins as if trying to unload his hatred of the system and of his subjugation to the opportunism of the oppressors.

Wirski watches him carefully and takes the truncheon back. In a physically violent encounter Winkiel blurts out that the existence of security files does not give the security officials the right to construct a screenplay to jeopardize the activists. He also adds that, thanks to the security forces, he was able to get in touch with inspiring people from the shipyard, and he no longer will work for the regime. At this moment Wirski becomes physically offensive. He grabs Winkiel by the collar and reminds him of his unfortunate accident several years ago. He tells him that a similar file exists on him, and, as the spectator infers from the way his words are phrased, on everybody in a totalitarian society. This physically explicit, powerful encounter expresses the frustration and helplessness of both opponents. The mutual hatred cannot be expressed in an elemental way, by physical struggle but instead has to give way to political means – the power of the word. Winkiel is let go. Like a schoolboy Winkiel runs downstairs with an outcry, "Get off me! At last I will be left in peace!"[82]

There is no place left for the audience to relate dialogically to the images on the screen in this scene. The "good" guy in this scene (Winkiel), and the "bad" guy (Wirski), are openly hostile, the feelings of revulsion and hatred exposed on their faces. Consequently, the audience breathes with relief when the smiling Winkiel enters the shipyard and calls the Warsaw *Radiokomitet* offices from the strike headquarters. Winkiel tells his chief's secretary he wants to resign.

This easy resolution of the conflict – in the form of escape on the part of Winkiel – enraged many spectators. Klopotowski claims, for instance, that "instead of revealing the symbolic images residing in the popular subconscious, Wajda decided to play on easy feelings."[83] However, as Klopotowski argues, "The spectators went along with Wajda because the film gives vent to feelings of hatred and hope pent up over the years. *Man of Iron* destroys the myth that the authorities only wanted the good of the people. For the first time it shows the ill will and egoism of the authorities, of whose existence the society had suspected the party and government agencies for decades."[84] In this sense, the spectator forgave Wajda the monological presentation of the authorities and accepted the monochromatic image as a political necessity.

The most surprisingly overt historical discourse in *Man of Iron*, following years of silence in the films and mass media in Poland, is the presence of the Catholic religion. Wajda captured in this film the significant role the Catholic Church played in supporting opposition movements and the Gdansk strike. By including documentary footage of the crowds in prayers, and the images of religious icons on the shipyard fence, Wajda emphasized the importance of Catholicism in Poland but also signified its ritualistic value. As the opposition grew, the significance of the Catholic religion meant not only an impressive spectacle but also a notable addition to the opposition's power, which undermined the authority of the government and constituted a parallel, powerful current of resistance. Wajda presents Catholicism not only as an impressive show with praying crowds and huge masses – an aspect of religion that seems especially tempting for a director trained as a painter – but also as a ritual in which the bad forces of the government are to be eliminated and the good forces in the form of the Catholic religion are to be revived. However, Wajda does not pay attention to other important aspects of religion in the film, such as its importance in the active support of the Polish opposition and the reasons this opposition sought support in religion. What was the role played by religion? Did the people in the shipyard pray for help or for moral support against the powerful fear that shadowed them? Or, rather, did prayer serve as a pretext for a demonstrations and as another kind of global behavior standing in contrast to the official May Day demonstrations or other demonstrations supporting the totalitarian system? These demonstrations were imposed on the general public, and refusal to take part in them brought open or hidden sanctions.

In fact, as many historical sources certify, Catholicism in Poland played an extremely important part in the formation of the political "other." The prayers had a sociotechnical impact of integration, compensation, and autotherapy. But also, because of its deeply ingrained importance at all levels of authority or education, culturally inscribed in all the strata of society, Catholicism in Poland served as a natural barrier against the oppressiveness of the party apparatus and party ideology. Paradoxically, the party members were usually deep believers themselves. This was the likely reason, why the rage over the death of the priest Jerzy Popieluszko[85] was shared by everybody, since the security officials violated not only the right of human life, but also widely shared beliefs concerning the inviolability of the priesthood. Police intervention in a church ceremony would always be understood as blasphemy, so numerous representatives of the authorities shuddered at the thought of imposing their force there. However, as history showed, and as Agnieszka Holland's film *To Kill a Priest* (1989), based on the murder of Popieluszko, illustrated, the authority of religion in Poland at that time and after the introduction of martial law was so great that it filled the oppressor with religious awe but also religious zeal to kill.

Man of Iron activates a magical concept of religion not only as a ritual but also as a supernatural force that aids the victory of the workers. This kind of interpretation is almost forced upon the spectator by Wajda's incorporation of the footage of the mass from a bird's-eye view. The spectator sees the praying masses from above; the sea of people and the murmur of their voices impose an interpretation of God-like omnipotence that was to help the strikers win. On the other hand, Wajda does not offer any power of enunciation to the church itself, which played an extremely important role not only in supporting Polish opposition movements but also in placating the militant Solidarity in its first phase. As Andrews comments on this situation:

> Solidarity, slowly organizing itself from the plant level upward, had a long way to go. At the top, differences arose as to what Solidarity should be and do. On one hand, Walesa followed a moderate policy of seeking to resolve problems through negotiations, an approach compatible with the Church's position. On the other hand, many young regional leaders and some KSS/KOR members and their associates, acting as union advisers at various levels, concluded that only a tough confrontation would compel the Government to negotiate a reasonable settlement ... Although many Solidarity members harboured genuine feelings of sympathy and gratitude toward intellectuals for their past support, they did not want to feel obligated to them or, for that matter, to the Church for their every decision.[86]

In this aspect, the role of religion, seems to be downplayed in the fictional scenario. The Catholic religion does not appear as a strong political voice, able to "work according to a long-term program of gradual change,"[87] but, rather, as a supernatural power having no contact with actual politicians, the real voices in the political reality of that time.

The introduction of religion in the film was noted by Western critics. For instance, Vincent Canby of *The New York Times* wrote that "the most interesting thing about *Man of Iron* is the way it dramatizes the immense political importance of Polish Roman Catholicism at this time."[88] Polish critics, Tadeusz Szyma[89] for instance, also noted the presence of religion in Wajda's film. In his opinion, the director's moderation in presentation of the theme causes the symbol of the cross to function with extreme power.

The multiplicity of historical glossia that Wajda uses to attack the spectator in his film and that reinforces his monological position sometimes produces the unsettling effect of a mosaic of political allusions and side remarks. It can be argued that this unsettling effect is caused by the disparity between the complicated mode of presentation and the simplicity of the message. This kind of impression is created especially in the eleventh sequence, when Winkiel is suddenly surrounded by representatives of the Gdansk Writers' Union, who want him to sign a group statement indicating solidarity with the striking workers and confirming opposition to the regime. Wajda based this scene on a real event, which marked an important moment of understanding and support for the working class on behalf of the intelligentsia. On the other hand, Wajda wants to show in this scene how Winkiel, a representative of a huge group of opportunist journalists who could not decide whether the shipyard strike was the real thing or just another clash with the totalitarian system, finally gives in to these enthusiasts, and, out of shame and slowly rising optimism, signs the statement. The camera lingers on Winkiel for a long time. Winkiel hopes at first that it is only a matter of an innocent signature on a piece of paper. Thousands of declarations were signed during the long and convoluted history of Poland, usually supporting the regime. Winkiel did not mind that. However, when he realized that the declaration stated openly that the main role of journalists in socialist Poland up to that time had been to confuse the public and to show a distorted picture of the realities of life, he hesitated and did not know how to react. "It is very ambiguous," reacts Winkiel to one of the most non-ambiguous messages in the journalistic discourse of the previous thirty-five years. Finally, Winkiel signs the paper with a look of resignation on his face. The scene functions as a reminder that such an event took place. It produces an impression, however, that Wajda wanted to present all the historical facts pertinent to the times the film was about, but that he failed to incorporate them neatly in the fictional discourse of the film.

In *Man of Iron* history imposes its monological power in the form of the immediacy of historical events that, with their raw reality, outshine their fictional interpretation. History dialogically intervenes into the act of spectatorship, as the viewing of the film coincides with the viewer's fresh perception of the changes in Poland in August 1980. After years of political "newspeak" in the media, spectators yearned for a truthful presentation of the events of August 1980.

Raw truth, in the form of scenes from documentary films and in the form of direct monologues and dialogues of the protagonists, overwhelmed the spectator. Finally, the spectator heard what he or she had wanted to hear about the political and social life in Poland for thirty-five years, since the implementation of socialism in 1945. No intervention on the part of censors was apparent; the film revealed a direct address to the public, which completely identified with the message, if not with all the aspects of its presentation. The fictional lives of the protagonists and the artistic intervention of the director were useful only in that they introduced the spectator into the process of truth revelation. Through the film's main protagonists, the spectators were able to enter the world of history in the making, and to dialogically relate to the presented facts with whatever they knew, imagined, or had heard about. Wajda's artistic confabulation served as an entry to the world of historical truth, which was, in fact, the truth of montage and artistic presentation. The monological, black-and-white version of the historical truth appealed to the spectator to such an extent that he or she enthusiastically accepted the film despite its artistic sketchiness, and inadequate narrative line and character development.[90] The spectator desired a monological truth about the events so much that he or she approved of the dispersed, uncertain, and artistically uneven presentation by Wajda as if it were the last word on the subject.

The Historical Discourse in *Danton*

Danton, a historical film that describes events of the French Revolution in the eighteenth century, depicts a time that is impossible for a spectator in the 1980s to experience. However, the way Wajda presents history relates his depiction to contemporary time on the one hand, and to the understanding of historical sources and populist legends on the other. In this sense, the dialogical interaction between the past and present functions as a constant clash between the presented and the imagined, the visual and the referred to. Moreover, *Danton* has to be read in the context of its reception in Poland and in France, the two countries in which the construction of the film's historical message implies a deep knowledge of Polish and French histories. These two issues, the reception of the film in Poland, and in France, will orient our discussion of the historical discourse in *Danton*.

Despite Wajda's continued denial that the film *Danton* does not refer to the Polish context,[91] such an interpretation was repeatedly presented in both the Polish and French press after the film's screening. For instance, in the film review in *Trybuna Robotnicza*, Ireneusz Leczek states, "Those who start the huge machinery of a social movement become its victims, thrust out by others. Private intentions mix with social ones. Naive activists operate alongside experienced political players yearning for power and money. All this is very close to recent Polish affairs. Consequently, my opinion is that *Danton* is much more Polish than it may seem."[92]

Accordingly, the Polish spectator, the author of this book included, persistently saw numerous Polish references in the film. The general interpretation of Robespierre's and Danton's motives was closely related to the Polish historical experience of the conflict between Jaruzelski and Walesa, respectively. Also, particular scenes in the film resembled Polish political culture. The third sequence, as well as the following ones, serves as an example of such an interpretation. The beginning scene of sequence number three, when angry citizens of the Republic wait in the rain to get bread and spies walk around listening to what they say, dialogically introduces the discourse of constant, persisting shortages in the food distribution in Poland in the 1960s and 1970s. Due to the lack of proper organization of distribution, most Poles spent their time in long queues complaining constantly about the government. The scene in the same sequence of the abduction of a young girl by the police after she has commented on the beauty of the passing prisoner introduces the discourse of terror during the first months of the introduction of martial law, so well known to the Polish spectator. Ordinary citizens could be interrogated on any charge and kept at the police station without any legal reason for up to forty-eight hours.

In the fourth sequence, on the other hand, the scene in which Robespierre reads Desmoulins's gazette, followed by the scene in which Desmoulins's printing plant is demolished, transports the Polish spectator to the early months of martial law, when police and the representatives of the Polish army could enter the apartment of a citizen under suspicion, carry out a brutal search, and, on finding printing materials or machines, could demolish them and turn the whole apartment upside down.

Robespierre's tense demeanor and brutal decisions place him on a par with Jaruzelski, who, at the time of martial law, pressured writers to conform to the standard symbols of loyalty to the regime, and reinstated party control over the intelligentsia. The brutal demolition of the plant, with the smashing of machines and window panes, is immediately followed by a scene presenting

Heron, the executor of Robespierre's order, leaving the plant with the paper in his hands. The printed material falling from his full hands is obediently picked up by young boys attracted by the turmoil in the plant. Thus, the brutality of the police of the revolution is placed within an ironical framework of impressionable young citizens of the Republic,[93] who see how the law of the Republic is implemented, and know that it has to be respected and obeyed.

The fifth sequence, when Robespierre is taken care of by the barbers, presents Robespierre as a pompous, stiff-necked individual, concerned about his appearance, a man who puts on his costume as armor against the outside world. This negative presentation of Robespierre does not give credit to the great historical person, who, according to professor Jan Baszkiewicz, the historical consultant for the film *Danton,* was an advocate of "a utopian, *sans-culotte* program of an egalitarian society who wanted to stabilize the revolution by introducing and strengthening its basic reforms in the years 1789–93."[94] In general, Robespierre is presented as a militant advocate of the revolution, obsessed with ideas of egalitarianism and populism. This kind of presentation dialogically interacts with the popular presentation of General Wojciech Jaruzelski in the Polish mass media. The stiff-necked, very private, stony-faced general was obsessively concerned about *raison d'état* and about the implementation of the repressive regulations of martial law. Like Robespierre, Jaruzelski also wore "a stiff corset" under his military uniform. He never changed his outward appearance during martial law or long after it. His image, similar to the image of Robespierre, is that of a solemn and formal politician, consistently following the outlines of his own policy. Surprisingly, Robespierre shows some human attributes when he disagrees with his confederates about the accusations against Danton. Similarly, Jaruzelski admitted in many interviews after the termination of the martial law that he considered martial law his own private tragedy. Both Robespierre and Jaruzelski seemed to consider the imposition of terror as a necessary painful condition for the service of the state.

Sequence six, on the other hand, which presents a meeting between Danton and his supporters in a Parisian street, dialogically relates to the Polish historical phenomenon of conspiracy, the constant subversive political activity against the oppressor. Over 100 years of partition in Poland and the domination of the Soviet Union after the Second World War produced determined insurgents endlessly debating possible political revolution. As in the time of the French Revolution, this subversive political activity had to be secret, so the scenes of whispering insurgents were strangely familiar.

Also, sequence number seven, which depicts the meeting of the National Convention, conjures the idea of the Polish Sejm and its notorious deliberations, during which the principal of the province could frustrate the directives of the government. The Sejm's debates continued endlessly in the sixteenth and seventeenth centuries, leading to chaos in the country and a lack of solutions for many of its problems. This political culture of constant deliberations, conspiracy, and political infighting was so inscribed in the Polish mentality that even the new union Solidarity could not withstand this tradition. Within the union itself, just after its commencement various factions and oppositions appeared.

The policy of introducing new decrees in order to silence political opponents (in sequence nineteen the decree introduced by The Committee for Public Safety and implemented during Danton's trial successfully silences Danton), and the methods of setting up opponent (Robespierre and his advocates fabricate false accusations against Danton and force Legendre to sign a false deposition about a plot planned by Desmoulins's wife and Danton's friends) are well known to the Polish spectator accustomed to the policies of conspiracy and the unfair and traitorous methods used by the authorities. The Polish public saw the film as a clear metaphor for its situation, where ideological and political so-called reasons of state were at variance with human needs, happiness and personal freedom.

That unavoidable temptation to see *Danton* in terms of Solidarity was corroborated by many critics. Danton, the popular spokesman, loudly demanding a spotlight for his own protection, echoes the very public perils of Lech Walesa, while the inflexible authoritarian, Robespierre, who seems bound to suppress him, looks like a perfect fit for Jaruzelski. Some critics[95] read whole areas of possible discourses into Wajda's film when they questioned whether the director intended *Danton* to be a metaphor for Polish events, with Danton as a surrogate Walesa and Robespierre as a stand-in for the military government or even the Soviet regime. Interviewed by filmmaker Marcel Ophuls in *American Film*, Wajda says "Poland was indeed in a revolutionary situation last year," and *Danton* attempts to describe "the atmosphere of revolution." David Sterritt goes as far as stating that:

It's possible that *Danton* has more biting political meanings and intentions than Wajda cares to let on, fearing for his status in the Polish artistic community (his next project is a stage production in Krakow) or his personal well-being. "There are moments in the history of our country when we can afford to make a political film that one is not ashamed to put one's signature to," he told Ophuls, adding that "right now, this is not the case in Poland."[96]

However, Philip Strick noted that the reference to the Polish context also signifies the film's universality, when he wrote: " ... such parallels as it may contain with events of the 1980s simply confirm the validity of the piece as a philosophical debate relating to the fortuitous (if cyclical) repetitions of history, applicable as much to current French politics (and duly applied, with some uproar, to the 1982 Socialist Party conference at Valence) as to the problems of Poland or anywhere else."[97]

The sequences analyzed above are just a few examples of numerous references that Polish spectators drew from the film and connected to the political situation at home. The time of the film's release – 1982, only a year after the implementation of martial law – encouraged such a reading of the film. The film was highly appreciated in Poland for its unconventional presentation and discussion of the political message that related to contemporary time. Moreover, the film was praised as another example of Wajda's Aesopian style, in which important political messages are communicated between the lines.

In France, conversely, *Danton* was received icily. Most of the controversy surrounding *Danton* was of a clearly political nature. President François Mitterand, after a special screening at the Cinémathèque Française, is said to have walked out as soon as the lights came on, hurrying through a crowd of journalists to not have to answer questions and reveal his displeasure. The reason was Wajda's questionable presentation of historical facts and particularly, his identification with Danton rather than with Robespierre. In the eyes of the French public, *Danton* was extremely pro-Danton, and very anti-Robespierre. Wajda seemed to be very lenient toward Danton's obvious corruption, his venality, his rabble-rousing, and quite contemptuous of Robespierre's thirst for virtue. As Marcel Ophuls asks in an interview with Wajda, "Admittedly, both (heroes of the French Revolution) had a great deal of blood on their hands. But should the virtuous, the incorruptible side of Robespierre be considered as nothing more than an infirmity, a psychoanalytic quirk, to be held up to ridicule?"[98]

In the opinion of this French critic, the fact that Wajda comes from a country that lived through countless revolutions should make him more inclined to a thoughtful and penetrating analysis of all the aspects of each of the leaders. Alas, as Ophuls mentions, there is no predisposition in Wajda to do that. Moreover, the expectations of what Wajda would do to present an interesting picture of the Revolution were very high. Ophuls himself admits that "For some reason, most of us expect artists and intellectuals from Eastern Europe, who have made their reputations behind what used to be known as the iron curtain, to remain sympathetic to the ideals of revolution, no matter how disenchanted and disillusioned they might have become with revolutions in their own time and their own countries."[99]

Ophuls, whose opinions match those of the representatives of French socialism, desired a different portrayal of the revolution and its leaders. His disillusionment also was the disillusionment of the French spectators of various political and cultural orientations who expected a more enthusiastic depiction of the revolution from the director, a former Resistance fighter.[100] The French spectator inscribed into his or her polemic with the film a similarity between Polish and French histories and a similar passion for the political and the emotional in history. Distressed by the incompatibility of these discourses, the French spectator asks:

> Why should any French Socialist today still expect a Polish film-maker to show any sympathy or even any understanding for the mentality of those leaders of the French Revolution whom he holds, rightly or wrongly, to have been responsible for the ravages of the guillotine? ... If after thirty years of Stalinist oppression, *Nomenklatura* corruption, broken promises and *Pravda* "truths," a man like Wajda decides to make Robespierre and Saint-Just into what some of us might consider to be caricatures, that's his privilege.[101]

Ophuls's opinion reflects the polemical opposition between the intentions of the film director and the spectator's response. The spectator may understand the artistic message, but not every spectator could approve of its ideological content. Thus, in the reception of the film, the clash between various aspects of reception produced a spectatorial tension impossible to pacify, both within the spectator trying to polemically unite the points of view of the two protagonists, and among spectators representing disparate points of view. As Ophuls sees it, Wajda infuses his Robespierre with all the negative aspects of Revolution; he charges him with "all the crimes of Stalinism."[102] In attacking the puritanism and ideological hypocrisy of the historical figure, Wajda, in the eyes of the French spectator, attacks the very idea of the revolution itself as embodied in Robespierre.

In *Danton*, the two political opponents also are dialogically displayed from an angle other than the historical one. An opposition between sexuality and a passion for ideas is displayed explicitly throughout the film, starting from the presentation of the naked boy in the bathtub, through explicit references to Danton's virility and promiscuity, up to an imperturbable Robespierre in front of women and other of life's pleasures. Ophuls sees this opposition between sex and politics, feelings and intellect, as Wajda's allegiance to Polish Romanticism. This Romanticism is understood by the French with a forbearing smile that covers a lack of sympathy for passionate Poles, for whom feelings were always the guiding principle in their political endeavors.

The tendentious presentation of the two historical opponents prompted by their deliberate or accidental depiction as replicas of Walesa and Jaruzelski led to a distorted presentation of the two leaders and of the historical facts of the French Revolution. The French critics reacted particularly strongly to the unfavorable presentation of Robespierre. Robespierre, who historians believe to have been a clever and knowledgeable politician, is degraded and humiliated in the film, the French critics stated. One such critic is Pierre Enckell in *Les Nouvelles Litteraires*, who claims that the film seriously devalued Robespierre and cleared Danton and Desmoulins:

Danton himself helped in establishing the terror. Also, as a minister, he condoned the September massacre of Royalist prisoners. On the other hand, Desmoulins, depicted as only a journalist, a few days earlier had brought about the guillotining of Herbert and 18 other people through his own ruthless campaigning. To show both of them as pacifist, liberal souls, desiring to propagate democracy, is more of a political act than a service rendered to the political truth.[103]

Also, Louis Mermaz, the leading activist of the Socialist Party in France and Chairman of the National Assembly, comments on the role of Robespierre:

Undoubtedly, in the period from March 1793 to July 1794, the Revolution reaches the culmination. The differences between Danton and Robespierre have certainly a deep, human and psychological aspect, but these are also two different notions of the future of the revolution, which clash with each other. Danton wants to enter into a compromise with the "bourgeois forces." Robespierre, on the other hand, wants to anchor the revolution in the masses. He shows his intentions in the spring and summer of 1794, when he brings about the acceptance of a series of economic and agrarian reforms which would create a social basis for the victorious classes.[104]

Polish film reviewers agreed with the opinions of the French critics in this matter. For instance, Jan Sajdak states:

> The French public opinion rightly states that Danton was a promi-
> nent figure with none too clean hands and that he liked to make
> money in every possible way. Sartre said openly, "We loved Danton
> as a tribune but we could not respect him as a man." Robespierre
> was a completely different man. He was an idealist with clean
> hands, commonly called "incorruptible." The Revolution and the
> Republic were his beloved only child, to whom he devoted his
> whole life. He it is who supports the plan of national education, the
> common obligation to provide a free education. As he considers
> war the best defense, he knows that war will enable him to crush
> counterrevolution. Robespierre considered terror as a necessary
> evil and he stated that terror can only be a tool in the hands of truly
> honourable people. It was no accident that his desire to clear cor-
> ruption from The Committee for Public Salvation and Safety led to
> his death. A real patriot, democrat and revolutionary died. He
> became immortal and was lionized in the newest research of Jaurès
> and Mathiez.[105]

Ostrowski, moreover, indicates that the French reviewers criticized the way Jacobins were presented in the film, "After the
film's first screening in France the French reviewers underlined
that Andrzej Wajda had produced a film 'completely incompatible
with the French Republican tradition,' because he presented the
Jacobins, considered the spiritual fathers of the contemporary
Socialist Party (in power at present), in a very bad light."[106]

The Left resented the distorted picture of the Great Revolution.
The left-wing press found Wajda's interpretation of the French
Revolution verging on caricature, and was especially offended by
the characterization of Robespierre. The right-wing critics, on the
other hand, praised the film's demonstration of the fact that dem-
agoguery and totalitarianism can lurk behind the façade of revolutionary ideals.

This specific representation of the two leaders of the revolution
leads, consequently, to a faulty presentation of history. Two critical
remarks are worth presenting in this discussion of the historical

discourse in *Danton*. In one of them, quoted by Ostrowski in his review of *Danton*, Louis Mermaz contends, "The film is misleading: in the final analysis, there is nothing wrong in this for those who have a modicum of knowledge. However, there is a risk that it will be completely incomprehensible to those spectators who did not learn history."[107]

Laurent Dispot from *Le Matin* is even more critical in his remarks, "The historical period the film deals with is very well known to school children. They would fail their history lesson miserably if they reproduced Wajda's version, without any reference to Herbertists or dechristianization; without mentioning the fact that France had been attacked and that the war had been the cause and the driving force of everything, of the protagonists' every statement, every decision and activity."[108]

The arguments of the French critics constitute parallel voices in the clarification of the film's political message. They contribute to the reading of *Danton* as a dense, polyphonous text in which Polish and French voices interact on many levels of interpretation. Moreover, *Danton* is a polyphonous film utterance in its dialogical contest with the spectator and with the play on which it is based (this play, by Stanislawa Przybyszewska, will be presented in chapter five). The images of the French Revolution actively engage with the images of political activities and historical events within the Polish context. These images also connect with the depiction of the French Revolution in *Danton*, which implies the existence of various voices cohabiting within this utterance. They include the voice of the Polish director, who presents a specific, Slavic interpretation of the Revolution; the voices of the Polish spectators, who inscribe their own, Polish interpretation into the film; and the voices of French spectators who introduce their own specific interpretation of the historical events in France.

Of the three films presented in this book, it is *Danton* that reveals the internal polemical understanding of the historical discourse to the greatest degree. The images in this film are like words combined with a sideward glance. In this situation, the spectator becomes an interlocutor, "the second speaker present invisibly."[109] Depending on the positioning of the spectator, different meanings emerge. Thus, history in *Danton* functions differently for different spectators. It serves as a reference point for the Polish spectator, since the meaning of the film is dialogically related to the spectator's understanding of Polish history. The French spectator, on the other hand, relates the film to his or her knowledge of the French Revolution, the legendary *personae* of Danton and Robespierre, and the reality of contemporary France. The historical is dialogically inscribed in *Danton* in the sense of a trigger that stimulates different responses in the spectators. The film functions within the sphere of social intercourse, where understanding the text becomes a pragmatic process that involves the participants of the communication exchange. This film especially justifies Bakhtin's statement that the meaning of an utterance comprises semantic relations "behind which stand (and in which are expressed) real or potentially real speech subjects, authors of the given utterances."[110] In this context the film becomes a link in a very thoroughly organized chain of communication.

Notes

1. For the explanation of the term "diegesis" see note 25 in chapter 1.
2. M.M. Bakhtin, *Dialogic Imagination: Four Essays*, ed. Michael Holquist and trans. Caryl Emerson and Michael Holquist (Austin: University of Texas Press, 1981), 19.
3. Ibid.
4. Julia Kristeva, *Desire in Language*, ed. Leon S. Roudiez, trans. Thomas Gora, Alice Jardine, and Leon S. Roudiez (New York: Columbia University Press, 1980), 68.
5. Ibid., 65.
6. William McClellan, "The Dialogic Other: Bakhtin's Theory of Rhetoric," in *Bakhtin and Otherness*, 245.
7. P.U. Hohendahl, "Introduction to the Reception Aesthetics," *New German Critique*, 10 (1977), 29–65.
8. H.R. Jauss, *Literaturgeschichte als Provokation der Literaturwissenschaft* [Literary history as a challenge to literary theory] (Frankfurt am Mein: Suhrkamp, 1970).
9. Ibid., 155.
10. H.R. Jauss, "Literary History As a Challenge to Literary Theory," *New Literary History* 2, no. 1 (1970), 9.
11. Heidegger as quoted by E. Rentschler in "Expanding Film Historical Discourse: Reception Theory's Use Value for Cinema Studies," *Cine-tracts. A Journal of Film and Cultural Studies* 4, no. 13 (1981–1982), 57–68.
12. R.T. Segers, "An Interview with Hans Robert Jauss," *New Literary History* 11, no. 1 (1979), 83.
13. Ibid., 86.
14. K. Mannheim, *Man and Society in an Age of Reconstruction: Studies in Modern Social Structure* (New York: Harcourt and Brace, 1940).

15. H.J. Schmidt, "Text-Adequate Concretizations and Real Readers: Reception Theory and Its Applications," *New German Critique* 17 (1979), 158.

16. Hayden White, *Theories of History: Papers Read at a Clark Library Seminar, March 6, 1976* (Los Angeles: University of California, 1978), 11.

17. Ibid., 24.

18. N. Davies, *A History of Poland: God's Playground* (New York: Columbia University Press, 1982), 577.

19. Ibid., 581.

20. The films seem to be constructed around Stalinism's distanced image similarly to what Bakhtin referred to in his interpretation of the epic, in which "contemporaneity is a reality of a 'lower order' in comparison with the epic past" (*The Dialogic Imagination*, 19).

21. Adam Mickiewicz, one of the most important poets of Polish Romanticism, propagated in his poems the ideas of freedom, truth, and honesty, which were especially dear to Poles during the period of partition.

22. Nicholas G. Andrews, *Poland 1980–81: Solidarity vs. the Party* (Washington, D.C.: National Defense University Press, 1985), 18.

23. As Coates notes, Gierek argues in his autobiography that KOR was allowed to develop by Stanislaw Kania, another party official who used it for his purpose (or rather, allowed it to live relatively unmolested), which was to undermine Gierek's own position (a private conversation with Prof. Paul Coates, McGill University, Montreal, March 1992).

24. Ray Taras, *Poland: Socialist State, Rebellious Nation* (Boulder and London: Westview Press, 1986), 64–73.

25. Timothy Garton Ash, *The Polish Revolution* (London: Granta Books, 1983), 41–47.

26. Andrews, *Poland 1980–81*, 27.

27. "Voivodship" is the biggest administrative unit in Poland. It is a Polish equivalent to, for instance, the Canadian province of Alberta, or the American state of Iowa. Each voivodship has its capital city, for instance Cracow for "wojewodztwo krakowskie" or "Cracow voivodship."

28. Andrews, *Poland 1980–81*, 38.

29. Solidarity's National Commission was elected during the Solidarity Congress in September 1981.

30. Andrews, *Poland 1980–81*, 264–265.

31. Suslow was an important political figure in the Politburo of Leonid Brezniew in the Soviet Union. The latter was the last old-style leader in the Soviet Union before Gorbachev brought some changes with his pierestroika. Brezniew was directly responsible for the intelligence work in Poland that led to the implementation of martial law and to the imprisoning of thousands of Solidarity members.

32. The following articles are examples only of a fierce debate in the media concerning the contents of the Suslov file: Waldemar Gontarski, "Teczka 'S'" [The suitcase "S"] *Wprost*, Warszawa, czerwiec, 1994. Piotr Cywinski, "Sprawa zycia, [A Matter of Life] *Wprost*, Warszawa, czerwiec 1994. Korespondencje z Rosji Krzysztofa Pilawskiego, "Co radziecki wywiad wiedzial o 'Solidarnosci'?" [Krzysztof Pilawski's correspondence articles from Russia "What did the Russian intelligence know about 'Solidarity' movement?"] *Nie*, Warszawa no. 24, 1994.

33. For the division of the films into scenes and sequences, see appendix.

34. Andrzej Wajda, "Cineaste Interviews," in *The Cineaste Interviews: On the Art and Politics of Cinema*, ed. D. Georgakas and L. Rubenstein (Chicago: Lake View Press, 1983), 10.
35. Lomnicki died in 1992 while directing a play in the theater.
36. The fragments shown during the projection in the projection room are in fact fragments of the excised footage from Burski's films.
37. Boleslaw Bierut was the president of the Polish Republic from February 1947 to his sudden death in Moscow in February 1956. He was a politician who followed Stalin in his every move, and Poland under his rule was a weak replica of the Stalinist Soviet Union. The same propaganda machine functioned in both countries, but also the same horror of security, with its trials and persecutions.
   Bierut died the same year that was later recognized as the year of political and ideological thaw. As Davies mentions, "The crisis of 1956 which rocked the whole communist world was launched by Krushchev's 'secret speech' to the Twentieth Congress of the Soviet Communist Party in Moscow recounting a limited selection of Stalin's crimes against the Party and the people." (Davies, *A History of Poland*, 583)
38. This opinion was presented by Z. Zaluski in his article "About *Man of Marble*," *Literatura*, no. 14 (1977), 10.
39. W. Godzic, "Political Metaphor – *Man of Marble* by Andrzej Wajda," in *Analyses and Interpretations: Polish Film*, ed. Alicja Helman and Tadeusz Miczka (Katowice: Uniwersytet Slaski, 1984), 114.
40. Birkut worked with two others as a three-man team. One of them gave him the bricks to be laid and the other gave him the mortar. Birkut's aim was to lay the bricks as fast as he could. After the Second World War the country had to be rebuilt. There was no other way to force the workers into undertaking such an enormous task with poor pay and insufficient food, without starting a huge propaganda machine based on the workers' competition. The more the worker worked, the more bricks he laid, the more respect he supposedly earned from his co-workers and the more privileges from the party authorities.
41. During the Stalinist regime, the workers slowly and reluctantly got used to the spectacles organized by the party. The anger and hidden awe on seeing officials from the higher echelons of the party slowly gave way to inertia and indifferent attendance at party meetings and festivities. In the Gierek years (1970–1980), the years in which the film was produced and, also, Agnieszka's time in the film, "the Party's reputation for honesty, fairness and morality slumped. It became known by word of mouth that Party and Government officials at the national, regional and local levels were taking advantage of the relaxed moral climate; they were feathering their own nests and using their positions and influence to do favors for their relatives and friends. Corruption increased, and a new class of privileged Party people emerged. Elitism among the higher echelons of the Party bred an arrogant attitude toward the people and a disdain for their concerns. The links between the Party hierarchy and the masses, especially the industrial workers, became rusty with disuse." (Andrews, *Poland 1980–81*, 22) The image of Party officials in *Man of Marble* has to be seen in the context of the abuse of power, and the constant humiliation of the people who knew about the abuse or suffered from it but could do nothing about it out of fear or resignation.
42. It is worth noting at this point that the practices Birkut was trying to show were not popular with the general public; the horrible race was detested by

hard-working people and treated as a propaganda trick to increase productivity and maintain a high level of readiness for work. The workers portrayed in
the film, aware of the degree of cynical manipulation, were reluctant to express
their opinion for fear of being deprived of scarce goods and privileges.
43. For instance, W. Wierzewski, "Nowe filmy polskie. Czas terazniejszy, czas
    miniony" [New Polish films: the present time and the past], *Kultura*, no. 53 (4
    March 1977), 8.
44. The presence of the social realism discourse in Wajda's films, especially *Man
    of Marble* and *Man of Iron*, will be discussed in the chapter devoted to the
    films' aesthetics.
45. Krzysztof Klopotowski is quoted by Boleslaw Holdys in the speech presented
    at The Jagiellonian University in Cracow on 13 October 1980, at the conference
    "Young Polish Cinema," reprinted in *Powiekszenie. Students' Film Monthly*
    (April, 1981) (Cracow: Jagiellonian University Press), 46.
46. Davies, *A History of Poland*, 578.
47. Cz. Milosz, *The Captive Mind* (New York: Vintage Books, 1981), 239.
48. The fact that Wajda chose Zakopane and not any other little town is significant
    for the film's symbolism and presentation of historical truth. It is also almost
    conspicuous in its postulation of a black/white opposition in the presentation
    of Birkut and Hanka. Zakopane became the first and most famous abode of the
    Polish new rich, who built luxurious villas in the beautiful Tatry mountains.
    Zakopane was (and still is) a very expensive ski resort, where both the party
    officials and private entrepreneurs met in a curious combination of money,
    contacts, and influence. The owners of the restaurants (such as Hanka's new
    husband) and the owners of small boarding houses made a lot of money rent-
    ing rooms to skiers. They were quietly tolerated by the authorities, who also
    made use of their services.
49. A similar kind of jargon was generally used on TV and on the radio as a
    famous *propaganda sukcesu* [success propaganda], when the reality presented
    in the media was only colorful, never black or gray. In this particular sequence
    Wajda introduces the historical discourse characterized by this style, which
    reached its height in the late 1970s.
50. Godzic, "Political Metaphor," 115.
51. As Coates notes, this idealistic presentation of the industrial landscape in *Man
    of Marble* could be compared with the industrial sublime of *Ziemia Obiecana*
    [Promised Land], another film by Wajda which shows the process of industri-
    alization, this time in nineteenth-century Lodz (private conversation with Prof.
    Paul Coates, McGill University, April 1992).
52. Wajda, *Cineaste Interviews*, 323.
53. Godzic Wieslaw, "Political Metaphor," 119.
54. Bakhtin, *The Dialogic Imagination*, 327.
55. Ibid.
56. Ibid., 299.
57. Ibid., 345.
58. On the discussion of historical discourse in general, consult Hayden White,
    Metahistory: The Historical Imagination in Nineteenth-Century Europe (Baltimore
    and London: The Johns Hopkins University Press, 1973).
59. According to Malgorzata Szpakowska, "Prawdy i nieporozumienia" [Truths
    and misunderstandings], *Kino* (1983), 9–12, the following materials were used
    in *Man of Iron*: materials from Polska Kronika Filmowa [Polish Film Chronicle];

materials from Telewizja RFN [German Television]; fragments of the films *Sierpien* [August] by Ireneusz Engler and Leon Kotowski, and *Robotnicy* [The Workers, 1980] by Andrzej Chodakowski and Andrzej Zajaczkowski.

60. Andrews, *Poland 1980–81*, 30.
61. Hayden White, *Tropics of Discourse: Essays in Cultural Criticism* (Baltimore and London: The Johns Hopkins University Press, 1978), 51.
62. See appendix for the division of the film into scenes and sequences.
63. Bakhtin, *The Dialogic Imagination*, 304.
64. Jack C. Ellis, *The Documentary Idea: A Critical History of English-Language Documentary Film and Video* (Englewood Cliffs, N.J.: Prentice Hall, 1989), 267.
65. Mariusz Muszkat, "Laury niezasuszone" [Undried laurels], *Tygodnik Solidarnosc*, no. 14 (21 August 1981).
66. Pawel Jedrzejewski, "Wajda na Linie" [Wajda on a tightrope], *Ekran*, no. 35 (30 August 1981), 12–13.
67. Jerzy Surdykowski, "Zelazem po marmurze" [With the iron on the marble], *Zycie Literackie*, no. 154 (8 September 1981).
68. Roman Jakobson, "Concluding Statement: Linguistics and Poetics," *Style and Language*, ed. T. Sebeok (Cambridge, Mass.: Massachusetts Institute of Technology Press, 1960), 371.
69. Peter Wollen, "Photography and Aesthetics," *Screen* 19, no. 4 (1978–79), 9–28; quoted by Paul Willemen, "Cinematic Discourse: The Problem of Inner Speech," in *Cinema and Language,* ed. S. Heath and P. Mellencamp (Frederick, MD: University Publications America, 1983), 162.
70. It is interesting to note that almost all Polish film reviewers reviewing the film immediately after its release commented first on the credibility of the images, and then reacted to its artistic power; the reviewers were emotionally concentrated on the enumeration of possible inconsistencies of the images with historical facts, and only secondarily mentioned the heart-rending impact of beautifully orchestrated scenes.
71. As Coates suggests, meetings with characters in the present are just pretexts for getting into their flashbacks to the past (punctuation marks, as it were) (private conversations with Prof. Paul Coates, McGill University, Montreal, April 1992).
72. Czeslaw Dondzillo, "Bez ochronnych barw" [Without protective colors], *Film*, no. 34 (23 August 1981), 3–5.
73. Ibid.
74. Muszkat, "Laury niezasuszone" [Undried laurels], ibid.
75. W. Wlodarczyk calls Milosz "najlepszy jak dotad polski tropiciel meandrow psychiki doby stalinowskiej" [the best Polish analyst so far of the twists and turns of the psychology of the Stalinist era] in W. Wlodarczyk, *Socrealizm: Sztuka Polska w latach 1950–1954* [Socialist Realism: Polish Art in the Years 1950–1954] (Krakow: Wydawnictwo Literackie, 1991), 7.
76. Jerzy Surdykowski, "Zelazem po marmurze" [With the iron on the marble], *Zycie Literackie*, no. 154 (3 September 1981), 5.
77. Ibid.
78. This interpretation is openly questioned by Coates, who postulates that a more complex discursive situation is present in *Man of Marble*. In fact, unquestionably, what is open to debate in *Man of Marble* is the question of the filmmaker's relation to "them" (for instance, Burski). However, "they" are clearly bad guys as well (private conversations with Prof. Paul Coates, McGill University, Montreal, April 1992).

79. Malgorzata Szpakowska, "Prawdy i nieporozumienia" [Truths and misunderstandings], in *Nowe Filmy* (Warszawa: Panstwowe Wydawnictwo Naukowe, 1981), 10.
80. Andrzej Bernat, "Powrot 'Czlowieka z zelaza'" [The return of "Man of Iron"], *Przeglad Katolicki* (19 March 1989).
81. Pawel Jedrzejewski, "Wajda na linie" [Wajda on a tightrope], *Ekran*, no. 35 (30 August 1981).
82. As early as the 1950s many members of Polish society decided that they wanted to be left in peace when they saw no escape from Stalinism. This social and cultural phenomenon is called internal emigration, and it constitutes both a political and emotional escape from the turmoil of the social life in Poland.
83. Krzystof Klopotowski, "'Czlowiek z zelaza.' Kontrowersje: Odpowiadam na zarzuty" ["Man of Iron." Controversies: a reply to objections], *Tygodnik Solidarnosc*, no. 14 (6 November 1981).
84. Ibid.
85. Jerzy Popieluszko was a priest sympathetic to Solidarity who was brutally murdered by the Polish Secret Police on 17 October 1984. The feature film by Agnieszka Holland, *To Kill a Priest* (1989), relates this event.
86. Andrews, *Poland, 1980–81*, 75.
87. Andrews, *Poland, 1980–81*, 72.
88. Vincent Canby, "Act of Bravery. *Man of Iron*," *The New York Times Film Reviews* (12 October 1981), C14, 3.
89. Tadeusz Szyma, "Czlowiek z zelaza" [Man of Iron], *Tygodnik Powszechny*, no. 28 (12 July 1981).
90. The analysis of the film's aesthetic impact will be discussed in the chapter devoted to aesthetics.
91. In one of the interviews Wajda says openly that the impression that his film refers to the Poland of the 1980s is "an unpleasant simplification. If we were to look for an analogy, we would have to refer it to a completely different epoch." M. Ostrowski, "Danton czy Robespierre" [Danton or Robespierre], *Polityka*, 5 February 1983. On the other hand, such denials could themselves be political in nature, to allow him to continue making films in Poland.
92. Ireneusz Leczek, "*Danton*. Rewolucja Francuska wedlug Wajdy" [*Danton*. French Revolution according to Wajda], *Trybuna Robotnicza*, no. 39 (16 February 1983).
93. I refer here to the scene at the beginning of the film in which a little boy is forced to learn by heart the dictates of the Declaration of the Rights of Man and the Citizen. The discourse of the historical past reminds the spectator of the political discourse of every totalitarian society, whether French at the time of the Revolution or Polish at the time of the screening, when the regime tries to educate young people to change their mentality and their understanding of reality and history. The time of Stalinism, with its ideological impositions, and the time of martial law in Poland, when the autonomous powers of university rectors and academic bodies were reduced and the Party tightened its supervision over academic research institutions, immediately came to the Polish spectator's mind.
94. This remark, together with an insightful analysis of the role played by Robespierre in the French Revolution, was presented by Prof. Jan Baszkiewicz in an interview conducted by Krzysztof Kreutzinger for a popular Polish weekly *Film*, dated 10 April 1983.

95. David Sterritt, "Danton," *Christian Science Monitor Film Review Annual*, 6 October 1983, 231.
96. Ibid.
97. Philip Strick, "Danton," *Monthly Film Bulletin* (September 1983), 242.
98. M. Ophuls, "The Provocation and Interrogation of Andrzej Wajda on the Matter of Danton as Performed by Marcel Ophuls," *American Film* 9, no.1 (October 1983), 24–98.
99. Ibid., 24.
100. As Wajda himself admits in the *Cineaste* interview, neither of these features ought to imbue Wajda with enthusiasm for revolution. His declared socialism, however, ought to have done so.
101. Ophuls, "The Provocation and Interrogation," 25.
102. Ibid., 94.
103. Pierre Enckell, "Un film historique n'est pas de l'histoire filmée" [A historical film is not a filmed history], *Nouvelles Litteraires* (7 January 1983).
104. Anne Chaussebourg, "Un entretien avec M. Louis Mermaz – La révolution n'est pas à l'ordre du jour en France"[The conversation with M. Louis Mermaz – the revolution is not on the agenda of France], *La Croix* (7 January 1983).
105. Jan Sajdak, "Dwaj adwokaci przed sadem historii" [Two lawyers facing the court of history], *Odra*, Wroclaw (1 May 1983).
106. Marek Ostrowski, "Danton czy Robespierre" [Danton or Robespierre], *Polityka*, Warszawa (5 February 1983).
107. Ibid.
108. Laurent Dispot, "L'Histoire escamotée" [The pilfered history], *Le Matin* (7 January 1983).
109. Mikhail Bakhtin, *Problems of Dostoevsky's Poetics*, 197.
110. Mikhail Bakhtin, "Problems of the Text," in *Speech Genres and Other Late Essays*, trans. Vern W. McGee, ed. Caryl Emerson and Michael Holquist (Austin: University of Texas Press, 1986), 124.

4

WAJDA AND HIS *DRAMATIS PERSONAE*

Wajda's *dramatis personae* – Agnieszka, Birkut, Burski, Maciek, Winkiel, Danton, Robespierre, and many others – reflect the director's own history and sociocultural positioning. These personae also reveal the multiple roles in a highly historicized and politicized Polish society entangled in problems of moral choice and forced to take sides in political struggles throughout the ages. As a film director, Wajda himself becomes on the one hand an initiator of and on the other hand a participant in the dialogue between his protagonists and the audience. He emerges from his films as a truly discursive author, disseminating his hesitant, polemic concepts among many interlocutors.

The three films reveal a certain continuity in the development of Wajda's *dramatis personae*. From a depiction of naiveté and youth in *Man of Marble*, the spectator is led to the maturity of position in *Man of Iron* (especially in Wajda's presentation of Agnieszka), and then to a broader ideological speculation in *Danton*. The *dramatis personae* serve in the first film as the carriers of the ideological position of youth; they change into men of iron in the second film, by becoming complex examples of revolutionary heroes; and, in the third film, they carry on their struggle to the bitter end by becoming both the victims and carriers of political terror. In *Danton*, the ideological and political dilemma – what to do with a revolution conceived to solve social problems – is transformed into a political debate on the incompatibility of ideals with a gruesome reality. Robespierre and Danton, both advocates of the same cause, turn in two different directions: Robespierre insists on introducing the principles of the Revolution, while Danton goes with the flow on a wave of love for the people he represents politically.

The interpretation of Wajda's *dramatis personae* is a passionate dialogical process of accommodation and rejection on the part of the spectator. The protagonists of his films are both on the screen and among the audience, their ideological positions intertwined with those of the disillusioned members of Polish society on the one hand, and with the members of French society (in the case of *Danton*) on the other. The director shows the *dramatis personae* in his films as individuals produced by social mediations. Given Wajda's approach, Bakhtin's understanding of the individual psyche as a locus of inner and outer speeches in a dialogical interaction proves useful in elucidating differences in the interpretation of the protagonists. According to Bakhtin, the self is completely and thoroughly permeated by the social and ideological:

> The individual, as possessor of the contents of his own consciousness, as author of his own thoughts, as the personality responsible for his thoughts and feelings, such an individual is a purely socioideological phenomenon. Therefore, the content of the "individual" psyche is by its very nature just as social as the ideology, and the very degree of consciousness of one's individuality and its inner rights and privileges is ideological, historical and wholly conditioned by sociological factors.[1]

With this theorization in mind, all the protagonists are discussed as conditioned by the social context, by the ways they represent different aspects of the society at large. Of all of them, Agnieszka seems to be the most significant presentation of the socially constructed character in Wajda's films. She appears in both *Man of Marble* and *Man of Iron*, and constitutes a meta-comment on the political development of a citizen of the Poland of the 1970s and the 1980s. Her personal growth from a naive but enthusiastic student, to a conscious thinker, to an unorthodox revolutionary who commits her life to the cause despite personal inconvenience and misery, is a significant achievement by Wajda. *Man of Iron* marks the moment of maturity in the development of her character. From a character whose social awareness starts to bloom in *Man of Marble*, Agnieszka changes into a grown character facing an open revolutionary struggle in *Man of Iron*. In the latter film her transformation is complete: she is a mother and a wife but also a strong, revolutionary activist, completely convinced of victory. Krystyna Janda, who plays the part of Agnieszka, explains the development of the part herself:

> My development is obvious in *Man of Iron*, which came four years after *Man of Marble*. My Agnieszka changed ... For example, I knew Agnieszka would not enter the shipyard, I knew that, as a woman, I should stay with the child. We considered for a long time whether I should participate in the strike. And Andrzej (Wajda) said, "No, because now you have to make yourself over into another symbol

– the mother who protects the future. Because that's how it ought to be. This is already the next stage in the historical development."[2]

Wajda's suggestions produced in *Man of Iron* a subdued, mature Agnieszka who displays her love for Maciek and her despair that she must leave him when he becomes involved in political activities. Moreover, she is presented as a tough political activist herself, and a mature, sarcastic political opponent. Her dialogue with Winkiel in a prison cell defines her as the toughest of them all, the activist who knows the weaknesses of her opponents and who is strong enough to joke about them and ridicule them. By this presentation, Agnieszka again denies the traditional role ascribed to women in the Polish film as "flowers to look at and admire which just floated across the screen and really didn't hold power."[3]

Agnieszka's role of a fighting revolutionary is further dialogized in her presentation as Mother Poland and as an icon of Solidarity. This representation is especially clear in the sequence depicting the scene in her apartment when she is offered help by Maciek's coworkers. Her calmness and dignified demeanor in this sequence dialogically clash with her earlier, more fierce performance in *Man of Marble*.

Agnieszka is the most prominent character in *Man of Marble* to function as Wajda's alter ego, but is also a symbol of the militant intelligentsia and its growing social consciousness. She is presented as an androgynous figure who finds herself in a masculine world. The presentation of Agnieszka as an independent woman meant that the film also provoked farfetched feminist analyses in the West, and thus brought a feminist "voice" to the film reception. This feminist interpretation in the context of the film, and in the context of Polish history, is partly explained by Janda in her interview with *Cineaste*:

> *Cineaste*: You have been called not only the icon of Solidarity but also of the emerging feminist consciousness in Eastern Europe. What makes your role really attractive is this feminist sensibility, which is really quite unprecedented in Polish film. You play very decisive women fighting not for some stereotypical set of values but for a deeply human individualism. You play strong, determined, independent-minded, and, above all, thinking women. How do you see your energetic activism on the screen as reflecting what Polish women today think?
> *Janda*: I really believe that this strength of character comes from our tradition. In our literature or other forms of cultural expression, women are much stronger than men. The woman in her role as the

mother figure is certainly cherished. In contrast, all our Romantic male heroes fail. They have their weaknesses; they want to kill the tsar but they catch fever. Kordian, Konrad, Gustav: they are all weaklings. These men have terrible doubts and problems. The women, even though they don't play principal roles, are really the ones who endure, who wait, who suffer, who really make do under trying circumstances. Women are marginal but strong. There are no winners in our tradition as far as the hero is concerned but the women hold their own.[4]

In the two films Wajda presents two different depictions of Agnieszka as a female protagonist: the more traditional one in *Man of Marble,* and a more controversial one in *Man of Iron.* In the latter, Agnieszka is depicted as an ideal mother and wife, patiently waiting for her activist husband to come out of prison, but also enduring the hardship and danger of activist work herself. *Man of Marble,* on the other hand, presents her as a strong, aggressive woman; this presentation was resented by many Polish spectators of the older generation. Janda herself admits:

No woman before acted like that in our films: such a role never existed. In *Man of Marble,* there is not a single moment when I am self-involved. Aside from a brief scene with my father when I express some personal doubts, I don't think about myself. I'm always forging ahead, attacking the matter at hand, pursuing an idea, taking care of someone else. I move forward, I make the decision.[5]

These two depictions of Agnieszka introduce a dialogical tension in the films that, among other tensions, indicates Wajda's conflicting intentions. On one hand he wants to create a political hero who could be the carrier of the political message, while on the other hand, he wants this hero to be a human being with doubts, a love life, and different roles to play in real life as a woman.

In general, the problem of depiction of female characters in Wajda's films demands a separate study. Already in these three films, however, Wajda's ambivalence in his presentation of women is striking. Agnieszka in *Man of Marble* and *Man of Iron,* Anna Hulewicz in *Man of Iron,* and Mme. Lucille Desmoulins in *Danton* are not classical female characters directed by subjugation to the patriarchal order and submission as determining factors in their lives. All these women are highly politicized, taking an active part in political events, risking their careers and freedom, and acting in a very masculine way. They are masculine in their actions and feminine in the way they treat their families, that is, as the most important aspect of their lives. This dialogical positioning of female characters in Wajda's films requires a separate historical and sociological debate far beyond the scope of this text, however. On another plane, reactions to the presentation of Agnieszka covered a broad range of responses, from outright denial by older spectators to an enthusiastic approval by younger ones. Agnieszka was resented particularly by older party members who, in their writings in the official publications of the 1970s, represented the position of state authority. These spectators felt indignant about everything connected with Agnieszka: the way she dressed, her constant smoking, her casual, free-wheeling life style, her cynicism, and her tone of voice. They associated Agnieszka with the cynical representatives of her age group who tried to build their career at any cost, the careerist intelligentsia who used their chutzpah in order to advance their career prospects. Symptomatic for the audience of this group of spectators is the review by Bozena Sycowna,[6] who, starting with Agnieszka's dress and finishing with her ideological position, presents an overall negative picture of her. Sycowna states:

Agnieszka is not a nice protagonist. In a jeans suit from top to bottom, in wooden sandals, often photographed with wide angle lens, she appears to be a monstrous figure. She decides to make a film about the 1950s not because this is the time of her father which she wants to recount. It is not entirely true. She acts from a very egoistic point of view as she wants to have a "catchy" story for her diploma film.[7]

In her review Sycowna describes the second sequence at the National Museum in Warsaw where Agnieszka, in a cheeky manner, opens the door to a cellar with the monuments from the 1950s, and eagerly surveys the marble figures. This scene is interpreted by Sycowna as an unnecessary intrusion into the world of the past. The author of the review considers Agnieszka too rude and too openly aggressive to be able to cover all the intricate contextualizations of that period. The emotional tone of Sycowna's review indicates how deeply she rejected Agnieszka as a Romantic seeker of truth and justice, far from the ideal hero who would seem appropriate, Sycowna believes, for the task set by Wajda. It is worth noting here that the Romantic hero in Polish Romantic and Post-Romantic literature was usually an idealized male individual who complied with the requirements for a well-behaved, nice person, not needlessly obnoxious, as Agnieszka sometimes was. Agnieszka, a young and unruly woman, did not match the old-fashioned expectations some older spectators held of the Romantic hero.

Sycowna also criticizes Agnieszka's attitude to her elderly cameraman, whom she should have contacted and talked to about those difficult years before starting the diploma film. In Sycowna's opinion, Agnieszka patronizes Mr. Leonard, treats him as a technical assistant, and disregards his uneasiness and his fear of the consequences of revealing the truth of those years. Agnieszka ignores Leonard's experience and takes the creative initiative into her own hands, as if claiming absolute access to the truth. The cameraman does not want to take a shot of the marble figure of the worker from the 1950s because, he says, "I want to reach a comfortable retirement." His reluctance to be a part of Agnieszka's film is dictated by fear of repercussions from the authorities. Neither the cameraman in the film nor the director state this openly. The message is extracted by the audience members through their own drawing of personal references. In this sense, they dialogically relate to intentional gaps in the screenplay left by the director.

Interpreters from the older generation were angered by Agnieszka's ignorance of the 1950s. The fact that some films were not presented to the public because of "technical reasons" was perfectly understood by the older generation, which comprehended this euphemism as a maneuver on the part of censors to reject films that could not be screened for ideological or political reasons. They interpreted Agnieszka's involvement as excitement over a hot theme. Her naiveté, they argued, made Agnieszka unaware of possible repercussions that could lead to the complete and ultimate breakdown of her artistic career. Agnieszka must have known from her father how difficult that time was (although many parents tried to spare their children and did not reveal the sordid facts about the 1950s). Michalek and Turaj write that, "The young knew little about Stalinism, the ruthlessness and fear as well as the intensity of ideological pursuit that marked the period. It had all been shrouded through the years and muffled in silence."[8]

This very tendentious interpretation of the dramatis persona of Agnieszka is counteracted by a strikingly different response demonstrated by the younger group of spectators, who saw in Agnieszka a youthful representation of a superwoman opening all the forbidden doors to reveal the truth of the 1950s. The symbol of her courage is the omnipotent camera (she declares the phallic possession of this object in the National Museum by taking it away from the older cameraman). Another symbol of this courage is her hair clasp, which serves as a passkey to the mysteries of the basement where Stalinist statues are kept. At this point during the film's screening in Polish cinemas, the audiences loudly encouraged Agnieszka to go on. This part of the audiences responded in particular to Wajda's revolutionary (radical?) intentions concerning the part. As Krystyna Janda explains in the already mentioned interview:

> When Andrzej Wajda first gave me the part in *Man of Marble*, he told me that in whatever I do, I had to enchant, anger or irritate, because I had to carry half the film. He told me that my role should announce to the world: "Watch out, here comes a generation that will not only open doors which were closed for so long. It will force them off their hinges." And he was absolutely right because my age group created Solidarity. He deliberately exploited my behavior and my personality to forge a new idea.[9]

Wajda could not anticipate the hostile reactions to Agnieszka, a Romantic hero, that were expressed by older spectators in the audience. He clearly intended her to function in a manner consistent with the Romantic line of film protagonists in Wajda's earlier films. In fact, Agnieszka is a link to Wajda's first Romantic hero, Maciek, from the film *Ashes and Diamonds* (1958). Maciek is an underground fighter and nationalist, devoted to the ideal of an independent Poland free from the Soviet influence. He is ordered to assassinate an old good Communist, Szczuka, a terrorist act intended to hamper the consolidation of party power and the process of political stabilization. He finally commits this senseless destructive murder, but he himself is soon killed, not in an act of retribution, but as the result of a misunderstanding on the part of some militiamen. Maciek represents youth and its idealism contaminated by death, brutal innocence. He carries with him the mystery of his generation, people who have matured too fast in a bloody struggle. It is hardly surprising that this figure, as magnificently interpreted by Zbigniew Cybulski, became a legend for the young people of the 1950s and the 1960s. In portraying the figure of Maciek, Wajda clearly meant to evoke the tradition of Polish Romantic culture with its theme of the nation as a martyr, symbolically crucified between the two villains, Russia and Germany.[10] Wajda, in a way a Romantic figure himself, undoubtedly identifies with both Maciek and Agnieszka in their quest for truth, an assumption that arises from Wajda's understanding of the role of the artist. As he states, "The Romantic artist had to transcend himself ... He had to be more than a maker; he had to be the conscience of the nation, a prophet, a social institution."[11]

In *Man of Marble*, Agnieszka plays not only the leading role in the film – that of the instigator of the action – but also the role of an ideological "double" or counterpart of the idealistic Birkut, the object of her search and the subject of the parallel discourse in the film. As Birkut's counterpart, Agnieszka dialogically relates to his lineage and his character development. Both Birkut and Agnieszka come from the same poor family background. Their curriculum vitae could be started in a similar way: "he/she came from a poor village near Cracow." Birkut is a country boy caught up in the social currents of a big construction site. He brings with him strength, skill, willingness, and a kind of country honor and truthfulness. Wajda turns him into a proletarian hero. Agnieszka is an educated woman of the 1970s, modern, with little direct emotional connection to the past. As she learns about Birkut, she begins to identify with him. Despite her feminine aggressiveness, her style, she is basically cast in the same mold as Birkut. They meet across a generation of time, bridging the gap of a quarter century in their desire to see lies repudiated. In their own ways, both Birkut and Agnieszka change from naive, idealistic heroes into disenchanted and disillusioned mature human beings. While Birkut is a helpless object of history manipulated by powers beyond his will, Agnieszka tries to exert some control over her life by revealing this manipulation to the world. These two characters, however, are only two elements in the complex social mosaic that Wajda presents in his film. The representation of reality that Agnieszka would like to craft as her own subjective, monologic view of that time is disrupted or supplemented by other monologues, including those of Witek, Birkut and his wife, the representative of the security forces, the young Stalinist director, and others.

Consequently, *Man of Marble* is not the monologue of Agnieszka relentlessly and bravely trying to pursue her ideas, but is a constant dialogue that seeks to disrupt the assimilation of differences sought by a monologic discourse. There is no single truth in the film and no single authorial message. This polyphony begins with the director, who seems to disappear behind the richness of the Polish glossia only to reappear as a many-voiced demiurge with his own complex experience as a citizen of Poland and an artist.

As if to make the dialogical character of *Man of Marble* even more vibrant, the dialogicity is reiterated and recapitulated in time and space. As the enunciator, Agnieszka moves within different times and different spaces, trying to coin a synthetic presentation of the 1950s in Poland. The protagonists of her film project engage in dialogical exchanges both with themselves in different times and spaces, and with other protagonists who criss-cross these spaces. Witek in 1970 asks Agnieszka whether she had already contacted Birkut, anticipating Birkut's private version of the events of 1950s. Every protagonist in the film has something to say about the dreadful time, but also relates his or her own experience to the time of the film, 1976, while Wajda situates the monologue of Agnieszka in the context of disillusionment with the Gierek regime. The spectators, on the other hand, depending on the time and place of their private viewing of the film, engage in their own dialogue with the film, and are emotionally and ideologically involved in the process of the film viewing. The meaning "in" the film becomes a discursive dimension of the dialogic which, like Volosinov's word, is:

> a two-sided act. It is determined equally by whose word it is and for whom it is meant. As word, it is precisely the product of the reciprocal relationship between speaker and listener, addresser, and addressee. Each and every word expresses the "one" in relation to the "other." I give myself verbal shape from another's point of view, ultimately, from the point of view of the community to which I belong.[12]

A multiplicity of voices, a fascinating display of character traits, and the narratological complexity of the parts she plays in the two films make Agnieszka the most plurivocal and most dialogically complex protagonist in the films discussed.

In contrast to the rich persona of Agnieszka, other characters, especially in *Man of Iron*, are flat and uninteresting. None of them seems to have much importance; cardboard cutouts, they exist merely to narrate history. Only Dzidek (played by Boguslaw Linda), a TV studio technician who long ago compromised his student idealism, seems ever to have faced any doubts or dilemmas. Sadly, Maciek, whose story the film *Man of Iron* tells, also seems entirely monological. In his attempt to present Birkut's son, Wajda appears to have set too great a goal for himself. Maciek had to match his father's uncompromising attitude, his honesty and virgin naiveté. In *Man of Marble*, while presenting Birkut, Maciek's father, Wajda dared introduce a grain of doubt, of comic relief, which made this tragic figure accessible to the spectator. In *Man of Iron* nothing like this happens. The tragic historical events overwhelm the psychological construction of the characters. Too much has to be said about the justification of the Gdansk agreement, too many historical circumstances have to be explained. The tragic and courageous hero of *Man of Marble* is not replaced by an equally dialogical character of the son, but by a monological cardboard cutout, boring in its univocal presentation.

As Szpakowska suggests in her article "Prawdy i nieporozumienia,"[13] Maciek symbolizes a series of dates: 1968, 1970, 1976, 1980, and a series of statements about complex relations between workers and intelligentsia. He also exemplifies a simplified juxtaposition of social roles: a naively enthusiastic student, a despairing son, a lonely rebel, a leader. Least of all is he a living man who hesitates, doubts, seeks a better solution, and makes decisions that are not always obvious to the onlooker. With mechanical regularity, Maciek Tomczyk always takes the side of an obviously good cause.

Maciek is without flaws, a monological giant. Although he breaks a chair during the inauguration speech of Edward Gierek in 1970, his rage seems to be justified since it is caused by the despair resulting from the death of his father, and by a general feeling of helplessness. After the event and after spending some time in a psychiatric asylum to avoid a harsher punishment from the authorities, Maciek becomes uncommunicative. His actions become monologically devoid of any human attributes. The spectator does not hear any discussions between him and anybody else, and rarely does Maciek show any feelings. He becomes the monological carrier of the revolutionary purpose that seems to arise more from a private act of revenge for the death of his father than from a mature political belief.

Maciek as a social construct was severely criticized at the time of the film's release. Wajda constructed this protagonist as a specific social hybrid: neither student nor worker. Maciek gives up studying and starts to work in the shipyard, partly as a sign of protest against the December events. However, Maciek is not convincing in the role of a revolutionary who goes *pomiedzy lud* (among the people) and tries to organize the masses. This phenomenon depicted in the film mirrors the revolutionary events in Tsarist Russia, where the masses were truly ignorant and needed the help of the intelligentsia to understand what the authoritarian system had done to them. The Polish workers were at a higher level of organization than Russian peasants had been. They did not need any Macieks, or disillusioned intelligentsia, to start their strikes. Only when the intelligentsia joined them as partners did they accept their advice and comradely help (as happened historically during the Gdansk strike, preceded also by the opposition work of KSS-KOR). The persona of Maciek is thus a victim of Wajda's narrative strategy, which forced the films' protagonists to be the carriers of the political message rather than living people.

Szpakowska suggests the reason that Maciek's character is so monologically dull is Wajda's lack of decisiveness in the way he presents the historical events of August 1980:

> One of the two: either historical chronicle or people. First, Wajda chose the chronicle but could not trust it to the end. He wanted to present a chronicle of events but he doubted whether it was enough. He made an overview of several years: authentic documents, and stagings of real events. Into the midst of political events he introduced the protagonists from his other film, added a sensational plot, a love story, gags and new cinematic ideas. He did not realize, however, that in the case of this film, all these endeavors, all artificiality and fiction could turn against him.[14]

Szpakowska's article indicates one of the many objections that Wajda faced from the critics and from the workers who protested his schematic presentation of Maciek. Instead of a cliché of a worker with a schematic life story Wajda could have presented a real man, tough and ugly in his contradictions, a living *man of iron*, trying to find his place in history. Maciek's ideal status turned him into an improbable icon of a worker. A real worker, by comparison, would often get drunk, perhaps would hit his wife, would curse and complain and get things done in a stubborn, inconspicuous way. A real worker's fight at that time needed a lot of psychological resistance because his life was one of constant insecurity, constant harassment at work and at home, and continual complaints from the family. Stress lasted sometimes for months on end, and rarely ended with such a spectacular reward as the Gdansk strike. Not surprisingly, spectators were quite outspoken in their criticism of Maciek. Klopotowski expresses his disappointment in the following words:

> Spectators found themselves in a false situation since they could not invest their feelings anywhere. Their hero was neither the main protagonist in the film, who provoked nothing but pity, nor Maciek, who seemed to them an epitomization of a dilemma of the intelligentsia:

to be promoted or to be honest. Maciek chose to be a worker; it was his lordly gesture. He has nothing in common with ordinary people. Maciek is similar to highly born revolutionaries who went "among the people" in the last century to prepare a coup d'état. Wajda seems to be attached to the type of post-nobility individualist ... If Maciek were to be real he would have to go to the "first line," pushing aside the real leaders.[15]

By devoting so little attention to this character's development in the film, Wajda risked a contradictory interpretation of this important dramatis persona. In fact, several film reviews attest to such ambiguity. On the one hand, Maciek was criticized as a person from the outside, not so much a real worker as someone whom Wajda cloaks with the respect and recognition accorded to the workers. On the other hand, with certain reservations the persona of Maciek epitomizes the suffering militant working class. The first aspect was quickly used by the opponents of the Solidarity movement to argue that the movement's nature was manipulated and structured by influences from "the other" – the intelligentsia disguised as a worker, probably supported by the West. This particular reading of the Solidarity movement was favored by the government mass media in their attempts to incapacitate this most important historical event in socialist Poland by portraying it as a subversive act supported by the West. Winkiel, in fact, was supposed to uncover evidence of a second line of CIA-financed counter-revolutionaries.

The second aspect, of Maciek representing the suffering militant working class, was highlighted in the Western press; the film was understood as a compensation for the effort of all the anonymous workers, a tribute to their courage and persistence. The Golden Palm award given at the Cannes Film Festival was Wajda's reward for the first attempt at a synthesis of the Gdansk event, and the presentation of the workers' stamina and courage. This mythologization of their fight was a gesture of gratitude for the years of humiliation and lies; for their persistence and their loneliness; for the tests of character that not everybody endured well; and for the personal tragedies followed by enforced silence.

Despite the title of *Man of Iron*, Maciek, the man of iron, is not the main figure in the film. The main hero in *Man of Iron* is the television journalist with no moral backbone, and his development is at the center of the spectator's attention. With his restless eyes and constant fear, Winkiel epitomizes the schizophrenic consciousness of the opportunistic strata of Polish society. The only aid that keeps his fears at bay is alcohol, served in copious quantities by party officials at every occasion. The film probably would have been more authentic had Wajda left Winkiel in the role of a passive observer. The spectator would then identify with him in joint, reverent admiration for the courage of the working class. By making Winkiel a scoundrel, though with potential for reform, Wajda alienated the spectator, who had nobody to turn to for the investment of his or her feelings of frustration. Klopotowski accurately expresses the spectators' disappointment, "For God's sake, gentlemen, where were your heart and reason when you settled accounts with TV flunkeys while the whole of Poland changed its historic direction?"[16]

Winkiel functions as little more than a simple structural device. He constitutes an interesting conglomerate of character features typical of those representatives of Polish society who mainly evoked revulsion and disgust. Surprisingly, this character is not as monological as he would seem at first glance: there are interesting traits in Winkiel that dialogically clash with his apparently monological constitution of a figure sponsored by the apparatus of power. As David Denby notes, "[Winkiel is] secretly in love with the idea of revolt, [but he is also] scared and vindictive; he won't let himself believe that the workers can win. He's a coward and buffoon – Falstaff to Maciek's Prince Hal – but he's also intensely sympathetic, and he gives the movie its soul."[17] This inner conflict in Winkiel is visualized in the dialogical tension between his "official" self, shown in the moments of fulfillment of his official journalistic assignment, and the Winkiel of triumph and relief when he hears the news about the success of the Gdansk talks.

With Winkiel in *Man of Iron*, as with Burski in *Man of Marble*, Wajda may be referring to elements of bad conscience in his own character. "I am no more innocent than anyone else," he has said, referring to an early Stalinist propaganda film he worked on as a young assistant director. More generally, Winkiel clearly stands for all artists and intellectuals, whom Wajda regards with a jaundiced eye. In a conversation in New York he said, "More than once I thought I knew where history was going, but I was wrong. The workers have more imagination." It was a worker at the Gdansk shipyard who gave his new film its title when he asked Wajda, "When are you going to make the film about us men of iron?" "Artists must be humble," said Wajda. "We are in public service. If we can fix up society we could make such wonderful films."[18]

The presentation of the characters in *Man of Iron* bypassed the expectations of the spectator. The spectator expected a film about the formation of the real leaders of the social movement and about the development of working class consciousness, the two phenomena that seem most important in the shipyard strikes. Deeply moved by the real events of the strike, the spectator expected a film about a real working class hero, such as Walesa, not Maciek, an unconvincing leader from the second lines, or Winkiel, an alcoholic journalist, or the ordinary workers, whose grievances they knew very well. What spectators wanted was a film about the heroes of their times, the leaders of their revolution. Although Wajda introduced those leaders in documentary footage and staged presentations in the film, and Lech Walesa, Anna Walentynowicz, and Tadeusz Fiszbach all play themselves, all of them, especially Walesa, function as icons rather than as characters who propel the drama. The introduction of the historical personae in the film dialogically functions in terms of the relation between history and reality, producing an overwhelming effect of authenticity. The spectator expected a documentary presentation of these historical figures' lives from the inside of the making of history, and was quite disappointed that the film had been shot from the viewpoint of the outsider, Winkiel, a representative of the intelligentsia, who pokes about in the workers' life stories. This was partly the situation of the director himself, as Klopotowski writes, "Wajda appeared at the shipyard at the very end of the events and for a moment only. Despite his sympathy for the strike, Wajda did not join the striking workers, and tried to learn what had happened only from the position of an onlooker."[19]

In both *Man of Marble* and *Man of Iron*, the *dramatis personae* enter a polemical relationship with the spectator, who accepts some aspects of the characters but does not identify with them unconditionally. In *Danton*, conversely, the spectatorial investment is almost total. At the time of the film's release in 1982, the spectator instantly identified with the figure of Danton who physically and ideologically resembled Lech Walesa, the Gdansk strike leader. Danton, played by Gérard Depardieu, is rough-hewn, streetwise, sensitive, and a charismatic blend of virility and dignity. His quicksilver Danton is believable as the revolution's most popular hero, a forgivable scoundrel, a public performer, a private intriguer, amusingly insouciant, passionately serious. Depardieu's Danton goes through an astonishing range of mood and personality changes. His opportunism, oratory, and sybaritic lust for life are offset by his live-and-let-live humanity, as the least polemical and bloodthirsty of the revolutionary powerbrokers. This presentation of Danton was widely interpreted as a symbolic surrogate for "the warm, cuddly Polish dissident"[20] (an obvious reference to Walesa). In this way, Depardieu's interpretation perpetuated the populist public image of Walesa widespread in the West.

On the contrary, Robespierre, Danton's opponent, is depicted as a pious fanatic whose religion is the revolution. The most dramatic scene in the film, in sequence number eight, stresses the contrast between the two. As Jack Kroll describes the scene in his review:

> In the scene of the dinner in the Restaurant Rosé the two former allies confront each other over an epicurean feast that Danton has prepared. Danton sniffs and coos gluttonously over the lavish dishes, as if trying to seduce the puritanical Robespierre into the sensual joy of liberty. Robespierre sits like an icy statue; the one swift sip of wine he takes shows the terrifying suppression of his own humanity.[21]

This dialogical clash in the formation of these *dramatis personae* is further reinforced by other voices that contribute to their complex interpretation. These include the voice of the historical sources and the voice of the text of Stanislawa Przybyszewska's play on which the film was based. For instance, in France, the persona of Danton was rejected by many spectators who expected a complex presentation that was more consistent with the historical sources. In absolute filmic terms (without the historical contextualization), Danton was accepted as a sybaritic popular leader of the masses, while Robespierre was rejected as Danton's relentless opponent. However, as I related in chapter three, on historical discourse in the film, both protagonists were severely criticized with reference to the lack of consistency in their historical representation.

An inconsistency on another level of analysis is discussed by Malgorzata Szpakowska who points to an inaccuracy in the adaptation of Przybyszewska's play:[22]

> While Przybyszewska presented the complicated affairs of many people, the tragic results of activities undertaken with honorable intentions in mind, unwanted pacts and the compulsion to struggle against one's closest friends, Wajda limited his presentation to an uncomplicated conflict of the protagonists. Thus, Przybyszewska wanted to show that history is complicated and Wajda showed that it is, in fact, simple.[23]

This monological simplicity of the dialogue between the two protagonists not only obliterated the complexity of the play itself but also undermined the importance of other *dramatis personae* in the film, as is noted by Bukowiecki, who wrote, "Because of that, several other outstanding historical personae had to be sacrificed. Only Philippeaux was left in the outstanding interpretation of Serge Merlin ... The others, however, seem to interfere with the main duel ..."[24] The reading of all the *dramatis personae* forms a complex, polyphonic coexistence of voices on many levels. The voices of the critics, historians, and politicians both in Poland and France form a mosaic of interpretations in which the historical truth, the director's intentions, and the the actors' personalities fight for the enunciatory power. Undoubtedly, the audiences sought answers to the issues of history, politics, and the formation of the political leaders. In this sense, *Danton's dramatis personae* engage in a fierce struggle of characters, presenting their positions both as politicians and as people. While Robespierre is monologically uniform in his approaches and his personal life, Danton is dialogically inconsistent, dispersed, suspended among the glossia that characterize his personal life of a sybarite and his political credo of doing everything for the people. Danton in the film does not invite the interpretation of Viscount Morley, a distinguished English politician and historian who claims that Danton's political objective was to "reconcile France with herself; to restore a society that, while emancipated and renewed in every part, should yet be stable, and above all to secure the independence of his country, both by a resolute defense against the invader, and by such a mixture of vigor with humanity as should reconcile the offended opinion of the rest of Europe."[25]

Danton epitomizes the Bakhtinian polemical discourse, in which the main *dramatis personae* are also the main glossia in the film's meaning. This formation of the film's meaning was considered to be its strength and its weakness. Leon Bukowiecki calls the film "an acting duel between Pszoniak and Depardieu,"[26], which is based on contrasts of ideological positions but also on the contrasts in the ways these are associated with the dramatis persona. As Bukowiecki notes:

> [Pszoniak's] terrifyingly cold, calculated Robespierre makes the spectator awe-struck. Nobody would like to find himself in the cogs of his political machinery. Whether it agrees with history is another matter. This kind of presentation was proposed by the scriptwriter, and Pszoniak is an ideal epitomization of his creative

suggestions. Next to him Depardieu, a bit embarrassed, somewhat jovial and "populist," loses as Danton, both as a protagonist and as an actor because neither the screenplay nor the play itself provided him with arguments.[27]

The match between the two historical opponents and the cool presentation of ideological positions makes Danton and Robespierre the most mature and least "Polish" of Wajda's *dramatis personae*. On the other hand, this match introduces an opposition of other layers in the film: the power of voice, the power of image, and the power of soundtrack that together, constitute a specific interrelation of glossia that forms the film's aesthetics.

To recapitulate: Wajda's main *dramatis personae*, Agnieszka, Birkut, Maciek, Winkiel, Danton, and Robespierre, combine the glossia most typical of everything Wajda was always interested in – inner passion, honesty, struggle for "the cause," nonconformism, and almost Dostoyevskyan internal conflicts. The other *dramatis personae* in his films function as supplementary or conflicting social voices that provide a necessary background for the internal struggles of the main protagonists.

Wajda presents the spectator with a multiplicity of positions and with a plethora of voices that make the spectator question the integrity of Wajda's intentions and the homogeneity of his thoughts; these positions make the spectator enter a passionate dialogue with his films. In this interpretation, the self, the agent of discourse, is not conceived as a closed-off, monad but as a fluid subject/site who constructs his or her discourse from the utterances of others. Statements are constructed in dialogue with previously uttered statements, ideas, and evaluations, and the agent of discourse must contend with a multiplicity of other meanings.

Notes

1. V.N. Volosinov, *Marxism and the Philosophy of Language*, trans. L. Matejka and I.R. Titunik (New York: Seminar Press, 1973), 34. Quoted by William McClellan, "The Dialogic Other: Bakhtin's Theory of Rhetoric," *Bakhtin and Otherness*, 242.
2. Michael Szporer, "Woman of Marble: An Interview with Krystyna Janda," *Cineaste* 18, no. 3 (1991), 14.
3. Ibid., 13.

4. Ibid., 12.
5. Ibid.
6. Bozena Sycowna, "Czlowiek z marmuru" [Man of Marble], *Powiekszenie*, Studenckie Centrum Kultury Uniwersytetu Jagiellonskiego Rotunda [The Student Cultural Center of the Jagiellonian University] (April 1981).
7. Sycowna, "Man of Marble," 36.
8. Boleslaw Michalek and Frank Turaj, *The Modern Cinema of Poland* (Bloomington and Indianapolis: Indiana University Press, 1988), 156.
9. Szporer, "Woman of Marble," 12.
10. It is worth noting that Polish literature is closely linked to the Romantic movement of the nineteenth century, embodying the nationalistic notion of rebellion against the state. Between the final partition of Poland by Russia, Prussia, and Austria in 1795, and the First World War, Poland existed only in history; there was no Polish state. The caretakers of Polish lore and letters prior to the First World War – figures like Stanislaw Wyspianski, a poet and a painter, and Stanislaw Reymont, a writer – constituted a Polish government of the soul in lieu of an autonomous political entity. In Poland, it is still considered to be the mission of the artist to do no less than mold history. Thus, both Maciek and Agnieszka can be seen as Romantic heroes, both of them trying to undo history in their own ways.
11. Michalek and Turaj, *The Modern Cinema of Poland*, 136.
12. V.N. Volosinov, *Marxism and the Philosophy of Language*, trans. Ladislav Matejka and I.R. Titunik (New York: Seminar Press, 1973), 86.
13. Malgorzata Szpakowska, "Prawdy i Nieporozumienia" [Truths and misunderstandings], in *Nowe Filmy* (Warszawa: Panstwowe Wydawnictwo Naukowe, 1981).
14. Ibid.
15. Krzysztof Klopotowski, "Pocieszmy Wajde" [Let's console Wajda], *Solidarnosc* [Solidarity] (21 August 1981).
16. Ibid.
17. David Denby, "Man of Iron," *New York Magazine* 14 (7 December 1981), 156–8.
18. Jack Kroll, "Man of Iron," *Newsweek* (28 December 1981).
19. Klopotowski, "Pocieszmy Wajde" [Let's console Wajda], ibid.
20. Gilbert Adair, "Danton," *Sight and Sound* 52, no. 4 (1983), 284.
21. Jack Kroll, "Danton," *Newsweek* (10 October 1983), 94.
22. The literary origin of the film, Przybyszewska's play *Sprawa Dantona*, will be discussed in the chapter on the films' aesthetics.
23. Malgorzata Szpakowska, "Danton," *Kino* (12 May 1983).
24. Leon Bukowiecki, "Danton i inni" [Danton and others], *Za i przeciw* (10 April 1983).
25. This opinion is related by Ostrowski in his review of *Danton*. Marek Ostrowski, "Danton czy Robespierre" [Danton or Robespierre], *Polityka*, Warszawa (5 February 1983).
26. Leon Bukowiecki, "Danton i inni" [Danton and others].
27. Ibid.

5

THE FILMS' DIALOGICAL AESTHETICS

The dialogic in the films is realized not only through a heteroglos-sia of voices fighting through the *dramatis personae* with the film director behind them, but within the dynamic of the cinematic image itself. The films' images demonstrate a whole array of cultural discourses that interact in the dialogical construction of the films' aesthetics. Among the cultural discourses in the three films discussed the following voices are especially vivid: the tradition of Eisenstein's montage; Socialist Realism; Polish Romanticism; the Hollywood tradition; and the theater tradition in Poland.

Consequently, although the films' aesthetics obey the screenplays' main narrative line, mostly they transcend the illustrative intention of the director and produce instead an independent artistic message, generating an artistic effect that goes far beyond the historical alone. In this chapter, I will show how various elements of the cinematic image – the *mise en scène*, color, music and sound – are integrated to form an aesthetic whole that represents the cultural discourses mentioned above.

In the presentation of Socialist Realism I will use numerous quotations from a book by Wojciech Wlodarczyk titled *Socrealizm* (Socialist Realism, 1991). Due to the change of power in Poland, this book could be published only recently. It illustrates the grim reality of Polish art under Stalinist rule. Since such materials are still rarely accessible in the West, I decided to translate critical sections of the text and include them in this chapter.

Eisenstein's Montage

The tradition of Eisenstein's montage is visible in many scenes created by Wajda. In order to produce a specific emotional impact, Wajda combines elements belonging to disparate semantic domains and, through montage, creates a unique, complex whole full of tensions.

Sergei Eisenstein's contribution to film is well known. His theory of dialectical montage revolutionized film production and the way film was interpreted. Eisenstein's influence in Eastern Europe was significant, appearing in films directed by such famous directors like Andrzej Wajda, Milos Forman, and Miklós Jancsó. Each of them considered dialectical montage an important intellectual concept contributing to the effect of heterogeneity and complexity in a transmitted message, and requiring from the spectator a significant intellectual input.

To summarize his theory briefly, Eisenstein saw film editing, or montage, as a process that operates according to the Marxist dialectic. This dialectic is a way of looking at human history and experience as perpetual conflict in which a force (thesis) collides with a counterforce (antithesis) to produce from their collision a wholly new phenomenon (synthesis). This new phenomenon is not the sum of the two forces but something greater than and different from both. The shot itself can be polysemous or univocal, but for Eisenstein it is montage that provides meaning by extracting dominant meanings from individual shots. Each shot is ultimately dependent for its meaning on juxtaposition, and thus upon the montage itself. Consequently, an increase of semantic potential within the shot can lead only to an increase of activity in the montage.

In his construction of the idea of montage Eisenstein used concepts related to Japanese haiku poems. He was greatly influenced by the epigrammatic form of this kind of poem, which he considered to be "little more than a hieroglyph transposed into phrases."[1] The method of the resolution of its meaning is analogous to the way it is done in the ideogram. As Eisenstein explains:

> As the ideogram provides a means for the laconic imprinting of an abstract concept, the same method, when transposed into literary exposition, gives rise to an identical laconism of pointed imagery. Applied to the collision of an austere combination of symbols this method results in a dry definition of abstract concepts. The same method, expanded into the luxury of a group of already formed verbal combinations, swells into a splendor of imagist effect.[2]

Eisenstein composed his shots like ideograms, as bundles of semantic clusters, tightly organized in their intra-frame construction. Like a line from a haiku poem, a single shot communicated a specific message, defined semantically and aesthetically. The combination of three or four such shots, like a combination of three or four lines from a haiku poem, produced a novel, meaningful unity that created a specific cinematic effect. In a brilliant transposition from poetry to cinema, Eisenstein considered haiku poems montage phrases, shot lists, which by mere juxtaposition produced an entirely new semantic entity. The responsibility to read this semantic unity properly falls on the reader of poetry. Haiku poems appeal to Eisenstein because the emotion in them is directed toward the reader. As Yone Nobuchi has said, "It is the readers who make the haiku's imperfection a perfection of art."[3]

A stress on juxtaposition and the sharing of meanings by juxtaposed images is what ties Eisenstein's montage to Bakhtin's *logos* as a dialogically vibrant entity, structured by outside influences, its meaning positioned between what is said and what is assumed by the reader. Jay Leyda explains in the translator's note to *The Film Sense*, Eisenstein "has discussed in detail certain means whereby the spectator's reactions can be fused with the creative process, producing a richer emotional expression of a film's theme."[4] This heavy reliance on the spectator and his or her ability to react properly to the juxtaposition of images binds Eisenstein, Bakhtin, and Wajda as creative thinkers who reveal a deep understanding of the potential lying in the polemical creation of meaning.

As the discussion of sequences in *Man of Marble* and *Man of Iron* reveals, the influence of Eisenstein's concepts was enormous in these films. In the sequences discussed, all the elements of a cinematic image cooperate to produce inner tension in the shot or in the sequence of shots. My suggestion is that the basic concept of montage was employed by Wajda to produce striking effects in film and to reveal social contradictions not only by concatenations of images per se but through the juxtaposition of image and sound, image and language, and image and music. Moreover, whole textual units taken from different films, especially from *Man of Marble* and *Man of Iron*, taken as a diptych, create the effect when juxtaposed of a dialectic clash of ideas characteristic of Eisenstein's theoretical reflections and his practical approach to making films.

The following scenes from *Man of Marble* serve as an illustration of Eisenstein's dialectical montage, when understood in its basic sense as the juxtaposition of shots. Two scenes in particular from the reconstructed films (sequence four) serve as examples of the dialectical clash of shots within one scene. In one of them the first shot presents a bulldozer flattening the ground to make way for new houses. This optimistic picture is later followed by a shot of the same machine cutting down beautiful blooming cherry trees. The concatenation of images produces a reaction of disbelief and distress in the spectator. The montage effect, through a combination of such semantically distinct images, is striking and upsetting. Another example of this kind, from sequence seven, shows an opposition of two worlds during the propaganda show in which Birkut performs his bricklaying techniques. The image of the older workers, tired and disinterested, looking with disbelief at the circus, is juxtaposed against the image of the party officials, dressed up and businesslike. The latter image is followed later by the image of the sick and mutilated hand of the worker shown in a close-up. This encounter of images creates the feeling of repugnance and hatred in the spectator, or, rather, it brings to the surface a feeling that had been present in the Polish spectator for almost two decades.

These two examples of the juxtaposition of shots are examples of Eisenstein's basic idea of montage only as a visual phenomenon. In this, Wajda directly relates to the great master of cinema. He even literally employs references from the originator of the montage concept. In particular, the scene of the fight for food in the film from the past leads the spectator into the discourse of Eisenstein's *Battleship Potemkin*.[5]

On another plane, however, the montage effect is present not only in the montage of images but in the montage of images and sounds, which together produce a new entity, a novel aesthetic object affecting the spectator in a different way than a concatenation of images alone. *Man of Iron* exemplifies a combination of sound and image that produces a striking, mostly frightening effect. For instance, in the scene of the procession with the dead body of the worker carried by his compatriots on the piece of board, the soundtrack superimposed on the visuals introduces a chilling reading. The soundtrack for this scene is composed of authentic recordings of the militia groups' short-wave radios that the militiamen used in monitoring the procession. The dry, crackling observation in the form of short, informative sentences such as, "a group of people are moving in the direction of street x," or "several hundred people are gathering in place y and should be dispersed," constitutes a frightening commentary to the solemnity of the procession. The image of the dead body of a worker is juxtaposed with an impersonal observation by the authority figures who are interested only in maintaining order and in avoiding another political confrontation. In the scene, there is tragedy, pathos, revolt, honor and despair, all dialogized through montage of visuals and sound.

Natural language in its written and oral manifestations is another important semantic element that reinforces the montage effect of the imagery in *Man of Iron*. Linguistic phrases form an integral part of the sequence but also contradict the semantics of the image, clash with the image or supplement it. The verbal signifiers are present in *Man of Iron* not only in specific phenomenal forms, such as soundtrack or as words within the field of the image (e.g., slogans on the walls of the houses), but they blend with images and sound. By stating this I would like to challenge those film analyses that, as Paul Willeman notes, "by restricting language to its phenomenal forms, (the currently dominant ideologies), promoting the notion of the audio-visual, assert that the orders of the figure and of the word are two homogeneous blocks that can only be juxtaposed, confronted or combined, but can never be merged in hybrid forms of signification, interpenetrating each other."[6] In my opinion, such a process of hybridization definitely takes place in the mind of the spectator, who derives the final meaning of the sequence from the merging of the two voices, the visual and the aural.

Man of Iron in particular relies on a hybridization of the visual and the aural by incorporating the linguistic component in various forms in different parts of the film. Beside slogans on the walls and documentary soundtrack, *Man of Iron* uses poetry to reinforce the political message. At the beginning, the film introduces a poem that functions as an opening to a linguistic framework, situating the fictional and factual message of the film in an artistic context. The film begins with Maja Komorowska, a great Polish actress, reading Czeslaw Milosz's poem "*Nadzieja*" (Hope), and it ends with a ballad about a shipyard worker killed in 1970, written by an anonymous author. These two texts give a monological interpretation to the cinematic dialectic on the screen; they alleviate the political and historical disruption and constitute a bitter commentary on the historical events. The linguistic sparsity and discipline of poetry binds the hope at the beginning of the film and the despair at the end of the film in an emotional condensation. The poems reflect feelings of hope based on religious belief, and events that, though they happened long ago, still have the same meaning; nothing can deny their importance and their factual existence. The poems delineate an emotional climate that dominates the whole film.

The poetic framework envelops a mosaic of other linguistic messages that illustrate the people's discontent and their hope for victory. These texts include the nervous outburst of the woman from the crowd in front of the shipyard, commenting upon food prices; workers' slogans heard from loudspeakers; the reminiscences of Mrs. Hulewicz; journalists' protests; and statements of the representatives of the authorities. Also, written linguistic messages infiltrate the film. The authorities' flyers distributed from airplanes clash with the workers' spontaneous slogans painted on the walls. Words dominate the film but do not entirely belong to particular *dramatis personae*. Rather, they describe various ideological positions, political attitudes, and different ways of seeing reality. By juxtaposing them, Wajda produces an invaluable accomplishment in that he arrests on the screen the historical coexistence of social attitudes. The cinematic image powerfully reveals not only the brutal verbatim quality of the linguistic message, but also the actors' faces and the grim background of the *mise en scène*; these reinforce the enunciative power of the natural language. What is even more important, the juxtaposition of these diverse semantic components of the image reveals new meanings in reality and shows how social reality does not match the slogans of the authorities' "newspeak."

Thus, the image voice, the aural voice, and the linguistic voice all cohabit in the same utterance, formulating the final meaning of the intended message. The three of them interact in a dialogical struggle. Through a symbolic opposition of image vs. sound, image vs. linguistic utterance, or all three engaged in a violent polemic, they create a cinematic unity full of internal contradictions and tensions.

Another element – music – is the aural component that especially reinforces the power of the images in Wajda's films. Music in *Man of Marble*, for instance, is indispensable for proper transmission of the cinematic message. It provokes and angers the spectator but also makes the process of identification with the images on the screen more effective. *Man of Marble* starts with songs of the 1950s, then proceeds to Andrzej Korzynski's dynamic musical score, which illustrates every scene in the film. Wajda is aware of the enunciative power of music and manipulates this element accordingly. As he himself notes, "Is music indispensable? As far as my own films are concerned – those in which I knew where I was going and what I wanted to achieve – I knew in advance what music would best support the story."[7] The director also realizes that some music should be as though it were non-existent, inaudible, a transparent discourse that merges ideally with the images on the screen. He writes, "Some people say that good film music is inaudible. That may be another way of complimenting the composer by saying that he has done his job so well one is not aware of the music as an outside element."[8]

This "inaudibility" of music is especially obvious in some sections of *Man of Marble* where music plays only the illustrative role. In *Man of Iron*, on the other hand, Andrzej Korzynski's score is mainly tense and spare, but it breaks through exuberantly when the occasion calls for it. However, in *Danton* music constitutes a clearly distinguishable voice. In Philip Strick's words, "an apparently anachronistic modern music composed by Jean Prodromides succeeds in capturing the essence of the picture: the sense of things tearing apart."[9] Music magnificently conveys the immediacy of the Terror through the grim, metallic orchestrations of the soundtrack, which sounds continually on the point of explosion. The executions, seemingly unattended, are "almost Bressonian matters of blades and blood in brief proximity."[10] A jagged, nervy score, with its opposition of the jarring sound of the imminence of terror, and full of life and toughness in the scenes with Danton, adds a discordant note of the dialogical clash of attitudes, emotions and judgements.[11]

As I proposed earlier in this chapter, Wajda seems to have used Eisenstein's idea of montage in larger textual units than shots. In *Man of Marble* and *Man of Iron*, whole scenes, when juxtaposed, reveal the same principle that Eisenstein's montage does. These extensions of montage technique to larger textual units than shots or scenes within one film, create an effect of thematic and aesthetic unity throughout these films, but also produce an effect of dialogization. An example of such an extension of the idea of montage to larger textual units is the concatenation of the last scene in *Man of Marble* and the first scene in *Man of Iron*. Even though the scenes are not placed side by side in one film, as is typical in Eisenstein's montage, the effect of juxtaposing these two scenes is that of a dialogical clash of two opposing sequences.

In the last scene in *Man of Marble*, Agnieszka and Maciek return to Warsaw to meet the TV producer and finish the film about Birkut. Maciek is living proof that Birkut exists. That proof is needed for the opportunistic film producer who invented the requirement that this proof be provided so that he could kill Agnieszka's diploma film. Agnieszka's triumphant return to the TV studio in Warsaw with Birkut's son at her side is juxtaposed with the humorous presentation of the TV producer, whose only reaction to this is to hide in the men's bathroom.

On the other hand, the last scene constitutes an amalgam of discourses in a curious blend of the fictional and the real. The film diegesis tells the spectator that Agnieszka will never finish her diploma film because nobody will ever let her. However, the film *Man of Marble* has been made, and after the three hours of the screening, the spectator sees the task completed. In the last scene, the fusion of the real (Wajda) and fictional (Agnieszka), a sort of absorption of Agnieszka into Wajda, seems absolute. Agnieszka/ Wajda, Wajda/Agnieszka triumphantly look from the screen with an expression on their faces of a sacred duty fulfilled.

The last scene functions on another level as well. It complies with the Hollywood principle of a movie with a happy ending, thus introducing a point of departure for reflections concerning the relation of Wajda to the American film industry, his fascination with Hollywood films (especially *Citizen Kane* by Orson Welles), and with American film technique. At the same time, the American trait is slightly mocked and appropriated by Wajda with a Polish, sarcastic sense of humor in *Man of Marble*. The last scene reveals the Hollywood paradigm of a patriarchal plot with him and her united by love, as he delicately takes control of the situation (Maciek puts his hand over Agnieszka's shoulder in a paternal gesture). This discourse of traditional family values and love re-emerges in the next film, *Man of Iron*.[12]

In *Man of Iron* the scene in this position ends in an abrupt and brutal way. The dialogical exchange of ambiguities in *Man of Marble* is replaced by a monological outburst of an open hatred for the system. Agnieszka describes this scene in her conversation with Winkiel, which takes place in prison. This time, the spectator is not left with a pleasant array of possibilities of interpretation but is bombarded with a literal presentation of the totalitarian monological imposition of authority. When the TV producer learns from Agnieszka that Birkut had been killed in Gdansk in 1970, a fact Agnieszka has no intention of hiding, he declares his final decision that the film will not be accepted from Agnieszka, and that she herself must never appear in the TV studio again.

The claustrophobic space of the TV producer's office constitutes a visual contrast to the feeling of openness in the TV studio corridor, which was supposed to lead the spectator into a polyphonous world of freedom of expression in *Man of Marble*. The spectator feels trapped in the small, cluttered office in *Man of Iron*, the ending to the triumphant walk in *Man of Marble*. The expectations of the spectator, raised so high in the first film, are squashed in the corners of the little office. The brightness and visual lightness of the last scene in *Man of Marble* gives way to the dark colors in *Man of Iron*. The blue and the white in the last scene of the first film are replaced by the brown and the yellow of the office, which throws the spectator down from his heavenly expectations to the dirt and dreariness of the bureaucrat's den.

The two scenes, one from *Man of Marble,* and the other from *Man of Iron,* constitute an aesthetic continuum that verbalizes the development of the political situation with aesthetic means. On the other hand, the juxtaposition of the two films itself forms a kind of dialogue, summoned forth by the to be continued tone of the last scene in *Man of Marble.* At the same time, the two scenes constitute two semantic units from two different films that, when juxtaposed, create a dialogical clash of meanings and expectations.

To recapitulate, Eisenstein's idea of dialectical montage influences Wajda's cinematography on many levels: the way the images are combined; the way sound and images work in unison to create a specific effect in the films; the way images and written representations of language operate; and the way larger textual units, such as whole sequences from different films, create unified semantic entities when they are combined. All these realizations of the idea of Eisenstein's montage permeate every aesthetic aspect of both *Man of Marble* and *Man of Iron.*

Socialist Realism

A significant cultural discourse manifested especially in *Man of Marble* and *Man of Iron* is Socialist Realism. Socialist Realism, an artistic version of Stalinism, produced a whole artistic school in the Soviet Union and in Poland that propagated the ideals of Stalin in painting, sculpture, literature, and film. All the artistic creations of this period (the Socialist Realist period is said to have been at its peak from 1950 to 1954), monologically impose the ideological credo of Stalinism. They propagate work, the cult of Stalin, and are uniformly based on a black-and-white dichotomy in character presentation. The character is either good or bad; or he or she is foreign, which means that he or she is either on the right or wrong side of the barricade. This code excludes any evolution in the character's development or any psychological explanation. The protagonist is a perfect construct of the Stalinist system and, in his or her activities, is totally subjugated to ideology and politics.

Both *Man of Marble* and *Man of Iron* exhibit this manifestation of Socialist Realist discourse. However, while *Man of Marble* does it in an ironical and self-mocking way, *Man of Iron* seems to exploit basic techniques of Socialist Realism in a monological imposition of its ideological stance. In *Man of Marble*, for instance, Birkut, though serious and monologically self-righteous in most of the film, allows for a moment of ironical self-doubt when he looks in disbelief at the marble figure of himself carved by a Socialist-Realist sculptor. Birkut almost winks at the spectator. In *Man of Iron*, however, Birkut's son changes into a monolithic, humorless, and inhuman giant who treats himself with utmost seriousness.

In this way, Wajda repeated the Socialist Realism paradigm of the strict division of roles, into good ones or bad ones without any psychological underpinning. In *Man of Iron*, there are no three-dimensional people, only one-dimensional abstractions that represent historical forces. According to this Socialist Realist interpretation, on the one side there is Maciek, a virtuous and courageous working-class protagonist. His enemies admire him; his friends and loved ones include salt-of-the-earth grandmothers and intellectuals who are drawn moth-like, to the light of his integrity. Even Lech Walesa stands in as best man at his marriage, which takes place in a church and signifies the ostensible communion of Church, working class, and intelligentsia. Against the idealistic hero, on the other hand, are arrayed a motley and assiduously villainous crew consisting of scheming bureaucrats, spineless newsmen, alcoholic police informers, and unscrupulous security police, all representatives of an oppressive and Machiavellian dictatorship. As Michal Glowinski notes, such a strict division of roles was characteristic for Socialist Realism:

> A strict division of roles was characteristic for Socialist Realism plots, regardless of whether in a "production" novel, a drama or a film. These parts were predetermined and pre-formulated, as in folklore. An enemy was always an enemy, easily recognized, even if he or she were in disguise; a hesitant intellectual was always a hesitant intellectual, even if he or she meant well and did not want to help the enemy in the realization of his nefarious plans; and, a positive hero was always a positive hero, even if, in the moments of weakness, he or she was over-eager or acted in a thoughtless way.[13]

Both *Man of Marble* and *Man of Iron* reveal such a division of roles, the latter film more emphatically. Much of *Man of Iron* is inspirational in tone, with Maciek and Agnieszka serving as the model for a new-style anti-Stalinist couple. In fact, the Maciek/Agnieszka couple in *Man of Iron* seems to recapitulate the Birkut/Hanka couple in *Man of Marble*, another example of an almost grotesquely schematic Socialist Realist construction. However, while the couple in *Man of Marble* is historically inscribed in the cultural fabric of the 1950s, the repetition of the same schema to illustrate the time of the 1970s and 1980s strikes the spectator as ironic.

Not only in the construction of character does the filmmaker more or less mockingly allude to the Socialist Realist discourse. Wajda also manipulates space in his shots in such a way that it resembles the construction of space in a Socialist Realist painting. As Wlodarczyk describes it for pictorial art in the Stalinist times, "A basic feature of composition of Socialist Realist paintings is that space is constructed in a specific way. Two devices are usually applied: a low-angle perspective which made the presented figures look enormous; and a deliberate deformation of the principles of linear perspective principles which made the figures stand out from the paintings' space in an unnatural way."[14]

An example of such a construction of an image is found in sequence sixteen, where Agnieszka is presented as a symbol of Mother Poland. The construction of the *mise en scène* places Agnieszka, the madonna with unborn child who is looked up to by Birkut's fellow workers with pious adoration, in the centre of the picture. However, Agnieszka looks monumental, statuesque, presented without any ironical comment. As Gilbert Adair notes, "In *Man of Iron* Agnieszka and Birkut's son was apotheosised – statufied, so to speak – as a pious, forward-straining hero out of a tradition that can be described only as Stalinist; and the fruit of their hard-working Stakhanovite loins was blessed in a pathetic little cameo appearance, by none other than Lech Walesa himself."[15]

In this shot Wajda creates almost a replica of a painting so typical of the Stalinist period, in which Stalin and his revolutionary heroes are presented as statuesque and monolithic figures. In this manner, Wajda refers directly to Poland's cultural past but also introduces an insidiously manipulative *mise en scène* that imposes a monological, sentimental reading. Similarly, most of the scenes of suffering are presented in *Man of Iron* in a conspicuously monological way. The aim is to establish priorities, as in a typical Socialist Realist drama. As Glowinski notes, "(In a Socialist Realist drama) the whole narration consists in establishing priorities, that is, in creating a world, each element of which undergoes an immediate valorization ... This need for assessment encompasses not only the protagonists but all other elements of the film narrative as well ... Everywhere, dichotomies appear."[16]

One of the examples of such a presentation is the scene of the search for the body of Maciek's father in a city morgue. The scene Wajda creates here is monologically grim and desperate. In the bluish interior of the morgue, Maciek and Mrs. Hulewicz are looking for Birkut's body. The bodies of all the victims are covered. Only their feet stick out with identifying labels on them. Thanks to an accident in the past, in which one of Birkut's feet was disfigured, both Maciek and Mrs. Hulewicz are able to recognize the corpse. The dressing of the body starts with the symbolic covering of the feet. Maciek, the son, takes off his own shoes and puts them on his father's feet. This scene, together with the scene of the burial of the father's body at sunset with the romantic but ominous sky in the background, Maciek's naked feet on the snow, and the menacing figure of the security official threatening the participants, creates a melodramatic effect that mixes sentimentalism with agit-prop and produces the unnerving effect of imposing the director's monological ideological credo onto the image.

In both scenes the composition of the *mise en scène* is distinctive. In the first scene, Birkut's feet are vividly exposed, while in the second one the wooden cross made from birchwood branches at the head of the freshly dug grave constitutes the locus of spectatorial engagement. In both scenes the most emotionally loaded elements are also most exposed, subjugating other elements of the picture to their emotional monologicity. "Composition" governs these images; in terms of painting, for instance, composition "disarms the painting from within, paralyzes it, overpowers its components ... It was forbidden in a Socialist Realism painting to develop another order than the "compositional" one, for instance, a color order, a light and shade order, a facture order, or cultivate a mood related to the spatial character of the painting."[17] This Socialist Realist scenario is clearly vivid in the discussed scenes, and it is also visible in other of Wajda's other images, especially those in the films within films in *Man of Marble*.

Finally, the film titles reiterate the monological, agit-prop function of the films. As Wlodarczyk notes, the title played an important role in Socialist Realist art:

The title, one of the most ideologically saturated elements of the work of art, and "initiating" and molding this work at the same time, is highly regarded and valued in Socialist Realism and its significance is clearly emphasized. The title tries to petrify the work of art and immobilize it in the ideological system, subjugating it to such a degree that, sometimes, the sense of the work of art is obliterated. In the years of the domination of the Socialist Realist doctrine, there could be no works without titles. The title imposed the interpretation guaranteed and required by the authorities. The title acted as an intermediary, a catalyst between the Socialist Realist work of art and the receiver. The title functioned as an ideological charge which the painter was obliged to place in a specific moment and place in a Socialist Realist painting.[18]

Both *Man of Marble* and *Man of Iron* clearly comply with the rules of the Socialist Realist title formation. However, while "man of marble" refers sardonically to the awful statues of Birkut made when he was a hero of communist labor, "man of iron" literally symbolizes the manufacture of Maciek's own character. The title of *Man of Marble* allowed for a dialogical exchange of presuppositions concerning Socialist Realism; the director assumed that the spectator functioned within the cultural and historical discourse of Stalinism and could relate to the film's irony in the presentation of Birkut as man of marble. The wink was literal especially in the scene when Birkut looks with awe at the marble figure of himself and then directs his eyes at the camera, smiling, as if communicating to the audience his own ironical commentary.

In *Man of Iron*, however, there is no place for irony. The title is literally reworded by the images of the iron cross Maciek builds for his father after his death; by the place where he works – the shipyard – where most elements of the ship are still welded in an old-fashioned way that imposes the association with iron and its treatment; and by the iron characterization of Maciek, who monologically imposes his inhuman unbending determination in ideological choices.

Socialist Realism is an important cultural discourse within which Wajda functioned as a film director (after all, Burski from *Man of Marble* constitutes Wajda's alter ego); its legacy is vivid in most film sequences. In this sense, the films moved but also irritated the spectator who discerned the presence of this discourse in every layer of the film. Another such discourse was that of Polish Romanticism which will be discussed below.

Polish Romanticism

All of Wajda's films, and particularly the three discussed here, are permeated with the discourse of Polish Romanticism, which complements the discourse of Socialist Realism, thus forming a curious blend of the sentimental, the romantic, and the pathos-laden. Polish Romanticism was a period in Polish culture that greatly influenced Poles not only at its beginning, sometime time after 1820, but also during the two world wars and up to the time of Solidarity. In the nineteenth century, Romanticism was the artistic outlet for the ideological ferment that was stirring the whole nation. The feelings of insecurity and injustice caused by the final partition of Poland by Russia, Prussia, and Austria in 1795 found an outlet in the Romantic movement, which embodied the nationalistic notion of rebellion against the state. Since Poland existed only in history between 1795 and the First World War, when there was no Polish state, the caretakers of Polish lore and letters before 1914 – figures like Adam Mickiewicz and Frederic Chopin, and later Stanislaw Wyspianski and Stanislaw Reymont – constituted a Polish "government of the soul" in lieu of an autonomous political entity. In Poland it is still considered the mission of the artist to do no less than mold history and substitute artistic work for impossible political action.

In this sense, Wajda as an author is not merely a bystander but an active participant in the history of his own country who tries to shape this history in his work. The Romantic protagonists he depicts in his films help him perform this task. As Maciej Karpinski states, "Wajda, as an artist with a mission, is a part of the Romantic inheritance."[19] Morawski concludes, "(Wajda's) conviction that the deepest artistic function is a critical attitude, drawing attention to negative episodes in history in the light of positive ones, makes him one of the most 'romantic' perpetuators of the Romantic tradition today. I would have no hesitation in describing him as a visionary, who seeks in the past, the best possible road to the future."[20] Romanticism gave rise to an important literary movement. Romantic poets such as Adam Mickiewicz and Juliusz Slowacki, transformed the language of expression of a whole generation. Their passionate, highly emotional poems and ballads awoke national consciousness and brought the attention of Poles to issues of patriotism and national identity. The leading theorist of Romanticism at that time, Maurycy Mochnacki, made it quite clear in his work of 1830 *O*

Literaturze polskiej XIX w (On Polish Literature of the 19th Century), that "one of Romanticism's main tasks was the awakening of national consciousness."[21]

The appearance of the first works of Romantic literature delivered a death blow to the concepts of the Classical School, since Romanticism rejected the rigid forms and cold reasoning. Romanticism meant passion and emotional involvement that counteracted the rigors of Classicism. Although very few groups among the young intelligentsia readily accepted the revolutionary ideology propagated by Romantic poets such as Mickiewicz, Romantic poetry made an immediate conquest of the hearts and minds of the educated population.

An important feature of Romanticism was an introduction of the "simple folk" as a political and cultural subject. The thoughts and desires of simple people were given priority in the literature and poetry of that time as a challenge to the culture of the salons. This trend was especially characteristic of Polish Romanticism in particular since it reflected the desire for liberation from both the constraints of Classicism and the Russian and German oppressors who held Poland in their grip during the partition of Poland.

Romantic themes such as the fate of the common people, the nourishing of national consciousness and the desire for freedom appear repeatedly in many of Wajda's films, for instance in *The Wedding*, and in the early *Ashes and Diamonds*. The three films discussed in this book are no exception. In *Man of Marble*, the common man is romanticized and glorified. Birkut is always presented in a favorable way. His image on the screen is surrounded by a halo of diffused orange light, and the contours are soft as if enveloping Birkut in the mist of the spectator's sympathy and understanding. Other scenes representing Birkut as a Romantic hero who fights for the fate of the simple man and suffers in the process reiterate this tone.

One of the most striking scenes that illustrates this Romantic discourse in *Man of Marble* is the scene that shows Hanka and Birkut moving from the apartment in Nowa Huta that they had obtained from the state. After his return from prison, Birkut is told that he no longer has a state apartment and must move to the slums on the outskirts of the city. The scene of the move is annoyingly romanticized. On the cart there are modest pieces of furniture, the table, chair and trunk, but the most important of Birkut's belongings seems to be a traditional red geranium, which Birkut and his wife handle with great care. This symbol of love for Polish peasant tradition seems to epitomize Birkut's love for truth and honesty. As a Romantic hero Birkut is presented in *Man of Marble* as a person suffering at the hands of the authorities but enduring this hardship with dignity and calm. The Romantic respect for common people is later recounted in *Man of Iron* in the heartbreaking recollections of Mrs. Hulewicz and, finally, in *Danton*, where the protagonist of the film is the epitome of the common people. The whole construction of Danton – not always clean, disheveled, with uncombed hair, uneasily wearing clothes that look too big for him, but passionate, robust, and impetuous – propagates the image of the common man that was popular in Polish Romanticism. The feelings and emotions in Romantic man, not necessarily his polished looks or refined speech, are crucial. As Walicki notes, this trait of Polish Romanticism was intensely criticized by Sniadecki, for instance, who wrote an article "On the Classical and Romantic Writings" in 1819 in which he "... fiercely condemned the Romantics, accusing them of mysticism, of glorification of the irrational superstitions of the country folk, and, last but not least, of undermining the social order by proclaiming the superiority of wild imagination over enlightened reason and healthy common sense."[22]

One of the most interesting elements of Polish Romanticism was its messianism. According to Walicki, messianism is "a type of religious consciousness closely bound up with millenarism, i.e., with the quest for total, imminent, ultimate, this-worldly, collective salvation. It is a belief in a redeemer, individual or collective, mediating between the human and the divine in the process of history."[23] Polish messianism as displayed in the writings and lectures of Adam Mickiewicz, was in fact a form of modern social utopianism that was religiously inspired and that consciously adopted the old millenarian patterns.

This kind of messianism is subliminally adopted by Wajda in the creation of his protagonists and in the passionate organization of the film message. The visionary aspect of Romanticism – the aspect of Messiah as the redeemer – is present in all three films. Agnieszka in *Man of Marble* tries to undo history and to open the eyes of the spectator to the historical truth. In the same film, Birkut openly believes in social utopianism, literally becoming a social worker after his fateful accident. In *Man of Iron*, Maciek devotes his life and the well-being of his family to organizing the opposition movement against the oppressive Communist system. Finally, Danton loses his head in an attempt to save the revolution. The

Romantic trait of the savior appears and reappears in each of these films, passionately present in the protagonists.

The religious element of Polish messianism is present especially in *Man of Iron*. This characteristic of Romanticism, as Walicki points out, is representative of its Polish variety:

> A full-fledged Messianism, national and religious at the same time, striving for an imminent and total regeneration of earthly life, was born in Poland after the defeat of the November uprising. The really new element in it – an element from which the entire structure of messianic thought could be derived – was the conviction that traditional faith was not enough, that Christianity should be rejuvenated or reborn, and that the fate of Poland depended on the universal religious regeneration of mankind.[24]

This element of Polish messianism is overpowering in *Man of Iron*. It is present in the images of Catholic masses, crosses, and cemeteries; in the scenes with obvious religious references (as in the scene of sharing bread by Anna Hulewicz and Winkiel); and in the scene of help being offered to the pregnant Agnieszka. It is also present in the soundtrack when the spectator is exposed to the religious hymns during the erection of the cross, during the mass, and at Winkiel's and Dzidek's departure from the house of Mrs. Hulewicz. Religious rituals like the wedding in the church, the Catholic mass, and the Catholic burial of the dead are openly related to the political and the ideological in a passionate dialogical relationship. The political and the religious merge in the presentation of the Romantic messiah.

Passion and feeling, the hallmarks of Romanticism, characterize the presentation of all the Romantic voices in the films: the religious, the messianic, and the populist. Sometimes, however, the films' Romantic emotionalism borders on the sentimental and campy. For instance, in *Man of Iron*, the presentation of Agnieszka as a symbol of Solidarity and Mother Poland is almost unnatural in its sentimentality. The scene combines all the necessary ingredients of the Romantic sauce: the messianic function, the populist tradition, and the religious elements, all merged in an elaborate shot of Agnieszka, the saint, humbly accepting money from the workers.[25] The spectator reacts impatiently to such a blatant use of national and religious symbols. However, whatever the effect on the audience, Polish Romanticism constitutes an important discourse in Wajda's films. It explains his films' sentimentalism, but also gives a reason for the ardent presentation.

Hollywood's Influence

The Romantic and the Social Realist discourses are interrelated in Wajda's films, producing a dialogical collage of voices accompanied by a discourse of Hollywood influence. As Wajda admits in his book *Double Vision. My Life in Film*, he was fascinated by Hollywood and openly acknowledged its influence in his own productions. He says, "We've all seen photos of D. W. Griffith or Eric von Stroheim on the set, striding, gesticulating, always on their feet: for me that expresses the American film of energy and action that I love and admire above all others."[26] There are direct references to this fascination for American film in *Man of Marble* when the TV producer tells Agnieszka that this is not the way to produce films in Poland. However, the film that specifically reveals itself as a voice of Hollywood discourse in *Man of Marble* is Orson Welles's *Citizen Kane* (1941), which critics such as Otis Ferguson[27] and David Bordwell[28] consider a departure from the Hollywood norm in form and style. Moreover, the film diverges from the usual practice of the classical Hollywood production by leaving some of the motivations of the protagonists ambiguous, an unheard of idea in the mainstream films of those times.

In numerous interviews Andrzej Wajda refers to *Citizen Kane* as his "inspiration"[29] and "the sort of marvelous, brilliant cinematic discovery that appears only from time to time (wspaniale, olsniewajace odkrycie kina jakie pojawia sie tylko raz na jakis czas)."[30] Indeed, the influence of this film is present in both the organization of the plots and in the cinematic techniques in *Man of Marble* and *Man of Iron*. Especially in *Man of Marble*, *Citizen Kane* is present in the way the plot is built; in how the satirical outlook on the issues of power is developed; and the camera work is used to create space. The same influence also is apparent in *Man of Iron* in a more serious and literal manner. While *Man of Marble* uses Orson Welles's journalistic technique in a clearly self-parodying manner, the same voice is used in a deadly serious manner in *Man of Iron* without any elements of parody, any attempts at "making digs at other voices," as Bakhtin would express it.

The voice of *Citizen Kane* as an important Hollywood reference especially in *Man of Marble* was noted by Western critics. Jan Dawson, in *Sight and Sound*, even refers to *Man of Marble* as "an East European *Citizen Kane*."[31] Like *Citizen Kane*, the film is concerned with the mechanics of mythology; it explores the creation of a public image while simultaneously pursuing its own investigation into the reality behind the official myths. It is also concerned with the power of the media in manipulating truth.

Like *Citizen Kane*, *Man of Marble* is many-layered and multidimensional. As in its model, *Citizen Kane*, the reminiscences that structure the narrative of *Man of Marble* all reveal something, usually ironic, about the characters and the kind of choices they have made. The plot of *Man of Marble* almost literally reproduces Herman Mankiewicz's plot of "the film about the life of a famous American, as seen from several different points of view."[32] Like *Citizen Kane*, *Man of Marble* is a mixture of flashbacks, crosscutting and contained discontinuity. Both films show refinement in their plot construction, where "chaotic as it seems at first, every loose end turns into an elegant bow."[33] As Thomson notes, "*Kane* confirms the way Hollywood films progress not like life but like a clever toy or a perfect construct … *Kane's* development grows out of cuts, slow dissolves, flashbacks, all of which were common, if not normally put together with such mannered ingenuity. They are also devices of dislocation making for an artificial coherence."[34]

In both *Man of Marble* and *Man of Iron*, Orson Welles's technique of producing elaborate flashbacks is further enriched by Wajda, who produces complex narratives within the mini-films that perform as flashbacks. These films within films are structured as different discourses evoking separate times and spaces. Thus, meanings clash not only within shots, scenes, and sequences, but also between the main body of the film and the inserted films of the fictional footage from the past in *Man of Marble*, and the footage from the past and actual newsreels in *Man of Iron*. The message of the whole film changes inasmuch as the inserted glossia constitute a semantic addition that reinforces the overall dialogical effect in the film.

In *Man of Marble*, the recreations of films from the 1950s are a brilliant accomplishment by Wajda, who produced a masterly collage of old newsreels and contemporary film produced with special color effects. Both the new and the old parts look as if they came from the same diegetic time, that of the 1950s. An example of such a film within a film is *Architects of Our Happiness*, a prize-winning documentary made twenty-four years earlier by the fictional director, Burski. *Architects* would be a parody if it were not such a precise re-creation of the era's socialist newsreel propaganda, albeit one that incorporates Burski. We see him on a reviewing stand as the effigies of Truman, Franco, and other enemies of socialism file past. To the upbeat Poland-on-the-march narration ("They sallied forth to join the struggle for a better future"), *Architects* dramatizes Birkut's official life, which, if one can judge from the optimistic workers' chorus, went on happily ever after. Wajda does not parody blatantly, but the edge of satire is unmistakable, trenchant. The same construction of the plot is present in *Man of Iron*. As he had used the technique of footage collage in *Man of Marble*, Wajda tried to introduce the technique of reminiscences from the past in *Man of Iron*. While it worked brilliantly in *Man of Marble*, in *Man of Iron* it seems like a catalogue of old tricks. The technique of reminiscences is too obviously the central thread of the whole film. The pattern is boringly repetitive: whenever somebody begins to reminisce, a close-up of his face is next, and a trip into the past inevitably follows. The cause-effect relation between consecutive shots is obvious in its mechanical tautology.

The discourse of *Citizen Kane* manifests itself in other ways as well. It is pervasive in the way Wajda uses space in both *Man of Marble* and *Man of Iron*. The use of wide-angle lenses and the creation of low-angle shots account for mannerist spatial distortions in both films. Actors lean aggressively into his lens; they appear very small or very large. "Space is opened out: The middle ground is stretched."[35] Undoubtedly, this technique is borrowed from Orson Welles, and especially from his brilliant cinematographer, Greg Toland. As Thomson notes:

> On *Kane*, all of Toland's skill and some of his unattempted dreams were adapted to Welles's visual interpretation. Depth and darkness embody the megalomaniac's view of his own plight, trapped at the center of an infinite but crushing space. The optics of the new wide-angle lenses Toland used distort the eye's normal vision ... Yet the pressure of space remains, and the relationship of the human figure to space – a key cinematic bond – exaggerates his tininess in the distance and his oppressiveness in the foreground. One feels an emotional force in those spatial relationships, and that is one of *Kane*'s glories.[36]

Similarly, in *Man of Marble*, the wide angle lens camera is the tool of Agnieszka's profession, which she literally drags with her wherever she goes. She is shot by Wajda with the wide angle lens camera; as a contemporary heroine of the Solidarity opposition she appears enormous and powerful.

Likewise, in the flashbacks in *Man of Marble* and in *Man of Iron*, the camera imposes its presence in low-angle shots. The films by Burski in *Man of Marble* and almost all the scenes in *Man of Iron* are shot with an excessive use of this technique. On one hand, this technique stresses the importance of the protagonists, and on the other it addresses the spectator in a highly emotional way. Copied, transformed, or ironically alluded to, the discourse of *Citizen Kane* is a source of frequent references and additional subtexts in the films. Especially in *Man of Marble* it transforms the overt literariness of Socialist Realism into a mocking parody of the genre.

The Polish Theater Tradition

Danton reveals the last cultural discourse discussed in this chapter, that of the theater tradition in Poland. In *Danton* Wajda's theatrical activities constitute an important contributing factor to the film's creation. In *Danton*, the spectator observes a dialogical clash between the cinematic and the theatrical, while the film director engages in a dialogue with himself as a film director, having produced a version of the same play in a Polish theater several years earlier.

The film *Danton* is based on Stanislawa Przybyszewska's play *The Danton Affair* (1937). The play[37] is primarily an intellectual drama on the philosophy of history, in which human issues are of secondary importance. Maciej Karpinski, a longtime friend of Andrzej Wajda's who has collaborated with the director on a number of theatrical productions, believes that in *The Danton Affair*, Przybyszewska stresses the ethics of a revolution inspired by reason and not passion, and not by its ultimate outcome, the emergence of Terror.[38] The French Revolution is used by Przybyszewska as an example of a historical confrontation of opposed ideals. While Robespierre adheres to principle, Danton embodies revolutionary compromise. Przybyszewska's text clearly shows her fascination with Robespierre. Although she realizes that Robespierre's devotion to revolutionary standards could turn at any point into a dogmatic absolutism "that would betray its initial idealism and bring destruction in its wake,"[39] her play leads through political discussions and masterly exegeses of ideological points, sanctioning Robespierre's clarity of argumentation, and, in general, the purity of the intellectual debate.

On the basis of this play, Wajda directed his own *The Danton Affair* in Teatr Powszechny (Popular Theatre) in Warsaw in 1975. The part of Robespierre was played by Wojciech Pszoniak, who was later cast in the same part in the film, and the part of Danton was played by Mieczyslaw Pawlik, who was later replaced by Gérard Depardieu in the film. A very rigid style of production (bare stage floor, a heavy wooden table as the basic prop) reinforced the strongly defined behavioral differences in the characterization. In this interpretation of Przybyszewska's work, all the characters are strongly individualized, with the main dramatic responsibility falling upon the two antagonists, Robespierre and Danton. As Karpinski notes, the acting styles of Pszoniak and Pawlik, who played the respective parts, had one thing in common, "a dominance, an undefinable sense of dangerousness that made their impersonation of the great historical figures truly convincing."[40]

The film *Danton* reveals a change in the interpretation of Robespierre and Danton, in which Robespierre turns into a dogmatic, cold advocate of the revolutionary idea while Danton becomes a charismatic champion of the populist cause. But the main principles of the dramaturgical construction of the plot remain the same on stage and on film. Like Przybyszewska's play and Wajda's theatrical production of 1975, the film concentrates on the two main personae in the drama, Danton and Robespierre. The whole aesthetic of the film is conditioned by the demands of the spoken word, which moves profusely between the two opponents. Consequently, *Danton* is played out in a series of mostly small, intimate, beautifully defined confrontations between the robust, commonsensical Danton and the steely Robespierre. The rigorous, formal theatrical construction of the film dialogically clashes with the power of the colors, the music, and the soundtrack, which transcend the severity of the theatrical production.

One of the consequences of this strict structuring of the scenes around emitted words is the film's lack of mass scenes. By cinematic standards, that invite huge crowd scenes and panoramic views, it must be said that Wajda's French Revolution is a modest spectacle. Scenes involving great numbers of people or horses are few and confined, with the result that the Convention sequences, with their packed assemblies, make a vivid display of government in turmoil. The court where Danton and his fellows rail against injustice is a packed, almost intimate place. Wajda has chosen to put the emphasis on high moments of chamber drama and on the opposite temperaments of his two protagonists. The film's power comes mostly from its faces and performances. The film's sequences show mainly close-ups of faces of the protagonists in a quick, rhythmical succession of shot-reverse-shots that ideally match the rhythm of the spoken word.

In this, Wajda seems to repeat his technique of a direct dialogue with the audience that he had already used in his first presentation of *The Danton Affair* in Teatr Powszechny in 1975. In this staging of the play, as Karpinski relates, Wajda dispensed almost completely with the conventional stage, which inevitably distances the audience from the action. Instead, he transported the action into the auditorium amongst the spectators. Seated on the chairs among the actors, the spectators actively participated in the play. A similar procedure of making the spectator an active participant in the events is used by Wajda in the film. Although Wajda was not able to place the spectators within the world of the film, he used the technique of a close-up with such refinement that the spectator felt he was a part of the conflict. Close-ups, shot-reverse-shots, and the display of the facial expression in the shots cause the spectator to be as emotionally and intellectually engaged in the process of viewing the film as audiences were engaged in the process of viewing the play. The facial expressions of the protagonists become the most important "word" in the film. The glassy, reptilian fervor of Wojciech Pszoniak is juxtaposed with Depardieu's unashamed play to the gallery. The film becomes a carefully orchestrated theatrical accomplishment of all the protagonists.

The theatrical facial expression constitutes the most straightforward voice expressing the political discourse in *Danton* complemented by passionate words and austere images. The film speaks constantly; the flow of words from the screen functions as a carrier of meaning for the film director but also as a trigger for a volatile discussion with the spectator, especially the Polish and the French spectators who respond to the film's assertions concerning their countries' distant and recent histories. The film is a celebration of the power of the spoken word. In *Danton* speech is action. Characters race through the night and burst into rooms, holding forth as they walk; they address large groups of people, small meetings, a cell, sometimes just another person. The film becomes a passionate argument about power, authority, and freedom: to speak well is to control history.

The film medium gives Wajda the possibility of reinforcing the dramaturgical structure of the opposing forces of the French Revolution through the use of color and the construction of the *mise en scène*. While the world of Robespierre and his preference for reason is presented in cool whitish and bluish colors, the world of the rustic Danton is rich in reds, yellows, and greens. In this application of color, Wajda clearly draws from his experience as a painter. Most of the *mise en scène* in *Danton* is constructed in a painterly manner. An example of such careful construction is Robespierre's room, which, unlike Danton's lively, colorful quarters, is cool and ugly. Robespierre's room functions as the epitome of the dogma of revolution; it is empty, rigid, and cruel in its bare necessities. Its bluish walls enclose modest furniture and sparse objects, forming an austere image that opens and ends the film and constitutes a rigid framework enclosing the deep, passionate conflict reigning in *Danton*. In the final scene of the film, the room constitutes an epilogue to the historical lesson of the revolution that ends in terror. Danton looks up to the room before going to the guillotine. He hopes to see Robespierre there, but he is not present. Danton shouts in the direction of the empty window that Robespierre will soon follow him. The room, therefore, functions as a comment on the imminence of the Terror, which will annihilate both the oppressed and the oppressor.

By contrast, Danton's revolution is the revolution of the masses, pulsating with the desire to live, eat well, drink, and make love. In Danton's quarters, passion and vitality reign. The predominant colors are red, brown, and orange; the rooms are cluttered with an abundance of objects. This vitality of Danton's persona, the life he lives and the ideas he propagates, is crushed at the end of the film by the image of Robespierre's room, which symbolizes the cruel reign of terror. The whiteness of the sheets covering Robespierre reveals the efficiency of terror, which embraces all the participants of the insanity of the revolution. The image of the sheets covering Robespierre at the end of the film brings in the discourse of martial law in Poland for the Polish spectator. The Polish spectator dialogically compares the inevitability of the Terror that ended the French Revolution with the inevitability of the martial law that ended the revolution in Poland. Both are associated with the color white: the sheets in Robespierre's bedroom, the snow when martial law was implemented on a December morning.

As Peter Greenaway does in all his films, so Wajda in *Danton* chose a color palette that is connected to the historical paintings of the period, specifically those of Jacques Louis David. Kevin Thomas comments on the use of color:

> Wajda had his superb cinematographer, Igor Luther, desaturate his stock to the extent that *Danton* seems a black-and-white picture shot in color, giving it the look of vintage prints that are essentially studies in black, white and gray with touches of red so rusty that it looks like dried blood. And for all the elegance of its period, *Danton*

has the authentic feeling of *La Nuit de Varennes*: People may wear silks and satins but there's lots of sweat and grime, and their drawing rooms, for all their crystal and tapestry, look shabby. You can all but smell the stink all that perfume was supposed to hide.[41]

By doing this, Wajda displayed the sensitivity of a painter, an art connoisseur, and an intellectual who understood that the true depiction of those times requires more than a mere presentation of historical facts in a spectacular manner. The sweat and the grime of the revolutionary effort constituted a parallel voice as important as the passionate words expressing political convictions.

To recapitulate, the theatrical and the cinematic elements create an absorbing mosaic of glossia that make the spectator indulge in the beauty of the presentation of the ideological conflict and in the cool, artistic images. Unlike *Man of Marble* and *Man of Iron*, however, *Danton* lacks Romanticism and passion. Wajda's *Danton* does not create the cinematic effect whereby the spectator may be influenced by the film enough to indisputably identify with the protagonist in the way he or she identified with Agnieszka or Maciek in the other films. *Danton*'s aesthetic leaves the spectator viewing the film unemotionally, but with prudent concern for artistic detail. However, in *Danton* Wajda reveals himself as a most plurivocal author who combines his experience as a painter, film director, and theater director to create a film that passionately presents the political argument in an artistically refined manner.

All three films discussed in this book reveal the five aesthetic discourses discussed in this chapter. *Man of Marble, Man of Iron,* and *Danton* all display traces of Polish Romanticism mixed with the propagandistic depictions of Socialist Realism and the theatrical positioning of the dialogues of the protagonists. All the films show the influence of Eisensteinian montage and the Wellesian approach to narrative and the creation of space within the *mise en scène*. Undoubtedly though, this latter artistic discourse is most recognizable in the first two films, while the theatrical tradition is most clearly discernible in *Danton*.

It would be interesting to see in which film sequence most of these discourses coalesce and form a tumultuous dialogical interplay of the Romantic, the pompous, and the propagandistic. In all three films there are scenes revealing this complexity of discourses, but the best choice for a comprehensive, dialogical analysis seems to be the second scene of the fifteenth sequence in *Danton*, depicting Robespierre posing for his portrait in David's studio.

The scene starts with the camera panning to a young naked boy who is posing for the painter David. This scene reminds the spectator of a similar one from *Man of Marble*, in which Birkut posed for a sculptor. However, unlike the cheerful and humorous scene in *Man of Marble*, in *Danton* the discourse of Socialist Realism mingles with the inevitability of the terror of revolution suggested by the disturbing music. The next shot shows an unfinished mural on the wall behind the young model, which reiterates the discourse of Socialist Realism. This is because Socialist Realism also required the production of huge wall murals that displayed celebrated contemporaries or the common people at work.

The next shot shows Robespierre trying on various costumes for his portrait as Caesar. This shot simulates the discourse of the Romantic tradition with its concept of the messiah, the savior of the nation. The discourse of messianism, however, clashes with an ironical presentation of Robespierre in this scene as he hesitates on the choice of the olive branch and other ornaments for his depiction in the mural. Moreover, the mode of presentation of Robespierre reminds the spectator of the low-angled presentation of Citizen Kane in Welles's film.

The grandiose depiction of Robespierre clashes with the sincere evocation of Judge Fouquier, who enters the studio and tries to convince Robespierre that the planned execution of Danton could produce unpredictable results. The moment is accompanied by somber music again. In reply, Robespierre shouts theatrically that the execution is for the good of the people, to which Fouquier has no answer and leaves the studio. Robespierre takes off his attire and orders David, the painter, to remove the portraits of the traitors from the mural. The scene ends with an image of a huge marble foot, a visible reminder of *Man of Marble* and the Stalinist discourse permeating that film's every layer.

The whole sequence reveals a dialogical interaction between the discourses of the Socialist Realism, the Polish Romanticism, *Citizen Kane,* and the discourse of the theatrical tradition. The pomposity of Social Realist paintings, the grandiosity of the Romantic messiahs, the somber presentation of *Citizen Kane,* and the passionate theatrical tradition of the Polish theater, all form a densely interwoven braid of glossia in which each of its elements exerts pressure on the others and interpenetrates it. The scene illustrates the Bakhtinian essence of the "word" with its internal dialogism "that penetrates its entire structure, all its semantic and expressive layers."[42]

Notes

1. Sergei Eisenstein, "From *Film Form*. The Cinematographic Principle and the Ideogram," in *Film Theory and Criticism*, ed. Gerald Mast and Marshall Cohen (New York and Oxford: Oxford University Press, 1992), 93.
2. Ibid., 92.
3. Ibid., 93.
4. Sergei Eisenstein, *The Film Sense* (San Diego, New York, London: HBJ Publishers, 1975), vii.
5. Wajda was greatly influenced by Pudovkin's "linkage of symbols" and by Eisenstein's "clash of symbols," terms introduced by Peter Klinge and Sandra Klinge, *Evolution of Film Styles* (Lanham, New York, London: University Press of America, 1983), v.
6. See Paul Willemen, "Cinematic Discourse: The Problem of Inner Speech," in *Cinema and Language*, ed. S. Heath and P. Mellencamp (Frederick, MD: University Publications of America, 1983), 142–3.
7. Andrzej Wajda, *Double Vision: My Life in Film* (New York: Henry Holt and Co., 1989), 114.
8. Ibid.
9. Philip Strick, "*Danton*," *Monthly Film Bulletin* (September 1983), 242.
10. Ibid.
11. In this acknowledgment of the importance of sound and music for the interpretation of film messages Wajda seems to have acknowledged Eisenstein's revolutionary statement concerning this issue, articulated in 1928. In "Sound and Image," a manifesto published on 5 August 1928, Eisenstein, Pudovkin, and Alexandrov correctly predicted, "Only the use of sound as counterpoint to visual montage offers new possibilities to developing and perfecting montage. The first experiments with sound must be directed toward its 'noncoincidence' with visual images. Only this method can produce the feeling we seek, the feeling which, with time, will lead to the creation of new orchestral counterpoint of image-vision and image-sound." The manifesto is quoted by David A. Cook in *A History of Narrative Film* (New York: W. W. Norton & Company, 1990), 281.
12. *Man of Marble* is full of multiple ironies, which function as additional glossia in the film. The film directs the spectator to the question of humor in Eastern Europe, its dialogical relation to the influences from the West, and its derisive quality. For instance, the last scene in *Man of Marble* suggests the following questions: Is Wajda mocking Hollywood or does the mockery fall short? Are the ironies all under control or are they implied by a sarcastic spectator conscious of Western snobbery? The answers to these questions fall beyond the scope of this book. The problem of humor in Eastern Europe requires a detailed analysis of the cultural and literary glossia that contribute to its qualities.
13. Michal Glowinski, "Fabryczne dymy i kwitnaca czeremcha" [Factory smoke and a blooming bird cherry], *Kino*, no. 5 (1991), 28.
14. Wojciech Wlodarczyk, *Socrealizm: Sztuka polska w latach 1950–1954 (Socialist Realism: Polish Art in the Years 1950–1954)* (Krakow: Wydawnictwo Literackie, 1991), 17.
15. Gilbert Adair, "*Danton*," *Sight and Sound* 52, no. 4 (1983), 284.
16. Glowinski, "Factory Smoke and a Blooming Bird Cherry," 29.
17. Wlodarczyk, *Socialist Realism*, 125.

18. Wlodarczyk, *Socialist Realism*, 121.
19. Maciej Karpinski, *The Theatre of Andrzej Wajda* (Cambridge, New York: Cambridge University Press, 1989), 119.
20. Stefan Morawski, "Glowny Topos Andrzeja Wajdy" [The Main Thesis of Andrzej Wajda], *Dialog*, no. 9 (1975). Quoted by Karpinski., 119.
21. Alexander Gieysztor, *History of Poland* (Warsaw: PWN, 1979), 379.
22. Andrzej Walicki, *Philosophy and Romantic Nationalism: The Case of Poland* (Oxford: Clarendon Press, 1982), 101.
23. Ibid., 241.
24. Ibid., 243.
25. Paul Coates suggests that this scene sinks less because of its iconography and more because of the workers' shy "this is our solidarity" statement. The spectator could have been annoyed by a timid flag-waving in this scene, which also reiterates the monological potency of the discourse of Solidarity (private conversation with Prof. Paul Coates, McGill University, Montreal, April 1992).
26. Andrzej Wajda, *Double Vision*, 92.
27. Otis Ferguson, "Welles and His Wonders," in *Great Film Directors: A Critical Anthology*, ed. Leo Brady and Morris Dickstein (New York: Oxford University Press, 1978), 760–5.
28. David Bordwell and Kristin Thompson, *Film Art: An Introduction* (Montreal: McGraw-Hill, 1990), 278–85.
29. Wanda Wertenstein, *Wajda mowi o sobie: Wywiady i teksty* [Wajda talks about himself: interviews and texts] (Krakow: Wydawnictwo Literackie, 1991), 246.
30. Wertenstein, *Wajda Talks About Himself*, 206.
31. Jan Dawson, "Man of Marble," *Sight and Sound* (Autumn 1979), 260.
32. David Thomson, "Orson Welles and *Citizen Kane*," in *Art As Film*, ed. P. Coates (Montreal: P.S. Presse, 1990), 35.
33. Ibid., 40.
34. Ibid.
35. Ibid., 43.
36. Ibid.
37. For further analysis of Przybyszewska's *The Danton Affair* and Wajda's theatrical production based on this drama, refer to the book *The Theatre of Andrzej Wajda* by Maciej Karpinski (Cambridge, New York: Cambridge University Press, 1989).
38. Karpinski, *The Theatre of Andrzej Wajda*, 34–57.
39. Ibid., 49.
40. Ibid., 53.
41. Kevin Thomas, "Danton," *Los Angeles Times* (14 October 1983), calendar, 2.
42. M.M. Bakhtin, *The Dialogic Imagination: Four Essays*, ed. Michael Holquist, trans. Caryl Emerson and Michael Holquist (Austin: University of Texas Press, 1981), p. 279.

✸ AFTERWORD

In my quest for a convincing interpretive methodology for film I came across a variety of theoretical fields in film theory, among them film semiotics, film linguistics, auteur theory, spectatorship theory, linguistic pragmatics, and reception theory. Finally, I approached Bakhtin's idea of dialogism which I found to be a unifying theoretical paradigm or mode of thinking applicable to film. *The Political Films of Andrzej Wajda: Dialogism in* Man of Marble, Man of Iron, *and* Danton is an attempt to analyze film within Bakhtin's concept of dialogism, which combines film language and film spectator in a mutual relationship. In this approach, film meaning becomes a negotiated entity, a product of a creative interaction between the image on the screen and the spectator in the auditorium. The final film meaning appears on the border between the seen, and the accepted, rejected or negotiated in the mind of the spectator.

Bakhtin's emphasis on the social and his profound feeling for the historical were the elements in his theory that especially appealed to me as an opportunity and a challenge in the analysis of the political films of Andrzej Wajda. The meaning of every image on the screen in these political films, where parable and a certain condensation of meanings are necessary to communicate the polemical structure of the image, is conditioned and formed by its historicity. This historicity is recaptured, and restored by the spectator in the active and dialogical construction of the message.

In my opinion, the political films of Andrzej Wajda in particular illustrate Bakhtin's understanding of language as an argumentative entity, a phenomenon that is meaningful *only* in relationship, only in the context of someone talking to someone else, even when that someone else is one's inner addressee. Andrzej Wajda's filmography can be considered an example of a specific, intimate relationship between the film, its director, the social and political conditions structuring the film, the spectator, and the spectator's background and needs.

Man of Marble, Man of Iron, and *Danton,* which I chose for this study, reveal multiple ways in which Bakhtin's dialogism can be manifested. They involve a dialogistic use of cultural and historical events within the film text, and they attain a realization of dialogism in the film form itself. In all these films, the concept of dialogism accounts for a multiplicity of discourses and for the process of merging these discourses with the discourses of the responding audience.

These three films look at political reality in post-war Poland with unbiased frankness. In their political content and conditions of production, Wajda's films are unique in that they propagate revolutionary notions but do not become overt tools of revolution, such as the films produced in the Soviet Union of the 1920s, or films produced in Latin America, where cinema has become a weapon in the service of revolution. Wajda's films combine elements of confrontation cinema, social problem film, and ideological film, all of which relate to different areas of the concept politics in film.

Man of Marble, Man of Iron, and *Danton* embrace a discourse that encompasses the history of contemporary Poland from the period after the Second World War to the time of the introduction of martial law in Poland in 1981. *Man of Marble* contains scenes from just after the Second World War that illustrate the enthusiasm incited by the country's new freedom and manifested in an ardent reconstruction of the country, but also the ever-present Stalinism and the growing role of the Communist Party in those times. *Man of Iron* encompasses the period of Gierek's rule, the growing power of opposition movements, the strikes in Gdansk in 1980, and the Gdansk agreement between the government and shipyard workers in August 1980. Although its diegesis reflects the times of the French Revolution, *Danton* dialogically refers to the introduction of martial law in Poland and debates the choice between the totalitarian power of reason and the passion of ordinary people in the formation of history.

History and politics are voiced through the films' protagonists who on the one hand reflect Wajda's historical and sociocultural positioning, and on the other reflect multiple types of beliefs in Polish society. Wajda's *dramatis personae* – Agnieszka, Birkut, Burski, Maciek, Winkiel, Danton, and Robespierre, represent political opinions of Poles, who are highly historicized and politicized, and who have been entangled in problems of moral choice in political struggles throughout the ages.

Wajda himself becomes on the one hand an initiator of, and on the other hand a participant in, the dialogue between his protagonists and the audience. In the sense of a post-Dostoevskian compilator or narrative voice, Wajda does not create the films' discourse in its totality; he only gives it a socio-ideological orientation and locates it in a historical context.

Several cultural discourses interact in the dialogical construction of the films' aesthetics. The dialogic in the films is realized not only through a heteroglossia of voices fighting through the *dramatis personae* and the film director who stands behind them, but within the dynamic of the cinematic image itself. Among the cultural discourses in the three films the following glossia are especially vivid: the tradition of Eisenstein's montage, Socialist Realism, Polish Romanticism, Hollywood's influence, and the theater tradition in Poland.

The films' aesthetics obey the screenplays' main narrative line. But the aesthetics mostly transcend the illustrative intention of the director and produce an independent artistic message generating an artistic effect that goes far beyond the political or the historical alone. Various elements of the cinematic image, the *mise en scène*, color, music, and sound, are integrated to form an aesthetic whole that represents the cultural voices mentioned above.

Not surprisingly, this analysis of the films revealed the nature of their audiences. As usual, when presenting the picture of society and its discontent, many elements had to be left out. Undoubtedly, Bakhtin's inspiring mode of thinking encouraged me to examine with a fresh eye the multiple complexities of the films' aesthetics, an issue I will definitely return to in future research. This, and many other topics which emerged during the work on the book, will, hopefully, constitute the themes of my next research projects.

I have finished this work with a feeling of sadness. In my attempt to create a picture of "the other" – the spectator with his or her capacity to extract meanings from the film – I was trying to recall my own "other," Poland, the country of my origin. Poland has always been a country in which political discourse constitutes the fabric of social and cultural life. Andrzej Wajda's political films illustrate this phenomenon in a powerful way.

❀ AFTERWORD
Film Synopses

Man of Marble

The film *Man of Marble* was produced in 1977. It was created by the director Andrzej Wajda on the basis of a screenplay by Aleksander Scibor-Rylski. The main parts in the film are played by Krystyna Janda and Jerzy Radziwillowicz. Other actors include Tadeusz Lomnicki, Michal Tarkowski, and Piotr Wojcik. The music was composed by Andrzej Korzynski.

Man of Marble is a film of precise construction and rhythm. It consists of two distinct parts. The division into thirteen sequences relates to the two temporal planes of the film, contemporary time and that of the recalled past. The essential part of the film consists of the first ten sequences, which deal with Agnieszka's work on her diploma film. In this part, flashbacks from the past play an important role in reiterating or reinforcing the diegetic equivalence of the two plots in the film. Agnieszka's plot is as important as Birkut's, a fellow Pole whose activities in the 1950s are the subject of Agnieszka's film. The former would not be able to exist without the latter. This mutual dependence functions on many planes in the film: on the diegetic plane, since Agnieszka's misfortunes with her diploma film are similar to Birkut's misfortunes in his life as a party member in the 1950s (both protagonists are driven by a desire to be honest and sincere in their lives); on the plane of character formation, since both protagonists reveal similar character traits (they are naive and outspoken at the same time); and, on the structural plane within the diegesis itself, since both of them constitute the axis along which other protagonists of the film meet. All the protagonists of the first ten sequences appear in the decade of the 1950s and in the decade of the 1970s, united by the persona of Birkut, and exhumed by the persona of Agnieszka.

The following is the construction schema of the film. The first section of the film is divided into two subsections, where particular sequences are titled according to the place of action. This schema takes into consideration both temporal realms, that of the time of Agnieszka and the time of Birkut, so that flashbacks and projections of old newsreels and Burski's films play an equally important part in the film's diegesis.

Film Schema
PART 1, SUBSECTION 1:

Sequence 1
The film starts from the documentary shots of Bierut during a May Day parade in the 1950s. Smiling workers parade in the streets of Warsaw. The next shot shows a huge portrait of a distinguished worker being taken down.

Sequence 2
In this sequence the TV producer and Agnieszka talk about Agnieszka's diploma film. Agnieszka wants to produce her diploma film about the period of her father's youth. The producer opposes Agnieszka's project because such a dangerous theme had never been presented on the screen. He wants Agnieszka to make a completely different film, about steelworkers and the results of the socialist economy, which would be more in line with party policy. Agnieszka insists on her project, since the theme she proposes could interest everybody. The TV producer refuses to give her forbidden film material, and reminds her that she has only twenty one days to finish the diploma film.

Sequence 3
This sequence takes the spectator to the National Museum in Warsaw, where Agnieszka and her film crew sneak into the museum and film the marble figure of Birkut despite a formal prohibition by the director of the museum.

Sequence 4
Location of the scene is a projection room in a TV studio during a projection of films from the 1950s. The projection starts by showing discarded footage from the film *The Beginning of a Town*. This footage presents the film director, Burski, taking shots of living conditions at a big construction site: the muddy boots of the workers, food lines, the destruction of the cherry orchard, construction equipment sinking in the mud, the throwing of food at a party official. The next film from the 1950s, *They're Building our Happiness*, shows Mateusz Birkut as a distinguished worker who

has contributed to the development of the country. The film is a brilliant collage of old footage and contemporary restagings of scenes from the 1950s. It shows Birkut's life as full of successes, from his origins in a small village near Cracow to his career as an exemplary worker and a union activist. Agnieszka finally sees the forbidden footage in which the huge portrait of Birkut is being taken down.

Sequence 5

This sequence introduces the spectator to the meeting with the film director, Burski. From the older cameraman, Mr. Leonard, Agnieszka learns that Burski's film about Birkut received a prestigious prize in the 1950s. Mr. Leonard feels that the theme Agnieszka is dealing with is potentially dangerous, and he expresses his doubts. Agnieszka does not offer comfort to the older cameraman, but asks him to shoot the whole film with a hand-held camera, not from the tripod. Agnieszka is next seen at the Okecie airport in Warsaw, where the director, Burski, is arriving from a film festival. She accompanies him to his house and on the way tells him about her plan to produce a film.

Sequence 6

The sequence presents the meeting between director Burski and Agnieszka. Burski describes the making of the film about Birkut at the construction site in Nowa Huta. He starts his description from a conversation with a party official, Jodla, who helped him in the creation of the new Stakhanovite. In this sequence Wajda shows a calculated and careful construction of a Stalinist myth by a cynical film director and a condescending party official despite initial opposition to the plan by more rational representatives of the party committee.

Sequence 7

This sequence shows the meeting between Michalak and Agnieszka. Michalak is a security officer who had taken care of Birkut in the 1950s. He accompanied him on all his propaganda shows, during which Birkut and two co-workers had to lay 35,000 bricks during a one-day shift. Michalak describes the sabotage in Zabinka Mala. During a typical propaganda show someone passes a hot brick to Birkut. Birkut drops the brick and screams with pain. The whole event is stopped and Michalak looks for the guilty party. On the way back from the show Michalak suspects Vincenty Witek, Birkut's friend, of sabotage. The next scene in the sequence shows

Birkut involved in social work in Nowa Huta. As Michalak explains, Birkut could no longer work as a bricklayer since his hands did not heal properly. A scene where Birkut helps the Nowa Huta workers move to a new apartment is immediately followed by a scene of Witek's visit to the security office in Nowa Huta. Witek has been called to the office for questioning concerning his presumed contacts with the West. As Birkut, who is waiting for his friend, realizes later, Witek has been detained in the office. Birkut goes to the central security office in Warsaw to save his friend. This scene marks the diegetic and ideological turning point in the film and ends the first subsection of the first part.

SUBSECTION 2:

Sequence 8
The sequence starts with a party meeting in Nowa Huta, to which Birkut comes directly after his trip to Warsaw. At the meeting he addresses his fellow workers with a desperate plea to save Witek. The workers dismiss his plea and start singing a party song. Birkut leaves the meeting hall alone. The next part of the sequence shows Birkut moving out of his new apartment in Nowa Huta. Birkut starts drinking, and after a binge with a gypsy troupe he throws a brick at the Cracow party headquarters.

Sequence 9
The ninth sequence starts from another conversation between Agnieszka and the TV producer. The TV producer is very dissatisfied with the results of Agnieszka's work and insists that she not touch upon forbidden subjects. Instead, he demands that she go to Huta Katowice and conduct an interview with Vincenty Witek, Birkut's former friend. The next scene in the sequence shows the projection room in the studio. Agnieszka examines the documentary material related to Birkut. The film *Skocznia Affair* is a description by Polska Kronika Filmowa (Polish Film Chronicle) of the political trial of three suspects. Among them is Vincenty Witek, accused of suspicious contacts with the West. During another part of the trial, Birkut, who is also accused of terrorist activities, recants the accusations he was forced to utter against Witek and openly mocks the whole trial.

Sequence 10
This sequence shows the meeting between Agnieszka and Witek in Huta Katowice. Witek, one of the managers of the construction site, takes Agnieszka for a ride in a helicopter and describes Birkut's

life after his return from the prison, where he was thrown after the trial. In a flashback Birkut is seen returning from prison, enthusiastically greeted at the railway station, and later looking desperately for his wife, Hanka.

Sequence 11
This sequence shows Agnieszka and her crew conducting an interview with Hanka in Zakopane. Hanka describes how Birkut came to Zakopane to find her, only to learn that she had betrayed him both as a husband and a comrade.

Sequence 12
Agnieszka is back in Warsaw. The introductory materials for her film are being seen by the TV producer and the commission. Agnieszka sits in the corridor, smokes a cigarette, and waits for the verdict. The TV producer leaves the projection room. He complains that Agnieszka found neither Birkut nor his son during her research. He tells Agnieszka that he cannot give her any more tape or equipment. When Agnieszka insists that she must finish the film she is given only two more weeks for final editing and sound. When she returns to the projection room, the projectionist shows her film about Birkut's participation in the national election.

PART 2:

Sequence 13
The sequence shows the meeting between Agnieszka and her father. Agnieszka tells him about the authorities' decision to take her film away from her. The father insists, however, that she finish the film without the equipment. He would like to see what happened to Birkut and how the whole story ended. Cheered up, Agnieszka leaves for Gdansk.

Sequence 14
The sequence shows the meeting between Agnieszka and Maciek at the Gdansk shipyard. Agnieszka explains the reason for her arrival and asks Maciek to come with her to Warsaw.

Sequence 15
The last sequence in the film presents Maciek and Agnieszka at the TV studio, going to meet the TV producer.

Sequence 13, which shows Agnieszka's conversation with her father, constitutes a kind of stillness, a pause in the action, a recharging of batteries. Sequence 14, at the Gdansk shipyard, indicates a new situation in the film diegesis; sequence 15, in the TV studio with Agnieszka and Maciek, indicates the beginning of a new diegesis, which later will be developed in another film, *Man of Iron*. There are certain regularities in the structure of this film. For instance, the retrospective events are symmetrically distributed and the camera movements reveal a certain structural order that serves the ideological premises.

In the first subsection of the film, Agnieszka's movement toward the camera in the TV studio scene serves as an introduction to the diegesis. In the second subsection, the opposite movement shows a turn in the development of the action. In sequence 15, on the other hand, the setting of the scene in the first subsection is repeated, signifying a classic closure but also an introduction to a new diegesis. Agnieszka and Maciek move in the direction of the camera, as if introducing another film.

Man of Iron

The film *Man of Iron* was produced in 1981. It was created by Adrzej Wajda on the basis of the screenplay by Aleksander Scibor-Rylski. The main parts in the film are played by Jerzy Radziwillowicz, Krystyna Janda, Marian Opania (playing the part of the journalist, Winkiel), Boguslaw Linda, and others. The music was composed by Andrzej Korzynski.

The film is a sequel to *Man of Marble*. It consists of several interviews carried out by Winkiel and numerous flashbacks referring to past events in the life of Maciek Tomczyk and Agnieszka. The following is the basic schema of the film.

Film Schema

Sequence 1
The film *Man of Iron* starts in Warsaw at the Polish Radio Studio. The recording of a radio broadcast is in progress. One of the most respected actresses in Poland, Maja Komorowska, recites Milosz's poem about hope and love. Winkiel, a journalist at the Polish Radio Studio, produces a broadcast with three women about the inconveniences of everyday life caused by the strike. Then he gets a telephone call from his supervisor in which he is informed that he has to see the chief of *Radiokomitet* (the Polish media organization)

immediately. The frightened journalist is taken there in a business car. At the chief's office, Winkiel is ordered to Gdansk, the heart of the revolution, and to produce a broadcast about the events. He gets a lot of money and radio equipment and is ushered to the door with a smile and a remark "everything remains between us."

Sequence 2
The next sequence takes the spectator to the railway station in Gdansk. On leaving the train, Winkiel is approached by an elderly man, the driver appointed to pick him up from the station and take him to the party official, Badecki.

Sequence 3
At the office of the official, Badecki, the spectator is introduced to the problematic of the strike. An interview is seen on a TV screen in Badecki's office. Tomczyk, the leader of the strike, is interviewed by a French crew about the circumstances of the strike, its beginning, and the reasons it started at all. Only a couple of minutes later does the spectator realize that the discourse of the strike is presented within the purview of authority. Wajda uses a skilful technique here, which he also used in his other film, *Wszystko na Sprzedaz* (Everything for Sale). The scene starts from events on a TV screen, forcing the spectator to remain within the reality of the reported events, and then the camera zooms out, into the room where the TV set is placed. The spectator has an impression that he is both a participant of the events reported on TV, and their commentator a couple of seconds later. From the scene of the interview the spectator is taken directly to Badecki's office. Next, there is an outright attack by Badecki on the striking workers and the opposition in general. In a brutally honest monologue, Badecki states that the interview can serve as introductory material for a smear campaign that Winkiel is supposed to start with his radio broadcast. Winkiel learns that he is supposed to concoct a broadcast that will destroy Maciek Tomczyk. When Winkiel expresses his surprise and revulsion, he is immediately reminded of an event from his past, when the same official helped to conceal evidence after Winkiel was involved in a fatal car accident in 1971.

Sequence 4
When Winkiel gets to his hotel room he realizes that someone has already been waiting for him there. It is captain Wirski from the security forces, who has brought the file on Tomczyk. Wirski presents Tomczyk as a reactionary with a suspicious-looking curriculum

vitae. Before Wirski leaves, Winkiel turns on the TV and listens to
a speech by the Communist Party First Secretary in Gdansk, who
warns the public against participating in the strike. With disgust
on his face, Winkiel listens to this unbearable monologue, the
monologue of "newspeak," of slogans and hidden threats. In response, he unscrews a bottle of whisky. Suddenly, the bottle slips
from his hands and crashes to the floor. Winkiel takes a hotel towel
and tries to save the remains of the alcohol by squeezing the towel
into a hotel cup.

Sequence 5

Winkiel goes to the hotel bar. He learns there that not only can he
not get alcohol, but he cannot contact Warsaw because the telephone lines have been cut. He also learns that the striking shipyard workers are in total control in Gdansk.

Sequence 6

Back in his hotel room, Winkiel witnesses from his window a
Catholic mass in front of the Gdansk shipyard. The next couple of
sequences show documentary shots of the huge mass held for the
workers and, next, the workers in front of the shipyard itself.

Sequence 7

Winkiel decides to go to the shipyard. The spectator is led with
Winkiel to the workers behind the shipyard gate, who complain
about their life, to the women in front of the gate, and to the erection of the cross in front of the shipyard commemorating the
workers' deaths in the demonstrations of 1970.

Sequence 8

At the shipyard gate Winkiel meets Dzidek, an aspiring engineer
he had met a long time ago. Dzidek will function as Winkiel's
guide in the world of the striking workers. He will also become
one of Winkiel's main sources of information about Tomczyk. As
the two men decide to go for a cup of coffee, the camera shows
the workers sitting on the wall of the shipyard, the loudspeakers
blaring with the speeches of the strike activists, and the general
atmosphere, which is that of a state of siege but also full of joy
and excitement.

Sequence 9

From the moment of their meeting in the studio, the film diegesis is
depicted in the form of two parallel temporal paths: the present and
the past. The present path relates the discourse of the society in

August 1980, during the strike. The past discourse contains numerous flashbacks explaining the development of Maciek Tomczyk as a political activist and referring to the historical events that shaped him. The first flashback takes the spectator into the demonstrations in Gdansk in 1970. Dzidek turns on the projector to show an illegal documentary film. At the same time, Winkiel turns on the tape recorder hidden in his jacket. He is going to register the subversive conversation and try to record derogatory information on Tomczyk. In the second flashback a conversation takes place between Birkut and Maciek, his son. It concerns Maciek's participation in the student demonstrations in 1968. Winkiel asks about Tomczyk, and Dzidek tells him about the events of 1968, when Maciek asked his father to influence workers to join the students in their demonstration against the authorities. The fictional flashback recalls Birkut, Maciek's father, and, at the same time, the protagonist of *Man of Marble*. Dzidek witnesses the quarrel between the two. Birkut does not allow his son to join the students who decided to go on strike in 1968 to support the liberal outbreak in Warsaw. He justifies his decision by supposing that there will probably be a provocation.

The third flashback leads the spectator to the demonstrations of 1970. The scene shows the room in the students' dormitory from which Maciek, Dzidek, and other students watch the demonstrating workers below in the street. This time it is the workers who call the students to demonstrate. Suddenly a woman enters and tells Maciek that his father has been killed. Maciek asks where his father is now. She tells him that he is at the overpass. Maciek comes nearer to her in a state of a shock. With a maternal gesture the woman folds a scarf around his neck. Maciek, in despair, lays his head on her shoulder. Next comes one of the most powerful scenes in *Man of Iron*, partly fictional and partly documentary. The fictional restaging of the procession of the workers with the body of a dead worker on the door board is accompanied by a documentary soundtrack recorded by the police. In the next scene, Maciek and his student friends arrive at the overpass to get the body of Maciek's father. The body is gone. In the meantime, the boys observe the police beating a worker. Before the boys run away, Wajda introduces another documentary scene of the police and their methods of interrogation.

In the fourth flashback, after the strikes of 1970 in Gdansk, the students listen to the inauguration speech of the newly appointed First Secretary of the Communist Party, Edward Gierek. The balanced, quiet voice of Gierek, providing an explanation for the bloody events, serves as a pacifier, a bitter candy after the killings. In this real TV footage, Gierek repeats the well-known phrases of all his predecessors, that specific conclusions should be drawn from these painful experiences of the last weeks. The students in the hall listen in silence but Maciek shows a completely different reaction. With a frown of disgust on his face Maciek rises from the chair, throws his jacket at the TV box and shouts "Nie chce, nie chce" (I don't want to). Two students take him away while others watch the scene in silence. When the police arrive the students politely report that their friend had a nervous attack and was taken away by ambulance.

The fifth flashback takes the spectator to the scene at the psychiatric hospital where Maciek was detained. Dzidek carries on a conversation with Maciek's doctor, who tells him that from the beginning Maciek was normal and healthy and needed no treatment. On leaving the hospital with Dzidek, Maciek tells Dzidek that he has decided to abandon his studies. When the film diegesis returns to the time of the strike we are still in the radio studio with Dzidek and Winkiel. Winkiel wants to know what happened to Maciek after this conversation. Dzidek replies that Maciek disappeared. Another flashback (the sixth), however, shows Maciek and Dzidek some years later in Gdansk. Dzidek is a young engineer with a diploma who has sent Gierek a congratulatory telegram; Maciek has finished his compulsory army service and works in the Gdansk shipyard. The meeting ends abruptly when Maciek tells Dzidek with anger to hang the telegram to the party secretary on the button of his jacket.

The conversation between Dzidek and Winkiel is resumed again in the studio. This time Winkiel wants to learn a little more about Maciek, whether he finished his diploma, and how long he worked in the shipyard. When he learns that Maciek was fired from the shipyard, his voice reveals excitement. "Because of the father?" "I don't think so," Dzidek answers. "Another surname, another shipyard." "It doesn't fit. I am trying to fit all that together" (Jakos mi to wszystko nie pasuje. Probuje cos sklecic). Suddenly Dzidek is suspicious, and asks, "What for?" "In 1970 I wrote something about his father. Maybe I will write about him now," Winkiel replies, showing his cards. Dzidek shows no reaction.

Sequence 10

Winkiel and Dzidek leave the studio. Winkiel goes to the shipyard fence hoping that he will be able to get into the shipyard. As one of the workers in the shipyard explains, however, access to the shipyard is forbidden even to the workers' mothers. Maciek's mother is one such person. She asks to see her son and is refused. Winkiel accidentally overhears the conversation and shows his sympathy.

Sequence 11
The next scene situates the diegesis of the film precisely during the eighth day of the strike. This information comes from the interview with a Japanese TV crew; people from that crew comment on the fact that the striking workers are showing symptoms of fatigue. From this scene Wajda leads Winkiel directly to the moment when he has to decide whose side he will take in this conflict. Winkiel is suddenly surrounded by the representatives of the Gdansk Writers' Union, who want him to sign a statement indicating solidarity with the striking workers and opposition to the regime. Winkiel reluctantly signs the letter.

Sequence 12
The next scene takes place in a TV studio where an interview is carried out with a real historical person, the First Secretary of the Communist Party in Gdansk, Mr. Fiszbach. Winkiel listens while standing in the open door of the studio. The interview continues when Dzidek approaches Winkiel and comments on Fiszbach's words about the threat of a civil war in Poland. He also promises that he has something else for Winkiel to see. This time it is a film that consists partly of fictional footage and partly of documentary footage. The fictional footage shows a scene in which Maciek reads the demands of the workers from the Interfactory Strike Committee (Miedzyzakladowy Komitet Strajkowy). The second part constitutes authentic documentary footage showing Walesa and the representatives of the government, among them Mieczyslaw Jagielski, Deputy Premier, marching in the direction of the negotiating hall. This part of the footage is followed by documentary scenes of the strike itself.

Sequence 13
The next scenes lead Winkiel to the meeting with Mrs. Hulewicz, Maciek's landlady. In the car that takes them to the meeting Winkiel further discloses his real character to Dzidek when he says that he is not a genuine journalist, but a mongrel, completely dependent on the will of his superiors. Winkiel almost decides not to carry out the interview and is convinced by Dzidek to do it only when

Dzidek promises Winkiel that he will get a coveted pass to the shipyard from Mrs. Hulewicz's daughter.

In the first flashback, Mrs. Hulewicz relates to Winkiel the scene of Birkut's death in 1970. She tells Winkiel how Birkut walked straight into a militia men's bullets as if he wanted to die. Although Mrs. Hulewicz ran to stop him, Birkut did not stop at all. Birkut was killed on the overpass. In the second flashback Mrs. Hulewicz and Maciek look for Birkut's body in the hospital's mortuary and they bury him secretly at the cemetery, after being warned by an official not to say a word to anybody.

The third flashback relates the process of looking for Birkut's grave on the first of November the following year. This is the Day of the Departed, devoted to the memory of the deceased when families traditionally gather at graves, light candles, and lay flowers. Birkut's grave is nowhere to be found. In response to that brutal and inhuman desecration of the grave, in the fourth flashback Maciek puts an iron cross at the place where his father died. In the fifth flashback, Mrs. Hulewicz refers to Maciek's discussions at the shipyard, where he tries to convince his fellow workers that they should officially support the strikes of 1976 in Radom.

Sequence 14
After leaving Mrs. Hulewicz, Winkiel goes to the shipyard. The next sequence takes place inside the shipyard, where Winkiel is let in by Mrs. Hulewicz's daughter, Anna. In the flashback that Anna Hulewicz relates, Maciek is seen putting up posters about the events in Radom and Ursus in Gdansk underpasses and streets. Suddenly, two security agents in civilian clothes force him to get into a private car with them. The scene of abduction is observed by a group of opposition members who happened to be nearby. After Maciek is released from prison, where he served three months, the same people talk to him on the beach.

Sequence 15
Winkiel leaves the shipyard. The moment of leaving the shipyard is immediately followed by religious hymns before a mass. The next shot shows Walesa himself reciting a prayer for the striking workers. The next scene places Winkiel at the hotel, where he listens to the prayers on the radio. Suddenly there is a telephone call summoning him to the restaurant where the chief of *Radiokomitet* (a probable reference to Maciej Szczepanski) is awaiting him. Winkiel who, unbeknownst to himself, had been disarmed, touched, drawn in by the discourse of truth in the workers, is brutally reminded

that he serves another master. He finishes the telephone conversation with the words "the wrong number" and tries to escape through the back door of the hotel. On his way he is stopped by one of the hotel personnel who is in the know, and he is asked to enter the restaurant.

The Szczepanski figure demands an answer to whether Winkiel has had any contact with the striking workers in the shipyard. When Winkiel tries to dodge the question the boss answers with a threat that Winkiel will be beaten someday if he does not answer correctly. The boss tells Winkiel that his first material will be on the air the following day. When Winkiel tries to interrupt with an objection that the material is not finished yet and that he needs some time for editing, the boss interrupts rudely and says Winkiel will not edit the material. Winkiel reacts violently, shouting that he does not want to carry out the assignment. In response to this, the boss blackmails him with the proofs of Winkiel's guilt. He tells him that he had already signed the papers for this assignment and there is no way back.

Sequence 16
Winkiel wants to do an interview with Agnieszka, who is in prison, but as an old acquaintance (he worked at the TV studio when Agnieszka was making her diploma film in Warsaw) he also wants to warn Agnieszka about a possible provocation regarding her husband, Maciek. The meeting between Agnieszka and Winkiel is organized by one of Winkiel's acquaintances from the security. Agnieszka describes her life with Maciek from the beginning, from her first meeting with him in Gdansk, through their unfortunate visit to the TV studio where Agnieszka brought Maciek as a proof that Birkut existed, up to the "silent revolution" in Gdansk. The next part of Agnieszka's monologue is an interplay of flashbacks and Agnieszka's commentaries, formally conducted by Wajda in a way similar to the interview with Mrs. Hulewicz. The first flashback takes the spectator to the scene at the TV studio in Warsaw, where Agnieszka took Maciek, Birkut's son, as living proof that Birkut existed.

The next flashback leads the spectator to the railway station in Warsaw. Maciek leaves Warsaw and asks Agnieszka to come with him to get acquainted with the people and the places where Birkut lived and worked. She would take photos, and they would be able to present them at an exhibition devoted to Birkut's memory. In this way, Agnieszka could finish her work on the film and provide a necessary closure to the diegesis of *Man of Marble*. Agnieszka agrees and goes with Maciek. The next flashback shows her at the Gdansk cemetery looking for Birkut's grave and leaving flowers at the gate of the cemetery – a symbolic gesture to show her respect for Birkut, whose grave could not be found, and for countless other victims of the 1970 massacre.

The next scene shows Maciek and Agnieszka preparing an exhibition of photographs in Maciek's house. The preparations are interrupted by the human relations officer from Maciek's workplace. The officer threatens Maciek, saying that his exhibition will have dire consequences. The next parts of Agnieszka's relation describe in detail the growth of love between the two of them, her return to Warsaw, their return to Gdansk and wedding at the church. The continuous interplay of flashbacks and Agnieszka's monologue is interrupted by a parallel insertion of documentary footage from the shipyard negotiations. During this scene Agnieszka calls the shipyard, but instead of Maciek's voice she hears the voices of Deputy Premier Mieczyslaw Jagielski and the representative of the Inter-Factory Strike Committee, Swiatlo, who are carrying out official talks at the shipyard.

When the telephone conversation with the shipyard ends, interrupted by the security agents at the police station, Agnieszka begins her description of her life as an opposition activist. The next flashback leads the spectator to the city trains in Gdansk, where both Agnieszka and Maciek distribute political leaflets. Then Maciek is tried and sent to prison. In another flashback the pregnant Agnieszka is seen working in a shop and accepting money from colleagues of Maciek. The next flashbacks show the return of Maciek, a brutal police search in his house, and, finally, Agnieszka leaving Gdansk with her newborn son. Only later, from the conversation with Winkiel does the spectator learn that Agnieszka went to her father.

Sequence 17
On his way out of the police station Winkiel passes the gym at the police headquarters, where Wirski, whom he had encountered earlier in the hotel, notices him and demands material on Maciek. Winkiel does not want to produce this material and leaves the gym relieved that he cut ties with the regime.

Sequence 18
Winkiel goes to the shipyard and calls the Warsaw *Radiokomitet* offices from the strike headquarters. He tells the secretary of his

chief that he wants to resign. The camera leads the spectator to the large negotiating room where the final agreement is being signed by a government representative and Walesa. On the way to the hall the spectator sees a triumphant Walesa and Maciek in a fictional shot; an enthusiastic Winkiel and Anna Hulewicz; and Agnieszka and Maciek finally meeting again after Agnieszka's stay in prison. The historical soundtrack relates the speech of Mieczyslaw Jagielski who talks about the painful negotiations and signals the act of signing the final agreement documents. The documentary footage continues in its presentation of Walesa before the shipyard facing a huge crowd of enthusiastic people and, later, shows Walesa on the shoulders of the workers and the crowds chanting "dziekujemy" (Thank you).

Sequence 19
Winkiel leaves the empty negotiating hall. He realizes that he had been denounced by Badecki's driver, who wants him to see Badecki in front of the shipyard. Winkiel leaves the shipyard. He approaches the car containing Badecki who, with a smile, tells him that the agreement is not important because it was signed under duress.

Sequence 20
The film ends with Maciek's monologue addressed to his father on the overpass.

Danton

Danton was shot in France in 1982. The screenplay was written by Jean-Claude Carrière on the basis of Stanislawa Przybyszewska's play *The Danton Affair*. The French actor Gérard Depardieu plays the part of Georges-Jacques Danton; the Polish actor Wojciech Pszoniak plays the part of Maximilien Robespierre. Polish actors also play the parts of the members of Robespierre's camp, while French actors perform in Danton's camp. The music was composed by Jean Prodromides.

In addition to Depardieu and Pszoniak, the cast includes Patrice Cherau as Camille Desmoulins, Danton's journalist-friend; Angela Winkler as Lucille Desmoulins, Camille's wife, who followed him to the scaffold; Boguslaw Linda as Saint-Just, and Roger Planchon as Fourquier Tinville, who prosecuted Danton and his associates in a rigged trial.

The film consists of twenty-three sequences. Most scenes are in the form of tableaux; each of them takes place in a closed, theatrical space, and involves the protagonists in an emotional exchange of ideas. The form of the film is directly conditioned by the screenplay which was based on Stanislawa Przybyszewska's play *The Danton Affair*. The theatrical composition of the scenes in the film makes the polemical power of the arguments presented on the screen even more pronounced. The important moments in the film are always connected with the speeches or responses to them by the film's protagonists.

Film Schema

Sequence 1
The film starts with the scene at a guardpost. The guards are checking the carts for aristocratic fugitives. Danton is in one of the carriages returning to Paris. He looks at the buildings and at the guillotine in the square.

Sequence 2
Robespierre's wife washes her little brother in the tub. She forces him to recite the Declaration of the Rights of Man and The Citizen. Robespierre is seen lying in bed; he looks sick, feverish.

Sequence 3
Angry people wait in a line in the rain for bread. Spies walk around them and listen to their complaints. A young prisoner is led to prison. A girl waiting in line comments on his beauty, which leads to her arrest later. Danton appears in the carriage nearby. He emerges from it and is greeted by enthusiastic crowds. This scene is watched by Robespierre from the window above the street.

Sequence 4
A member of the Committee for Public Safety reads Desmoulins's newspaper *Vieux Cordelier* to Robespierre. Robespierre orders the printing shop demolished. The next scene presents the demolition of Desmoulins's printing shop. Desmoulins opposes this act of vandalism. Heron tells him that he is no longer allowed to say anything. The remains of the printed material are picked up by young boys in front of the shop.

Sequence 5
The scene presents Robespierre being taken care of by his barbers at the same time as the printing shop is being demolished. This is

followed by the appearance of Saint-Just and his remarks about Danton and Desmoulins. Saint-Just suggests that there may be an overthrow of the government in the future because of Danton. Robespierre goes to the Tuileries, to the meeting of the Committee of Public Safety, where the question of Danton is being discussed. Billaud Varenne accuses Danton and his friends of counterrevolutionary activities. Robespierre does not agree to put Danton on trial although he does not believe him. Collot and others present arguments against Danton. Amar, the Chief of Police, arrives with the documents denouncing Danton.

Sequence 6
The sequence presents Danton and Fabre discussing the situation in the arcades. Danton learns about the conspiracy against him. He is still convinced that nothing can happen to him because all of Paris is behind him. Desmoulins and others approach Danton and tell him the paper that Danton supports has been closed. Philippeau, a representative of the centrist Jacobins, wants to talk to Danton about a possible overthrow of the government. Danton opposes this move since he is against a bloodbath.

Sequence 7
The sequence presents a meeting at the National Convention. Bourdon attacks the methods of the secret police and its chief, Heron. One of the members of the Committee of Public Safety relates this speech to the committee. Its members blame Danton for the demand to arrest Heron. Robespierre decides to meet Danton and wants to have a meeting arranged. Robespierre and Saint-Just talk about a meeting with Danton. Saint-Just suspects that Robespierre is afraid of Danton. The members of the Convention run to Danton sitting outside the Convention hall drinking wine, and celebrate the victory with him. Amidst the turmoil Danton is warned of the committee's accusation of treason.

Sequence 8
In this sequence Danton prepares the parlor of the restaurant for a meeting with Robespierre; he fusses about the food, the wine, and the choice of flowers; he also gets rid of other guests in the adjacent rooms of the restaurant. The meeting between Danton and Robespierre takes place. In the discussion, Danton and Robespierre reveal distinct differences in their outlook on revolution. Danton considers Robespierre's policy inhuman and destructive. Robespierre, on the other hand, considers Danton's accusations childish.

Robespierre wants Danton to join his Committee and Danton refuses. The two leaders do not reach any agreement. Danton is seen later in the evening walking in the arcades, where he is joined by Fabre, who urges him to take action. The more radical Fabre wants Danton to overthrow Robespierre. Danton refuses, saying that he does not want a bloodbath. He turns to the approaching women to get rid of Fabre.

Sequence 9

Camille Desmoulins and Lucille, his wife, talk about what has happened at the Convention. Lucille is frightened. She senses that something bad may happen soon. Robespierre, who is Desmoulins's close friend, comes to his house to convince him that he should make a speech at the Convention stating that Danton was using him. Desmoulins refuses and throws Robespierre out. On the way to and from Desmoulins's room Robespierre meets Lucille. Lucille, frightened, realizes that both she and her husband are lost.

Sequence 10

The Committee of Public Safety members meet to discuss the question of Danton. Robespierre sets the time of Danton's arrest for 3:30 A.M. that day. The list of the accused is produced. The sequence is composed of a number of scenes in which each member of the committee presents his opinion. Saint-Just writes an indictment. All of the members of the committee (with one exception, Varenne) sign the list of the accused. The list includes Desmoulins.

Sequence 11

Danton comes home in the evening. Desmoulins, who had been waiting for his return, accuses Danton of treason. Danton realizes that Robespierre has visited Desmoulins and concludes that their arrest is imminent. He sits at the fire and contemplates the options. The list of the accused is being completed by Robespierre and his people. The accused are being rounded up in their living quarters. Danton sits in his house at the fireplace. A young man sent by Lindel (a member of the Committee of Public Safety) comes in to warn Danton that he will be arrested soon. Danton tells his mistress to run away and take the money with her. Danton gets arrested in his house by policemen.

Sequence 12

The Convention Hall is full. People talk angrily. A young man announces that Danton has been arrested. The Committee of Public Safety members enter the Convention Hall. Legendre takes the stand and demands that Danton be heard in the Convention Hall. Other speakers want to defend Danton as well. Saint-Just pushes potential speakers away from the rostrum, and tears up the pieces of paper with the names of other speakers. People shout, "Down with the dictator." Robespierre gives a demagogic speech against Danton.

Suddenly, Bourdon says that he was fooled by Danton for a long time. In this way he cuts himself off from Danton. He finishes his deposition by intoning "La Marseillaise." When he leaves Lucille Desmoulins, who heard his declaration, slaps him in the face.

Sequence 13
In the temporary prison Desmoulins talks to Philippeau about their arrest. Danton, detained in the same place, explains to Desmoulins that the trial has nothing to do with political justice. He tries to justify his behavior in order to convince Desmoulins that he deliberately made the arrest happen to open the eyes of the people about the committees. Somebody comes with information that the Convention has accepted the charges against them and they have to go to the main jail. Danton still believes that the trial is simply a political duel. Robespierre comes to this temporary prison to see Desmoulins. Desmoulins refuses to see him. Robespierre gets only laughter from all the prisoners.

Sequence 14
On 2 April the prisoners, along with the thieves, are tried by the Revolutionary Tribunal. Danton protests this. Vadier, the main judge, does not allow the press to take notes. The judge reads the indictment. Danton produces his great speech and demands a public trial. Next door to the court the judge and the members of the Committee speculate about how to shut Danton up.

Sequence 15
Robespierre and his wife are in their room. Robespierre is tense, and does not want to talk. Robespierre is in David's studio, choosing poses for his portraits. Fouquier, the judge who is conducting Danton's trial, comes and tells Robespierre that they are in trouble. Robespierre explains that they must have Danton dead because the good of the Republic is at stake. He then approaches David and orders him to remove the traitor, Fabre, from the mural he has painted.

Sequence 16
Danton addresses the people in court but is interrupted continually. The judge uses the decree that the accused is not supposed to

address the observers in the hall. The observers react violently to this refusal. Consequently, the guards are called and order is restored. Danton then speaks in complete silence until he loses his voice.

Sequence 17
Danton goes to the main prison, La Conciergierie, with other convicts. He is bidden farewell by the people on the way, except for a man who spits in his face and says that there is some justice if people like Danton are also condemned to death. In the prison Danton is locked in the same cell as the others.

Sequence 18
On 4 April the members of the committee make Legendre sign a false deposition about a plot planned by Desmoulins's wife and Danton's friends. Robespierre and the members of the Committee talk about introducing a new law that forbids the accused (especially Danton) to speak at all during the trial.

Sequence 19
During the trial at the convention Danton states that the trial is rigged and that the committee wants to get rid of him. The delegates of the nation come in with the new decree which bars Danton from speaking. The accused leave the court. Lucille Desmoulins holds her naked baby high in the air and calls her husband's name.

Sequence 20
The guillotine is washed. On 5 April the verdict is read by the members of the court in the empty hall of the convention. Lucille Desmoulins faints when she hears that all the accused are condemned to death and their belongings will be confiscated.

Sequence 21
The guillotine is being prepared for the next "killing session." Danton and his colleagues have their hair cut in the prison before death. Danton and the other prisoners are led out of prison with their hands tied behind their backs. They are put on carts. David, sitting on the wall near the prison, draws the convicts. Outside prison, Danton looks up to the window of Robespierre's apartment.

Sequence 22
The guillotine is at work; the blade moves and the blood pours. Robespierre wakes up suddenly as if he had a bad dream. Danton climbs the scaffold. He asks the executioner to show his head to the crowds.

Sequence 23
Saint-Just enters Robespierre's apartment, sits on the bed of the sick Robespierre, and tells him that he has to accept his role of dictator. Robespierre, very sick, takes the sheets from his face and states that democracy is an illusion. Saint-Just leaves. The guillotine is washed after the killing. Lucille Desmoulins ties the red ribbon round her neck in the foreground. A little boy, the brother of Robespierre's wife, recites the decrees to Robespierre while he listens in horror. The image and sound fade.

❀ SELECT BIBLIOGRAPHY

Abrams, Meyer Howard. *The Mirror and the Lamp: Romantic Theory and the Critical Tradition*. New York: Norton, 1958.

Adair, Gilbert. "Danton." *Sight and Sound* 52, no. 4 (1983): 284.

Allen, Robert C. "Film History: The Narrow Discourse." *1977 Film Studies Annual: Part Two*. Pleasantville, N.Y.: Redgrave (1977): 10–11.

Andrew, Dudley. "Hermeneutics and Cinema: The Issue of History." *Studies in the Literary Imagination* 19, no. 1 (1986): 21–38.

————. *Concepts in Film Theory*. New York: Oxford University Press, 1984.

Andrews, Nicholas G. *Poland 1980–81: Solidarity vs. the Party*. Washington, D.C.: National Defense University Press, 1985.

Arnheim, Rudolf. *Film As Art*. London: Faber and Faber, 1958.

Ash, Timothy Garton. *The Polish Revolution*. London: Granta Books, 1983.

Bakhtin, Mikhail. *Problems of Dostoevsky's Poetics*. Ed. and trans. Caryl Emerson. Minneapolis: University of Minnesota Press, 1984.

————. *Speech Genres and Other Late Essays*. Ed. Caryl Emerson and Michael Holquist. Trans. V.W. McGee. Austin: University of Texas Press, 1986.

————. *The Dialogic Imagination: Four Essays*. Ed. M. Holquist. Trans. C. Emerson and M. Holquist. Austin: University of Texas Press, 1981.

————. "Discourse Typology in Prose." *Readings in Russian Poetics: Formalist and Structuralist Views*. Ed. L. Matejka and K. Pomorska. Ann Arbor, Michigan: Michigan Slavic Publications, 1978.

———— and Pavel Mikolovitch Medvedev. *The Formal Method in Literary Scholarship: A Critical Introduction to Sociological Poetics*. Trans. Albert J. Wehrle. Cambridge, Mass.: Harvard University Press, 1985.

Balio, Tino. *United Artists: The Company Built by the Stars*. Madison: University of Wisconsin Press, 1976.

Barsky, Robert F. and Michael Holquist, eds. *Bakhtin and Otherness: Social Discourse. International Research Papers in Comparative Literature* 3, nos. 1 and 2 (1990).

Barthes, Roland. *The Pleasure of the Text*. Trans. R. Millar. New York: Hill and Wang, 1975.

Benjamin, Walter. *Understanding Brecht*. London: Verso, 1983.

Bennett, Tony. "Texts, Readers and Reading Formations." *The Bulletin of the Midwest Modern Languages Association* 16, no. 1 (1983): 3–17.

Benveniste, Emile. "De la subjectivité dans le langage." *Problèmes de la linguistique générale* 1, Paris: Gallimard, 1966.

Bettetini, Gianfranco. *The Language and Technique of the Film*. The Hague: Mouton, 1973.

Bialostosky, Don H. "Dialogics As an Art of Discourse in Literary Criticism." *PMLA* 101, no. 5 (1986): 788–797.

Bordwell, David. "Our Dream Cinema: Western Historiography and the Japanese Film." *Film Reader* 4 (1979): 45–62.

————. *Making Meaning: Inference and Rhetoric in the Interpretation of Cinema.* Cambridge, Mass.: Harvard University Press, 1989.

———— and Kristin Thompson. *Film Art: An Introduction.* New York: McGraw-Hill, 1990.

Brady, Leo and Morris Dickstein. *Great Film Directors: A Critical Anthology.* New York: Oxford University Press, 1978.

Branigan, Edward R. *Point of View in the Cinema.* Berlin, New York, Amsterdam: Mouton Publishers, 1984.

Bren, Frank. *World Cinema I: Poland.* London: Flicks Books, 1986.

Browne, Nick. "The Politics of Narrative Form: Capra's Mr. Smith Goes to Washington." *Wide Angle* 3, no. 3 (1993): 4–11.

Buscombe, Edward. "A New Approach to Film History." *1977 Film Studies Annual. Part Two.* Pleasantville, New York: Redgrave, 1977.

Clark, Katerina and Michael Holquist. *Mikhail Bakhtin.* Cambridge, Mass.: Harvard University Press, 1984.

Coates, Paul. *The Story of the Lost Reflection.* London: Verso, 1985.

————, ed. *Art As Film.* Montreal: P.S. Presse, 1990.

Davies, Norman. *A History of Poland: God's Playground.* New York: Columbia University Press, 1982.

DeLauretis, Teresa. *Alice Doesn't: Feminism, Semiotics, Cinema.* Bloomington: Indiana University Press, 1984.

Deleuze, Gilles and Felix Guattari. *Anti-Oedipus: Capitalism and Schizophrenia.* Trans. R. Hurley. Minneapolis: University of Minnesota Press, 1983.

————. *A Thousand Plateaus: Capitalism and Schizophrenia.* Trans. Brian Massumi. Minneapolis: University of Minnesota Press, 1987.

De Saussure, Ferdinand. *Course in General Linguistics.* New York: McGraw-Hill, 1966.

Eagleton, Terry. *Literary Theory: An Introduction.* Minneapolis: University of Minnesota Press, 1983.

Edwards, Paul, ed-in-chief. *The Encyclopedia of Philosophy 4.* New York, London: The MacMillan Company and the Free Press, 1967.

Eisenstein, Sergei. "From Film Form. The Cinematographic Principle and the Ideogram." *Film Theory and Criticism.* Ed. Gerald Mast and Marshall Cohen. New York and Oxford: Oxford University Press, 1985.

Ellis, Jack C. *The Documentary Idea: A Critical History of English-Language Documentary Film and Video.* Englewood Cliffs, New Jersey: Prentice Hall, 1989.

Elsaesser, Thomas. *New German Cinema: A History.* New Brunswick, N.J.: Rutgers University Press, 1989.

Ferro, Marc. *Cinema and History.* Detroit: Wayne State University Press, 1988.

Fiske, John. *Understanding Popular Culture.* Boston: Unwin Hyman, 1989.

Foucault, Michel. "What is an Author?" *Language, Counter-Memory, Practice: Selected Essays and Interviews.* Trans. D. Bouchard and S. Simon. Ithaca: Cornell University Press, 1977.

————. *Power/Knowledge.* Ed. Colin Gordon. New York: Pantheon, 1980.

————. *Politics, Philosophy, Culture.* Ed. L.D. Kritzman. New York: Routledge, 1988.

Freund, Elizabeth. *The Return of the Reader: Reader-Response Criticism.* London and New York: Methuen, 1987.

Friedman, Lester. "The Necessity of Confrontation Cinema: Peter Watkins Interviewed." *Literature/Film Quarterly* 11, no. 4 (1983): 237–248.

Furhammar, Leif and Folke Isaksson. *Politics and Film.* Trans. K. French. New York, Washington: Praeger Publishers, 1971.

Gadamer, Hans Georg. *Truth and Method.* Trans. G. Barden. Ed. J. Cumming. New York: Continuum, 1975.

———. *Philosophical Hermeneutics.* Berkeley: University of California Press, 1976.

Georgakas, Dan and Lenny Rubenstein, eds. *The Cineaste Interviews: On the Art and Politics of Cinema.* Chicago: Lake View Press, 1983.

Gidal, Peter. *Structural Film Anthology.* London: British Film Institute, 1976.

Giejsztor, Alexander. *History of Poland.* Warsaw: PWN, 1979.

Godzic, Wieslaw. "Political Metaphor – *Man of Marble* by Andrzej Wajda." *Analyses and Interpretations: Polish Film.* Ed. Alicja Helman and Tadeusz Miczka. Katowice: Uniwersytet Slaski, 1984.

Goldfarb, Jeffrey C. *On Cultural Freedom: An Exploration of Public Life in Poland and America.* Chicago and London: University of Chicago Press, 1982.

Gomery, Douglas. "The Picture Palace: Economic Sense or Hollywood Nonsense?" *Quarterly Review of Film Studies* 3, no. 1 (1978): 23–36.

Gotz, Wolfgang. "Textverarbeitung: Ueberlegungen zu einer Kategorienbildung in einer strukturalen Literaturgeschichte." *Sozialgeschichte und Wirkungsaesthetik.* Ed. P.U. Hohendah. Frankfurt am Main: Athenaum Verlag, 1967.

Habermas, Jurgen. *The Political Discourse of Modernity.* Cambridge, UK: Polity Press, 1987.

Heath, Stephen. "Film and System: Terms of Analysis I and II." *Screen* 16, nos. 1–2 (1975), 7–77.

———. "On Screen, in Frame: Film and Ideology." *Quarterly Review of Film Studies* 1, no. 1 (1976): 251–265.

———. *Questions of Cinema.* Bloomington: Indiana University Press, 1981.

——— and P. Mellencamp. *Cinema and Language.* Frederick, MD: University Publications of America, 1983.

Hebdige, Dick. *Subculture: The Meaning of Style.* London: Methuen, 1979.

Helman, Alicja and Tadeusz Miczka, eds. *Analyses and Interpretations: Polish Film.* Katowice: Uniwersytet Slaski, 1984.

Herrmann, Anne. *The Dialogic and Difference: "An/other woman" in Virginia Woolf and Christa Wolf.* New York: Columbia University Press, 1989.

Hirst, Paul. *On Law and Ideology.* Atlantic Highlands, N.J.:Humanities Press, 1979.

Hohendahl, Peter U. "Introduction to Reception Aesthetics." *New German Critique* 10 (1977): 29–65.

Holub, Robert C. *Reception Theory: A Critical Introduction.* London: Methuen, 1984.

Husserl, Edmund. *Ideas Pertaining to a Pure Phenomenology and to a Phenomenological Philosophy.* The Hague: M. Nijhoff, 1982.

Ingarden, Roman. *The Literary Work of Art: An Investigation on the Borderlines of Ontology, Logic and the Theory of Literature.* Evanston, Ill.: Northwestern University Press, 1973 (First printed in Polish, 1931).

Iser, Wolfgang. *The Act of Reading: A Theory of Aesthetic Response.* Baltimore: Johns Hopkins University Press, 1978.

———. *The Implied Reader: Patterns of Communication in Prose Fiction from Bunyan to Beckett.* Baltimore: Johns Hopkins University Press, 1974.

Jacobs, Lewis. *The Rise of the American Film.* New York: Teachers College Press, 1939.

Jakobson, Roman. "Concluding statement: Linguistics and Poetics." *Style and Language.* Ed. T. Sebeok. Cambridge, Mass.: MIT Press, 1960.

Jauss, Hans Robert. *Literaturgeschichte als Provokation der Literaturwissenschaft.* Frankfurt am Mein: Suhrkamp, 1970.

————. "Literary History as a Challenge to Literary Theory." *New Literary History* 2, no. 1 (1970): 7–37.

Kaplan, E. Ann, ed. *Women in Film Noir.* London: British Film Institute, 1980.

Karpinski, Maciej. *The Theatre of Andrzej Wajda.* Cambridge, New York: Cambridge University Press, 1989.

Kempson, Ruth. *Semantic Theory.* Cambridge: Cambridge University Press, 1977.

Kirkpatrick, Betty. *The Cassell Concise English Dictionary.* London: Cassell, 1989.

Klinge, Sandra and Peter Klinge. *Evolution of Film Styles.* Lanham, New York, London: University Press of America, 1983.

Knight, Arthur. *The Liveliest Art.* New York: Mentor, 1957.

Kornatowska, Maria. *Leaders and Amateurs* [Wodzireje i Amatorzy]. Warszawa: Wydawnictwa Artystyczne i Filmowe, 1990.

Kracauer, Siegfried. *From Caligari to Hitler: A Psychological History of the German Film.* New Jersey: Princeton University Press, 1947.

Kristeva, Julia. *Desire in Language.* Ed. Leon S. Roudiez. Trans. Thomas Gora, Alice Jardine, and Leon S. Roudiez. New York: Columbia University Press, 1980.

Kuntzel, Thierry. "Film Work 2." *Camera Obscura* 5 (1980): 7–68.

Lawson, Sylvia. "Towards Decolonization: Some Problems and Issues for Film History in Australia." *Film Reader* 4 (1979): 63–71.

Le Grice, Malcolm. *Abstract Film and Beyond.* London: Studio Vista, 1977.

Levinson, Stephen C. *Pragmatics.* Cambridge: Cambridge University Press, 1985.

Londsbury, M. "'The Gathered Light': History, Criticism and the Rise of the American Film." *The Quarterly Review of Film Studies* (QRFS) 5, no. 1 (1980): 49–85.

Loy, Martin. *Browning's Dramatic Monologues and the Post-Romantic Subject.* Baltimore and London: Johns Hopkins University Press, 1985.

Lyotard, Jean-François. *The Differend: Phrases in Dispute.* Trans. G. Van Den Abbeele. Minneapolis: University of Minnesota Press, 1988.

MacBean, James Roy. *Film and Revolution.* Bloomington: Indiana University Press, 1975.

Mannheim, Karl. *Man and Society in an Age of Reconstruction: Studies in Modern Social Structure.* New York: Harcourt and Brace, 1940.

Margolis, H.E. *The Cinema Ideal: An Introduction to Psychoanalytic Studies of the Film Spectator.* New York and London: Garland Publishing Inc., 1988.

Marsh, Rosalind. *Images of Dictatorship: Portraits of Stalin in Literature.* London and New York: Routledge, 1989.

Marx, Karl. *Collected Works,* vol. 5. New York: International Publishers, 1976.

Mast, Gerald. "Film History and Film Histories." *Quarterly Review of Film Studies* 1, no. 3 (1976): 297–314.

————. *A Short History of the Movies.* New York: Pegasus, 1971.

Matejka, Ladislav and Krystyna Pomorska, eds. *Readings in Russian Poetics: Formalist and Structuralist Views.* Ann Arbor, MI: Michigan Slavic Contributions, 1978.

Maynard, Richard. *Propaganda on Film: A Nation at War.* Rochelle Park, N. J.: Hayden Book Company, 1975.

Metz, Christian. *Language and Cinema.* The Hague: Mouton, 1974.

————. *Film Language: A Semiotics of the Cinema.* Trans. Michael Taylor. New York: Oxford University Press, 1974.

Michalek, Boleslaw and Frank Turaj. *The Modern Cinema of Poland.* Bloomington and Indianapolis: Indiana University Press, 1988.

Milosz, Czeslaw. *The Captive Mind.* New York: Vintage Books, 1981.

Modleski, Tania. "The Terror of Pleasure: The Contemporary Horror Film and Postmodern Theory." *Studies in Entertainment: Critical Approaches to Mass Culture*. Ed. Tania Modleski. Bloomington: Indiana University Press, 1986.

Morley, David. *The "Nationwide" Audience*. London: British Film Institute, 1980.

Morson, Gary Saul, ed. *Bakhtin: Essays and Dialogues on His Work*. Chicago: University of Chicago Press, 1986.

Mukarovsky, Jan. "Dialog a Monolog. Listy filologické LXVIII" [Dialogue and monologue. Philological Letters LXVIII). *Kapitoly z ceske poetiky I* [Theses of Czech Poeteic I). Prague: Svoboda, 1948.

Mulvey, Laura. "Visual Pleasure and Narrative Cinema." *Screen* 16, no. 3 (1975): 8–18.

Nichols, Bill. "Critical Approaches to Film Then and Now." *Cineaste* 5, no. 2 (1972): 8–14.

———. *Ideology and the Image*. Bloomington: Indiana University Press, 1981.

Ophuls, Marcel. "The Provocation and Interrogation of Andrzej Wajda on the Matter of *Danton* as Performed by Marcel Ophuls." *American Film* 9, no. 1 (1983): 24–98.

Palmer, R. Barton. *The Cinematic Text: Methods and Approaches*. New York: AMS Press, 1989.

Paul, David W., ed. *Politics, Art and Commitment in the East European Cinema*. London: MacMillan, 1983.

Polan, Dana. "The Text Between Monologue and Dialogue." *Poetics Today* 4, no. 1 (1983): 145–52.

Ponzio, Augusto. "The Relation of Otherness in Bakhtin, Blanchot, Lévinas." *RSSI (Recherches Sémiotiques* [Semiotic Inquiry]), 7, no. 1 (1987): 1–18.

Propp, Vladimir. *Morphology of the Folktale*. Austin: University of Texas Press, 1968.

Rentschler, Eric. "Expanding Film Historical Discourse: Reception Theory's Use Value for Cinema Studies." *Cine-tracts: A Journal of Film and Cultural Studies* 4, no. 13 (1981–82): 57–68.

Rickey, Carrie. "Man of Iron." *Village Voice*, 23–29 September 1981.

Rock, Paul and Mary McIntosh, eds. *Deviance and Social Control*. London: Tavistock Publications, 1974.

Roffman, Peter and Jim Purdy. *The Hollywood Social Problem Film: Madness, Despair and Politics from the Depression to the Fifties*. Bloomington: Indiana University Press, 1981.

Rollins, Peter C. "Ideology and Film Rhetoric: Three Documentaries of the New Deal Era (1936–1941)." *Hollywood As Historian: American Film in a Cultural Context*. Ed. Peter C. Rollins. Lexington, Kentucky: University Press of Kentucky, 1983.

Rubenstein, Lenny. "Danton." *Cineaste* 13, no. 1 (1983): 36–37.

Saniewski, Wieslaw. "Kino polskie lat siedemdziesiatych: Dyskusja redakcyjna" [Polish Cinema of the Seventies: Editors discussion]. *Film na Swiecie*, no. 9, 1979.

Sarris, Andrew. *The American Cinema: Directors and Directions 1929–1968*. New York: Dutton, 1968.

———. *Politics and Cinema*. New York: Columbia University Press, 1978.

Scharff, Stefan. *The Elements of Cinema: Toward a Theory of Cinesthetic Impact*. New York: Columbia University Press, 1982.

Schmidt, Henry J. "Text-Adequate Concretizations and Real Readers: Reception Theory and Its Applications." *New German Critique* 17 (1979): 157–169.

Segers, Rien T. "An Interview with Hans Robert Jauss." *New Literary History* 11, no. 1 (1979): 83–96.

Seiter, Ellen, ed. *Remote Control: Television, Audiences and Cultural Power*. London, New York: Routledge, 1989.

Silverman, Kaja. *The Acoustic Mirror: The Female Voice in Psychoanalysis and Cinema.* Bloomington: Indiana University Press, 1988.

Stam, Robert. *Subversive Pleasures: Bakhtin, Cultural Criticism and Film.* Baltimore and London: Johns Hopkins University Press, 1989.

———. "Bakhtinian Translinguistics: A Postscriptum." *The Cinematic Text: Methods and Approaches.* Ed. Barton R. Palmer. New York: AMS Press, 1989.

———. *Reflexivity in Film and Literature: From Don Quixote to Jean-Luc Godard.* Irvington: Columbia University Press, 1991.

Szanto, George, H. *Theatre and Propaganda.* Austin and London: University of Texas Press, 1978.

Szporer, Michael. "Woman of Marble: An Interview with Krystyna Janda." *Cineaste* 18, no. 3 (1991): 12–16.

Taras, Ray. *Poland: Socialist State, Rebellious Nation.* Boulder and London: Westview Press, 1986.

Todorov, Tzvetan. *Genres in Discourse.* Trans. Catherine Porter. Cambridge: Cambridge University Press, 1990.

Tudor, Andrew. *Theories of Film.* London: Secker and Warburg, 1974.

Urmson, J.D. and Jonathan Rée, eds. *The Concise Encyclopedia of Western Philosophy and Philosophers.* London: Unwin Hyman, 1989.

Volosinov, Valentin Nikolaievich. *Marxism and the Philosophy of Language.* Trans. Ladislav Matejka and I.R. Titunik. New York: Seminar Press, 1973.

———. *Freudianism: A Marxist Critique.* Trans. I.R. Titunik. New York: Academic Press, 1976.

Wajda, Andrzej. *Double Vision: My Life in Film.* New York: Henry Holt and Co., 1989.

Walicki, Andrzej. *Philosophy and Romantic Nationalism: The Case of Poland.* Oxford: Clarendon Press, 1982.

Webster, A. Merriam. *New Collegiate Dictionary.* Springfield, Mass.: G.and C. Merriam Company, 1981.

Weed, Elizabeth, ed. *Coming to Terms: Feminism/Theory/Politics.* New York: Routledge, 1989.

Wertenstein, Wanda. *Wajda mowi o sobie: Wywiady i teksty* [Wajda Talks about Himself: Interviews and Texts]. Krakow: Wydawnictwo Literackie, 1991.

Wertsch, James V. *Voices of the Mind: A Sociocultural Approach to Mediated Action.* Cambridge, Mass.: Harvard University Press, 1991.

White, Hayden. *Theories of History: Papers Read at a Clark Library Seminar, March 6, 1976.* Los Angeles: University of California, 1978.

———. *Metahistory: The Historical Imagination in Nineteenth Century Europe.* Baltimore and London: Johns Hopkins University Press, 1973.

———. *Tropics of Discourse: Essays in Cultural Criticism.* Baltimore and London: Johns Hopkins University Press, 1978.

Willemen, Paul. "Cinematic Discourse: The Problem of Inner Speech." *Cinema and Language.* Ed. S. Heath and P. Mellencamp. Frederick, MD: University Publications of America, 1983.

Williams, Raymond. *Marxism and Literature.* Oxford: Oxford University Press, 1977.

Wlodarczyk, Wojciech. *Socrealizm: Sztuka polska w latach 1950–1954* [Socialist Realism: Polish Art in the Years 1950–1954]. Krakow: Wydawnictwo Literackie, 1991.

Wollen, Peter. *Signs and Meaning in the Cinema.* London: Secker and Warburg, 1974.

———. "Photography and Aesthetics." *Screen* 19, no. 4 (1978–79): 9–28.

Zavarzadeh, Mas'ud. *Seeing Films Politically.* Albany: State University of New York Press, 1991.

❄ INDEX